CONTROL AND DYNAMIC SYSTEMS

Advances in Theory and Applications

Volume 23

CONTRIBUTORS TO THIS VOLUME

BERNHARD ASSELMEYER
TAMER BAŞAR
LAWRENCE E. BERMAN
J. BERNUSSOU
J. C. GEROMEL
THOMAS J. HOLMES
KENNETH M. KESSLER
SHIGERU OMATU
P. N. PARASKEVOPOULOS
VIKRAM R. SAKSENA
JASON L. SPEYER
KAZUNORI YASUDA

CONTROL AND DYNAMIC SYSTEMS

ADVANCES IN THEORY AND APPLICATIONS

Edited by
C. T. LEONDES

School of Engineering and Applied Sciences
University of California
Los Angeles, California

VOLUME 23: DECENTRALIZED/DISTRIBUTED CONTROL AND DYNAMIC SYSTEMS
Part 2 of 3

1986

ACADEMIC PRESS, INC.
Harcourt Brace Jovanovich, Publishers
Orlando San Diego New York Austin
London Montreal Sydney Tokyo Toronto

ACADEMIC PRESS RAPID MANUSCRIPT REPRODUCTION

ACADEMIC PRESS, INC.
Orlando, Florida 32887

United Kingdom Edition published by
ACADEMIC PRESS INC. (LONDON) LTD.
24–28 Oval Road, London NW1 7DX

LIBRARY OF CONGRESS CATALOG CARD NUMBER: 64-8027

ISBN 0-12-012723-7

PRINTED IN THE UNITED STATES OF AMERICA

86 87 88 89 9 8 7 6 5 4 3 2 1

CONTENTS

The Linear–Quadratic Control Problem

Jason L. Speyer

A Ritz-Type Optimization Method for Optimal Control Problems and Its Application to Hierarchical Final-Value Controllers

Bernhard Asselmeyer

CONTRIBUTORS

Numbers in parentheses indicate the pages on which the authors' contributions begin.

Bernhard Asselmeyer[1] (295), *D-7132 Illingen, Federal Republic of Germany*

Tamer Başar (1), *Department of Electrical and Computer Engineering and the Coordinated Science Laboratory, University of Illinois, Urbana, Illinois, 61801*

Lawrence E. Berman (59), *Systems Control Technology, Inc., Palo Alto, California 94034*

J. Bernussou (123), *LAAS/CNRS, 31400 Toulouse, France*

J. C. Geromel (123), *FEC/UNICAMP C. P. 6122, São Paulo, Brasil*

Thomas J. Holmes (59), *Systems Control Technology, Inc., Palo Alto, California 94034*

Kenneth M. Kessler (59), *Systems Control Technology, Inc., Palo Alto, California 94034*

Shigeru Omatu (195), *Department of Information Science and Systems Engineering, University of Tokushima, Tokushima 770, Japan*

P. N. Paraskevopoulos (165), *Division of Computer Science, Department of Electrical Engineering, National Technical University of Athens, Athens, Greece*

Vikram R. Saksena (1), *AT&T Bell Laboratories, Holmdel, New Jersey 07733*

Jason L. Speyer (241), *Department of Aerospace Engineering and Engineering Mechanics, University of Texas, Austin, Texas 78712*

Kazunori Yasuda (139), *Faculty of Engineering, Kobe University, Kobe 657, Japan*

[1]Present address: Bayer AG, D-50g Leverkusen, Federal Republic of Germany.

PREFACE

In the series *Control and Dynamic Systems* this is the second volume of a trilogy whose theme is advances in techniques for the analysis and synthesis of decentralized or distributed control and dynamic systems. The subject of decentralized but coordinated systems is emerging as a major issue in industrial and aerospace systems, so this is an appropriately significant theme for this series at this time. These three volumes will thus comprise the most comprehensive treatment of the theory of this broad and complex subject and its many potential applications to date. It is in the various complex real-world applications that many practitioners may find these three volumes particularly useful. This includes chapters on many computational issues and techniques appearing in the textbook literature for the first time.

The first chapter in this volume, ''Multimodeling, Singular Perturbations, and Stochastic Decision Problems,'' by Vikram R. Saksena and Tamer Başar, constitutes a unique presentation in the textbook literature of the extensive efforts over a number of years of the fundamentally important work conducted by the co-authors and their associates integrated with the works of others. One of the major issues in decentralized but coordinated systems is that of the allocation of time-critical resources. The next chapter, by Lawrence E. Berman, Thomas J. Holmes, and Kenneth M. Kessler, constitutes a unique presentation in the textbook literature of rather powerful techniques for dealing with the complex issues in this broad problem area. The third chapter, ''Parametrical Optimization Approach for Decentralized Regulation of Discrete Systems,'' by J. C. Geromel and J. Bernussou, presents techniques which do not require any information exchange among subsystem controllers, and it should constitute a fundamental reference source for practitioners in many important applied situations. The following chapter, ''Decentralized Optimal Control for Large-Scale Interconnected Systems,'' by Kazunori Yasuda, deals with the major issue of reliable or robust decentralized control systems. The following chapter by P. N. Paraskevopoulos deals with the important considerations in model reduction for large-scale systems, another issue of major consideration in decentralized control systems. The next chapter, ''Optimal Estimation Theory for Distributed Parameter Systems,'' by Shigeru Omatu, constitutes a unique textbook treatment by a leading research worker in an area prominent on the international scene. Jason L. Speyer's many significant contributions in a diverse number of areas of major applied importance make it especially appropriate that he contribute the next chapter in this volume, which deals with a comprehensive and insightful treatment of the linear quadratic control problem, so fundamental to many areas of control and dynamic systems, including decentralized control. The volume concludes with ''A Ritz-Type Optimization Method for Optimal Control Problems and Its Application to Hierarchical Final-Value Controllers,'' by Bernhard Asselmeyer, which presents powerful techniques for dealing with an important class of problems in decentralized control systems.

When the theme for this trilogy of volumes, of which this is the second, was decided upon, there seemed little doubt that it was most timely. However, because of the substantially important contributions of the authors, all volumes promise to be not only timely but of substantial lasting value.

Multimodeling, Singular Perturbations, and Stochastic Decision Problems

VIKRAM R. SAKSENA*

AT&T Bell Laboratories
Holmdel, New Jersey

TAMER BAŞAR**

Department of Electrical and Computer Engineering
and the Coordinated Science Laboratory
University of Illinois
Urbana, Illinois

*This author's work was performed during his stay at the University of Illinois, Urbana-Champaign.

**Work of this author was supported in part by the Joint Services Electronics Program under Contract N00014-79-C-0424 and in part by the Department of Energy, Electric Energy Systems Division, under Contract DE-AC01-81RA-50658 with Dynamic Systems, P.O. Box 423, Urbana, Illinois 61801.

I. INTRODUCTION

The problem of efficient management and control of large-scale systems has been extremely challenging to control engineers. There are essentially two main issues of concern: the *modeling issue* is complicated due to the large dimension of the system, and the *control design issue* is complicated due to the presence of multiple decision makers having possibly different goals and possessing decentralized information. Efforts to understand the inherent complexities have led to the concept of nonclassical information patterns [1]. This concept expresses a basic fact that a decision maker has neither complete nor instantaneous access to other decision makers' measurements and decisions. A related but perhaps more basic fact is expressed by the multimodeling concept [2]. This concept accounts for the many realistic situations when different decision makers have different information about the system structure and dynamics and therefore use different simplified models of the same large-scale system. These models may differ in parameter values, signal uncertainties, and, more critically, in their basic structural properties.

A strong motivation for the multimodeling approach is found in multiarea power systems. The decision maker in one area uses a detailed model of his area only and some lower-order "equivalent" of the rest of the system. The decision makers in other areas behave in a similar way and as a result each has his own view of the same large-scale system. The main advantage of such an empirical decomposition is that it leads to distributed computations and less communication between the controllers because each decision maker would only require measurements of the variables appearing in his own reduced-order model. Many crucial problems (instability, suboptimality, etc.) arise because the strategies designed with such inconsistent models are then applied to the actual system.

We investigate, in this chapter, the effect of multimodeling inconsistencies on the design and implementation of multicontroller strategies under certain quasiclassical information patterns. The approach taken is perturbational. If the model inconsistencies are small, it is natural to expect that their effect on the designed strategies and on the actual system performance would be in some sense small. If this were not the case, the designed strategies would not be applicable to realistic systems whose models are never exactly known. We consider this low sensitivity property a *sine qua non* condition for any control design and, in particular, for the design of large-scale systems controlled from multiple control stations.

Another fundamental property of our perturbational approach is that it concentrates on modeling errors caused by reducing the model order. Such order reductions are achieved by separating the time scales, that is, by considering slow and fast phenomena separately. A typical situation is when the decision maker in one area neglects the fast phenomena in all other areas. In geographically dispersed systems this practice is based on the experimental observation that faster phenomena propagate to shorter distances than the slower phenomena. For example, in a multimachine transient the slower oscillatory modes are observed throughout the system, while faster intermachine oscillations are of a more local character [3].

A tool for analyzing the change in model order is the so-called singular perturbation method which converts the change of model order into a small parameter perturbation [4]. This parameter multiplies the derivatives of the fast state variables and when it is set to zero the fast phenomena are neglected. The fast phenomena are treated separately in the fast time scale where the slow variables are "frozen" at their quasi-steady-state values. This two-time-scale approach is asymptotic, that is, exact in the limit as the ratio of speeds of the slow versus the fast dynamics tends to zero. When this ratio is small, approximations are obtained from reduced-order models in separate time scales. This way the singular perturbation approach alleviates difficulties due to high dimensionality and ill-conditioning resulting from the interaction of slow and fast dynamic modes.

The chapter is organized as follows. In Section II, we study the fundamental problem of modeling and control of singularly perturbed systems driven by Wiener processes under various cases of continuous and sampled observations. An extension of the single-parameter model, which realistically captures the multimodeling situation, is formulated in Section III using multiparameter singular perturbations. In Section IV, we obtain multimodel solutions to Nash and team problems under certain quasi-classical information patterns, and establish their relationship with the solutions of the full problem. We summarize the results with some concluding remarks in Section V.

To highlight the ideas, we have adopted an informal style for the presentation and discussion of the main results. More rigorous treatment can be found in quoted references.

II. MODELING AND CONTROL OF STOCHASTIC SINGULARLY PERTURBED SYSTEMS

A. *WELL-POSEDNESS OF DIFFERENT MODELS*

The optimal control of stochastic singularly perturbed systems with white noise inputs leads to difficulties not present in deterministic problems. This is due to the idealized behavior of white noise which "fluctuates" faster than the fast dynamic variables. To illustrate the problem of optimally controlling a stochastic fast dynamic system, consider the following standard LQG formulation:

system dynamics: $$\epsilon\, dz = Az\, dt + Bu\, dt + G\, dw, \tag{1a}$$

measurement process: $$dy = Cz\, dt + dv, \tag{1b}$$

cost function: $$J = E\left\{z'\Gamma z + \int_0^T (z'Qz + u'u)\, dt\right\}. \tag{2}$$

Here, $\epsilon > 0$ is the small singular perturbation parameter; $w(t)$ and $v(t)$ are standard Wiener processes independent of each other, and all matrices are time invariant, with $\Gamma \geq 0$, $Q \geq 0$. We will further assume that A is a stable matrix, that is, $\mathrm{Re}\,\lambda(A) < 0$.

The optimal control u^* which minimizes the cost J is obtained in the usual manner by applying the separation principle, so that

$$u^* = -B'K\hat{z} \tag{3}$$

where K satisfies the Riccati equation

$$\epsilon\dot{K} = -A'K - KA - Q + KBB'K, \quad K(T) = \Gamma/\epsilon. \tag{4}$$

The vector $\hat{z}(t)$ denotes the optimal estimate of $z(t)$ given the past observations, which for any given $u(t)$ is the output of the Kalman filter

$$\epsilon\, d\hat{z} = A\hat{z}\, dt + Bu\, dt + PC'(dy - C\hat{z}\, dt), \quad \hat{z}(0) = E[z(0)] \tag{5}$$

where $P(t)/\epsilon$ is the error covariance of $\hat{z}(t)$, satisfying

$$\epsilon\dot{P} = AP + PA' + GG' - PC'CP, \quad P(0) = \epsilon\,\mathrm{Cov}(z(0)), \tag{6}$$

which does not depend on u(t). The resulting minimum value of the cost, J^*, is given by

$$J^* = \epsilon\hat{z}'(0)K(0)\hat{z}(0) + \frac{1}{\epsilon}\,\mathrm{tr}[P(T)\Gamma] + \frac{1}{\epsilon}\int_0^T \mathrm{tr}[CPKPC' + PQ]\,dt. \tag{7}$$

Notice from (6) and (7) that $\mathrm{Cov}(z - \hat{z}) = O(1/\epsilon)$ and $J^* = O(1/\epsilon)$. Hence as $\epsilon \to 0$, both the covariance of the estimation error and optimal cost diverge, even though the feedback gain of the optimal control law given by (3) remains finite (outside the endpoint boundary layer). This is because, in the limit as $\epsilon \to 0$, the fast variables z themselves tend to white noise processes, thus losing their significance as physically meaningful dynamic variables. Hence the problem formulation given by (1) and (2) is ill-posed. More detailed analysis of this formulation in the filtering and control context may be found in [5,6].

One way to circumvent the difficulty encountered above is to appropriately "scale" the white noise terms in the model. Let us now investigate ramifications of the following more general formulation:

The state dynamics description is replaced by

$$\epsilon\,dz = Az\,dt + Bu\,dt + \epsilon^{\alpha}G\,dw, \quad \mathrm{Re}\,\lambda(A) < 0 \tag{8a}$$

and the measurement process is

$$dy = Cz\,dt + \epsilon^{\beta}\,dv \tag{8b}$$

where α, β are some positive constants to be chosen. The cost function J is the same as before.

Now the optimal control is given by

$$u^* = -B'K\hat{z} \tag{9}$$

where K(t) satisfies (4).

The optimal estimate $\hat{z}(t)$ is obtained from the Kalman filter

$$\begin{aligned} \epsilon\, d\hat{z} &= A\hat{z}\, dt + Bu\, dt + M(t)(dy - C\hat{z}\, dt), \\ \hat{z}(0) &= E[z(0)] \end{aligned} \tag{10}$$

where M(t) is the filter gain given as

$$M(t) = \epsilon^{1-2\beta}PC' \tag{11}$$

and P(t) is the error covariance of $\hat{z}(t)$, satisfying

$$\begin{aligned} \epsilon\dot{P} &= AP + PA' + \epsilon^{2\alpha-1}GG' - \epsilon^{1-2\beta}PC'CP, \\ P(0) &= \mathrm{Cov}(z(0)). \end{aligned} \tag{12}$$

The minimum value of the cost, J^*, is given by

$$\begin{aligned} J^* &= \epsilon\hat{z}'(0)K(0)\hat{z}(0) + \mathrm{tr}(P(T)\Gamma) \\ &\quad + \epsilon^{1-2\beta}\int_0^T \mathrm{tr}(CPKPC')\, dt + \int_0^T \mathrm{tr}(PQ)\, dt. \end{aligned} \tag{13}$$

Let us now examine the behavior of P(t), M(t), and J^* for various values of α and β, in the limit as $\epsilon \to 0$. The limiting behavior of P(t) and J^* is governed primarily by the parameter α, while the limiting behavior of M(t) is governed by both parameters α and β. Notice that the behavior of K(t) is unaffected by the scaling.

A straightforward examination of (12) reveals that for $\alpha < 1/2$, P(t) diverges as $\epsilon \to 0$, which implies from (13) that J^* also diverges as $\epsilon \to 0$. (Note that $\beta > 0$ by hypothesis.) When P(t) diverges, the filter gain M(t) may or may not diverge as $\epsilon \to 0$, depending on the value of β. If $\beta > 1/2$, however, in addition to $0 < \alpha < 1/2$, M(t) always diverges as $\epsilon \to 0$.

This particular case ($\alpha < 1/2$, $\beta > 1/2$) corresponds to the situation where the observations become noise-free in the limit as $\epsilon \to 0$, and therefore the filter gain becomes unbounded.

When $\alpha > 1/2$ and β is any positive constant, it readily follows from (12) and (13) that P(t) and J^* go to zero as $\epsilon \to 0$. If at the same time $\beta < 1/2$, then M(t) also goes to zero as $\epsilon \to 0$. This case ($\alpha > 1/2$, $\beta < 1/2$) corresponds to the situation when the observations become too noisy in the limit as $\epsilon \to 0$, thus driving the filter gain to zero.

Hence the range of scaling ($\alpha, \beta > 0$; $\alpha \neq 1/2$, $\beta \neq 1/2$) leads to ill-posed formulations. This implies that it is not possible to give a physically meaningul interpretation to the limiting solution. (Of course for any fixed $\epsilon > 0$, the problem is well defined.) The only meaningful formulation is obtained when $\alpha = \beta = 1/2$. In this case P(t), M(t), and J^* remain bounded and nonzero and yield a well-defined stochastic control problem in the limit as $\epsilon \to 0$.

The above analysis has indicated that in order to obtain a well-defined stochastic control problem, the process and observation noise need to be scaled in an appropriate manner. To gain further insight, let us directly examine the limiting behavior of the stochastic process

$$\epsilon\, dz = Az\, dt + \sqrt{\epsilon} G\, dw, \quad \text{Re}\, \lambda(A) < 0, \quad GG' > 0. \tag{14}$$

Clearly, without the scaling term, z(t) converges to white noise in the limit as $\epsilon \to 0$. If, with the above scaling, z(t) converges to something which is physically meaningful, then this would provide a strong justification for the model (8), with $\alpha = 1/2$.

Solving for z(t) from (14) we obtain

$$z(t) = \frac{1}{\sqrt{\epsilon}} \int_0^t e^{A(t-\tau)/\epsilon} G\, dw(\tau) \tag{15}$$

where we have assumed, without loss of generality, that $z(0) = 0$. Now

$$\mathrm{Cov}(z(t)) = E\left\{\left[\frac{1}{\sqrt{\epsilon}}\int_0^t e^{A(t-\tau_1)/\epsilon} G\, dw(\tau_1)\right] \times \left[\frac{1}{\sqrt{\epsilon}}\int_0^t e^{A(t-\tau_2)/\epsilon} G\, dw(\tau_2)\right]'\right\}$$

$$= \frac{1}{\epsilon}\int_0^t e^{A(t-\tau)/\epsilon} GG' e^{A'(t-\tau)/\epsilon}\, d\tau$$

$$\triangleq W_\epsilon(t) \tag{16}$$

where $W_\epsilon(t)$ satisfies, for each $\epsilon > 0$, the linear matrix differential equation

$$\epsilon \dot{W}_\epsilon = AW_\epsilon + W_\epsilon A + GG'.$$

Since $\mathrm{Re}\,\lambda(A) < 0$, we clearly have the limit (excluding boundary layers)

$$\lim_{\epsilon\to 0} \mathrm{Cov}(z(t)) = W \tag{17}$$

where W is the positive definite (because $GG' > 0$) solution of the Lyapunov equation

$$AW + WA' + GG' = 0. \tag{18}$$

This implies that $z(t)$ converges in distribution to a zero mean constant Gaussian random vector whose covariance W satisfies (18) (see also [7,8]). The above convergence is indeed physically meaningful, and therefore we are justified in using (14) to model a fast stochastic dynamic system.

Physically, the above analysis has indicated that in order to meaningfully estimate and control a fast dynamic system, the influence of the random disturbances has to be "limited" in some sense.

B. SINGULARLY PERTURBED SYSTEMS WITH CONTINUOUS MEASUREMENTS

Let us now consider the full (with both slow and fast variables) stochastic singularly perturbed optimal control problem

$$dx = (A_{11}x + A_{12}z + B_1u)\ dt + G_1\ dw, \tag{19a}$$

$$\epsilon\ dz = \left(\epsilon^{\beta}A_{21}x + A_{22}z + B_2u\right)\ dt + \epsilon^{\alpha}G_2\ dw, \tag{19b}$$

$$dy_1 = (C_{11}x + C_{12}z)\ dt + dv_1, \tag{20a}$$

$$dy_2 = \left(\epsilon^{\nu}C_{21}x + C_{22}z\right)\ dt + \epsilon^{\nu}\ dv_2, \tag{20b}$$

$$J = E\left\{x'(T)\Gamma_1x(T) + 2\epsilon x'(T)\Gamma_{12}z(T) + \epsilon z'(T)\Gamma_2z(T) + \int_0^T \left(x'L_1'L_1x + 2\epsilon^{\delta}x'L_1'L_2z + \epsilon^{2\delta}z'L_2'L_2z + u'u\right) dt\right\}. \tag{21}$$

The parameters α, β, ν, δ represent the relative size of the small parameters within the system, with respect to the small time constants of the fast subsystem. The inclusion of a separate observation channel y_2 for the fast subsystem is essential, since otherwise for $\alpha > 0$ the fast variables cannot be estimated meaningfully from the slow observation channel (signal-to-noise ratio tends to zero). The stochastic processes $w(t)$, $v_1(t)$, and $v_2(t)$ are standard Wiener processes independent of each other and the Gaussian random vector $[x(0), z(0)]$. We also assume that $\text{Re}\ \lambda(A_{22}) < 0$. The optimal solution to the problem posed by (19)-(21) can be obtained by invoking the separation principle:

$$u^* = -\left[\left(B_1'K_1 + B_2'K_{12}'\right)\hat{x} + \left(B_2'K_2 + \epsilon B_1'K_{12}\right)\hat{z}\right], \tag{22}$$

$$d\hat{x} = \left(A_{11}\hat{x} + A_{12}\hat{z} + B_1u^*\right) dt + \left[P_1C_1' + \epsilon^{\alpha-\nu}P_{12}C_2'\right] d\sigma, \tag{23a}$$

$$\epsilon\, d\hat{z} = \left(\epsilon^{\beta} A_{21}\hat{x} + A_{22}\hat{z} + B_2 u^*\right) dt + \epsilon^{\alpha}\left[\epsilon P_{12}' C_1' + \epsilon^{\alpha-\nu} P_2 C_2'\right] d\sigma \tag{23b}$$

where the innovations process $\sigma(t)$ is defined by

$$d\sigma(t) \triangleq \begin{bmatrix} dy_1 \\ \epsilon^{-\nu}\, dy_2 \end{bmatrix} - \begin{bmatrix} C_{11} & C_{12} \\ C_{21} & \epsilon^{-\nu} C_{22} \end{bmatrix}\begin{bmatrix} \hat{x} \\ \hat{z} \end{bmatrix} dt \triangleq \begin{bmatrix} dy_1 \\ \epsilon^{-\nu}\, dy_2 \end{bmatrix} - \begin{bmatrix} C_1 & \epsilon^{-\nu} C_2 \end{bmatrix}\begin{bmatrix} \hat{x} \\ \hat{z} \end{bmatrix} dt. \tag{24}$$

The control gain matrices satisfy

$$-\dot{K}_1 = K_1 A_{11} + \epsilon^{\beta} K_{12} A_{21} + A_{11}' K_1 + \epsilon^{\beta} A_{21}' K_{12}' + L_1' L_1 - (K_{12} B_2 + K_1 B_1) \times \left(B_1' K_1 + B_2' K_{12}'\right), \quad K_1(T) = \Gamma_1 \tag{25a}$$

$$-\epsilon \dot{K}_{12} = K_1 A_{12} + K_{12} A_{22} + \epsilon A_{11}' K_{12} + \epsilon^{\beta} A_{21}' K_2 + \epsilon^{\delta} L_1' L_2 - (K_{12} B_2 + K_1 B_1) \times \left(B_2' K_2 + \epsilon B_1' K_{12}\right), \quad K_{12}(T) = \Gamma_{12} \tag{25b}$$

$$-\epsilon \dot{K}_2 = K_2 A_{22} + A_{22}' K_2 + \epsilon K_{12}' A_{12} + \epsilon A_{12}' K_{12} + \epsilon^{2\delta} L_2' L_2 - \left(K_2 B_2 + \epsilon K_{12}' B_1\right) \times \left(B_2' K_2 + \epsilon B_1' K_{12}\right), \quad K_2(T) = \Gamma_2. \tag{25c}$$

The filter covariances satisfy

$$\dot{P}_1 = A_{11} P_1 + P_1 A_{11}' + \epsilon^{\alpha} A_{12} P_{12}' + \epsilon^{\alpha} P_{12} A_{12}' + G_1 G_1' - \left(P_1 C_1' + \epsilon^{\alpha-\nu} P_{12} C_2'\right) \times \left(C_1 P_1 + \epsilon^{\alpha-\nu} C_2 P_{12}'\right), \quad P_1(0) = \mathrm{Cov}(x(0)), \tag{26a}$$

$$\epsilon\dot{P}_{12} = \epsilon A_{11}P_{12} + \epsilon^{\alpha}A_{12}P_2 + P_{12}A_2' + \epsilon^{\beta-\alpha}P_1A_{21}'$$
$$+ G_1G_2' - \left(P_1C_1' + \epsilon^{\alpha-\nu}P_{12}C_2'\right)$$
$$\times \left(\epsilon C_1P_{12} + \epsilon^{\alpha-\nu}C_2P_2\right), \quad P_{12}(0) = \epsilon^{\alpha}\,\mathrm{Cov}(x(0),\, z(0)) \tag{26b}$$

$$\epsilon\dot{P}_2 = A_{22}P_2 + P_2A_{22}' + \epsilon^{1-\alpha+\beta}A_{21}P_{12} + \epsilon^{1-\alpha+\beta}P_{12}'A_{21}'$$
$$+ G_2G_2' - \left(\epsilon P_{12}'C_1' + \epsilon^{\alpha-\nu}P_2C_2'\right)$$
$$\times \left(\epsilon C_1P_{12} + \epsilon^{\alpha-\nu}C_2P_2\right), \quad P_2(0) = \epsilon^{1-2\alpha}\,\mathrm{Cov}(z(0)). \tag{26c}$$

The performance index will be finite if $\epsilon^{2\delta}$ Cov(z) is finite. But

$$\mathrm{Cov}(z) = \epsilon^{2\alpha-1}P_2. \tag{27}$$

Hence, we require that

$$\delta \geq (1/2) - \alpha \tag{28}$$

in order to have a finite cost. Furthermore, a well-defined formulation also requires that

$$0 \leq \alpha = \nu \leq \beta \leq 1/2. \tag{29}$$

The restriction $\alpha = \nu$ is crucial, otherwise, either the fast variables are not observed due to very noisy observations ($\alpha > \nu$), or they are observed noiselessly ($\alpha < \nu$) in the limit as $\epsilon \to 0$, and if $\beta > 1/2$, the coupling between x and z becomes negligible. The constraint $\beta \geq \alpha$ ensures that the state z is predominantly fast, and relaxing it causes no conceptual difficulties.

Note that when $\alpha = \beta = \nu = 0$, it is required that $\delta = 1/2$ to yield a finite cost. In this case the fast variables are of no interest as far as the control is concerned, and serve only as a model for a wide-band disturbance to the slow variables.

The important case is when $\alpha = \nu = 1/2$ and $\delta = \beta = 0$, since this results in a full weighting of the fast variable. For this problem, it can be shown that [9]

$$\lim_{\epsilon \to 0} u^* = u_s + u_f, \quad 0 < t < T, \tag{30}$$

where

$$u_s = -R_0^{-1}\left(N_0'L_0 + B_0'K_0\right)\hat{x}_s, \tag{31}$$

$$d\hat{x}_s = \left(A_0\hat{x}_s + B_0u_s\right) dt + \left(P_0C_0' + G_0D_0'\right)V_0^{-1}$$
$$\times \left[dy - C_0\hat{x}_s\, dt + (1/\sqrt{\epsilon})C_2A_{22}^{-1}B_2u_s\, dt\right], \tag{32}$$

$$-\dot{K}_0 = K_0\left(A_0 - B_0R_0^{-1}N_0'L_0\right) + \left(A_0 - B_0R_0^{-1}N_0'L_0\right)'K_0$$
$$+ L_0'\left(I - N_0R_0^{-1}N_0'\right)L_0 - K_0B_0R_0^{-1}B_0'K_0, \quad K_0(T) = \Gamma, \tag{33}$$

$$\dot{P}_0 = A_0P_0 + P_0A_0' - \left(P_0C_0' + G_0D_0'\right)V_0^{-1}$$
$$\times \left(C_0P_0 + D_0G_0'\right) + G_0G_0', \quad P_0(0) = \mathrm{Cov}(x(0)), \tag{34}$$

$$A_0 \triangleq A_{11}, \quad B_0 \triangleq B_1 - A_{12}A_{22}^{-1}B_2, \quad N_0 \triangleq -L_2A_{22}^{-1}B_2,$$
$$L_0 \triangleq L_1, \quad R_0 \triangleq N_0'N_0, \quad C_0 \triangleq C_1 - C_2A_{22}^{-1}A_{21},$$
$$D_0 \triangleq -C_2A_{22}^{-1}G_2, \quad G_0 \triangleq G_1, \quad V_0 \triangleq I + D_0D_0', \tag{35}$$

$$u_f = -B_2'\overline{K}_2\hat{z}_f, \tag{36}$$

$$\epsilon\, d\hat{z}_f = \left(A_{22}\hat{z}_f + B_2u_f\right) dt + \overline{P}_2C_{22}'$$
$$\times \left\{dy_2 - C_{22}\hat{z}_f\, dt - \sqrt{\epsilon}\left[C_{21} - C_{22}A_{22}^{-1}A_{21}\right]\hat{x}_s\, dt\right.$$
$$\left. + C_{22}A_{22}^{-1}B_2u_s\, dt\right\}, \tag{37}$$

$$\overline{K}_2A_{22} + A_{22}'\overline{K}_2 + L_2'L_2 - \overline{K}_2B_2B_2'\overline{K}_2 = 0, \tag{38}$$

$$A_{22}\overline{P}_2 + \overline{P}_2A_{22}' + G_2G_2' - \overline{P}_2C_2'C_2\overline{P}_2 = 0. \tag{39}$$

Notice that u_s and u_f are obtained on solving a reduced-order slow control problem and an infinite-time fast control problem, respectively. These problems can be solved independently of each other. It is interesting to note that the fast filter is driven by the slow variables as well. Hence the implementation of the filters is not independent, but sequential in nature. The near-optimality result (30) is valid only for $t \in (0, T)$, because the boundary layer terms have been neglected.

C. SINGULARLY PERTURBED SYSTEMS WITH SAMPLED MEASUREMENTS

So far we have examined the modeling and control aspects of stochastic singularly perturbed systems when the measurement process is continuous in time. We shall now examine the same aspects when the measurement process consists of discrete samples. Two types of sampled observations will be considered. In the first case, sampled values of the state in additive noise are observed, and in the second case sampled values of a continuous-time measurement process are observed. These types of observations play an important role in multiagent decision problems as we shall see later.

It is a well-known fact that the open-loop dynamics of any system of the form (19) with $\alpha = 1/2$, $\beta = 0$, can be transformed into a block-diagonal form where the pure slow and fast variables are explicitly displayed [10]. Hence, without loss of generality, we shall assume that the system to be controlled is given by

$$dx = (A_1 x + B_1 u)\, dt + G_1\, dw, \tag{40a}$$

$$\epsilon\, dz = (A_2 z + B_2 u)\, dt + \sqrt{\epsilon}\, G_2\, dw, \quad \text{Re}\, \lambda(A_2) < 0. \tag{40b}$$

The performance index will be given by[†]

$$J = E\left\{x(T)\Gamma_1 x(T) + \epsilon z'(T)\Gamma_2 z(T) + \int_0^T \left(x'Q_1x + z'Q_2z + u'u\right) dt\right\}. \quad (41)$$

We now consider two cases of sampled observations.

Case 1. Noisy Measurements of Sampled Values of State. The observations consist of sampled noisy measurements of the state. Specifically, the observations

$$y(j) = C_1x(t_j) + C_2z(t_j) + v(j) \quad (42)$$

are available at sampled time instant t_j where $j = 0, 1, \ldots, N - 1$ and $0 = t_0 < t_1 < \cdots < t_{N-1} = T$. Let $\theta = \{0, 1, \ldots, N - 1\}$. Then the random vectors $\{v(j), j \in \theta\}$ are assumed to have independent Gaussian statistics with $v(j) \sim N(0, R_j)$, $R_j > 0$, $j \in \theta$. Their statistics are also assumed to be independent of the Wiener process $w(t)$ and the Gaussian vector $[x(0), z(0)]$.

A near-optimal solution to the problem defined by (40)-(42) can be shown to be given by

$$u_0 = u_s + u_f \quad (43)$$

where

$$u_s(t) = -B_1'K_1\Psi_1(t, t_j)\hat{x}_s(t_j), \quad t \in [t_j, t_{j+1}), \quad j \in \theta, \quad (44)$$

$$-\dot{K}_1 = A_1'K_1 + K_1A_1 + Q_1 - K_1B_1B_1'K_1, \quad K_1(T) = \Gamma, \quad (45)$$

[†] *A more general formulation would include cross terms involving slow and fast variables. Here we are avoiding this in order not to obscure the essentials of the following analysis by notational complexity. We should note, though, that such a restriction leads to no conceptual loss of generality.*

$$\dot{\Psi}_1(t, t_j) = \left(A_1 - B_1B_1'K_1\right)\Psi_1(t, t_j), \quad \Psi_1(t_j, t_j) = I,$$
$$t \in [t_j, t_{j+1}), \quad j \in \theta, \tag{46}$$

$$\dot{\hat{x}}_s(t) = A_1\hat{x}_s(t) + B_1u_s(t), \quad \hat{x}_s(0) = E[x(0)],$$
$$t \in [t_{j-1}, t_j), \quad j = 1, 2, \ldots, N,$$
$$\hat{x}_s(t_j) = \hat{x}_s\left(t_j^-\right) + S_1(j)\Big[y(j) - C_1\hat{x}_s\left(t_j^-\right)$$
$$+ C_2A_2^{-1}B_2u_s\left(t_j^-\right)\Big], \tag{47}$$

$$\dot{\Sigma}_s = A_1\Sigma_s + \Sigma_sA_1' + G_1G_1', \quad \Sigma_s(0) = \mathrm{Cov}[x(0)],$$
$$t \in [t_{j-1}, t_j), \quad j = 1, 2, \ldots, N, \tag{48}$$
$$\Sigma_s(t_j) = \Sigma_s\left(t_j^-\right) - S_1(j)C_1\Sigma_s\left(t_j^-\right),$$

$$S_1(j) = \Sigma_s\left(t_j^-\right)C_1'\left[C_1\Sigma_s\left(t_j^-\right)C_1' + C_2\Sigma_fC_2' + R_j\right]^{-1}, \tag{49}$$

$$A_2\Sigma_f + \Sigma_fA_2' + G_2G_2' = 0, \tag{50}$$

$$u_f(t) = -B_2'K_2\Psi_2(t, t_j)\hat{z}_f(t_j),$$
$$t \in [t_j, t_{j+1}), \quad j \in \theta, \tag{51}$$

$$A_2'K_2 + K_2A_2 + Q_2 - K_2B_2B_2'K_2 = 0, \tag{52}$$

$$\epsilon\dot{\Psi}_2(t, t_j) = \left(A_2 - B_2B_2'K_2\right)\Psi_2(t, t_j), \quad \Psi_2(t_j, t_j) = I,$$
$$t \in [t_j, t_{j+1}), \quad j \in \theta, \tag{53}$$

$$\epsilon\dot{\hat{z}}_f(t) = A_2\hat{z}_f(t) + B_2u_f(t), \quad \hat{z}_f(0) = E[z(0)],$$
$$t \in [t_{j-1}, t_j), \quad j = 1, 2, \ldots, N, \tag{54}$$

$$\hat{z}_f(t_j) = \hat{z}_f\left(t_j^-\right) + S_2(j)\Big[y(j) - C_1\hat{x}_s\left(t_j^-\right) - C_2\hat{z}_f\left(t_j^-\right) + C_2A_2^{-1}B_2u_s\left(t_j^-\right)\Big], \tag{55}$$

$$S_2(j) = \Sigma_f C_2'\left[C_1\Sigma_s\left(t_j^-\right)C_1' + C_2\Sigma_f C_2' + R_j\right]^{-1}.$$

If u^* is the optimal solution to the problem (40)-(42), then it can be shown that

$$\lim_{\epsilon\to 0} u^* = u_0, \quad 0 < t < T,$$
$$\lim_{\epsilon\to 0}\left(J(u^*) - J(u_0)\right) = 0. \tag{56}$$

Case 2. Sampled Values of Continuous Noisy Measurements. The measurement process is a continuous-time stochastic process described by

$$\bar{y}(t) = \int_0^t [C_1x(s) + C_2z(s)]\, ds + q(t) \tag{57}$$

where $q(t)$ is a standard Wiener process independent of $w(t)$ and the Gaussian vector $[x(0), z(0)]$.

Let $0 = t_0 < t_1 < \cdots < t_{N-1} < t_N = T$ and $\theta = \{0, 1, \ldots, N - 1\}$. The measurement process is not observed on the entire time interval $[0, T]$, but only its sampled values at time instants $t_1, t_2, \ldots, t_N$ are observed. Therefore, the only observation in the subinterval $[t_j, t_{j+1})$ is

$$\bar{y}(t_j) = \int_0^{t_j} [C_1x(s) + C_2z(s)]\, ds + q(t_j), \tag{58}$$

which is made at the beginning of that subinterval. In the time interval $[0, t_1)$, no observations are made and only the prior statistics of the random quantities are available.

Let

$$y(j) = \bar{y}(t_j) - \bar{y}(t_{j-1})$$

$$= \int_{t_{j-1}}^{t_j} [C_1 x(s) + C_2 z(s)]\, ds + v(j) \tag{59}$$

where $v(j) = q(t_j) - q(t_{j-1})$ is a discrete-time Gaussian white noise process with mean zero and variance $R_j = (t_j - t_{j-1})I$. Clearly the sigma-algebras generated by $\{\bar{y}(t_i),\ i = 1, 2, \ldots, j\}$ and $\{y(i),\ i = 1, 2, \ldots, j\}$ are equivalent.

A near-optimal solution to the problem defined by (40), (41), (59) can be obtained as

$$u_0 = u_s + u_f \tag{60}$$

where

$$u_s(t) = -B_1' K_1 \Psi_1(t, t_j)\hat{x}_s(t_j), \qquad t \in [t_j, t_{j+1}),\quad j \in \theta, \tag{61}$$

$$-\dot{K}_1 = A_1' K_1 + K_1 A_1 + Q_1 - K_1 B_1 B_1' K_1, \qquad K_1(T) = \Gamma_1, \tag{62}$$

$$\dot{\Psi}_1(t, t_j) = \left(A_1 - B_1 B_1' K_1\right)\Psi_1(t, t_j), \quad \Psi_1(t_j, t_j) = I, \qquad t \in [t_j, t_{j+1}),\quad j \in \theta, \tag{63}$$

$$\dot{\hat{x}}_s(t) = A_1 \hat{x}_s(t) + B_1 u_s(t), \quad \hat{x}_s(0) = E[x(0)], \qquad t \in [t_{j-1}, t_j),\quad j = 1, 2, \ldots, N, \tag{64}$$

$$\hat{x}_s(t_j) = \hat{x}_s\left(t_j^-\right) + S_1(j) \times \left[y(j) - \int_{t_{j-1}}^{t_j} \left[C_1 \hat{x}_s(r) - C_2 A_2^{-1} B_2 u_s(r)\right] dr\right],$$

$$\dot{\Sigma}_s = A_1\Sigma_s + \Sigma_s A_1' + G_1G_1', \quad \Sigma_s(0) = \text{Cov}[x(0)],$$

$$t \in [t_{j-1}, t_j), \quad j = 1, 2, \ldots, N,$$

$$\begin{aligned}\Sigma_s(t_j) = \Sigma_s\left(t_j^-\right) - S_1(j) &\times \Bigg[\int_{t_{j-1}}^{t_j} C_1\phi_s(r, t_{j-1})\, dr \\ &\times \Sigma_s(t_{j-1})\phi_s'(t_j, t_{j-1}) \\ &+ \int_{t_{j-1}}^{t_j} C_1 \int_r^{t_j} \phi_s(r, p)G_1G_1'\phi_s'(t_j, p)\, dp\, dr\Bigg],\end{aligned} \tag{65}$$

$$\begin{aligned}\hat{R}_j = &\int_{t_{j-1}}^{t_j} C_1\phi_s(p, t_{j-1})\, dp\, \Sigma_s(t_{j-1}) \int_{t_{j-1}}^{t_j} \phi_s(r, t_{j-1})C_1'\, dr \\ &+ \int_{t_{j-1}}^{t_j} C_1 \int_{t_{j-1}}^{p} \phi_s(p, r)G_1G_1' \int_r^{t_j} \phi_s'(l, r)C_1'\, dl\, dr\, dp \\ &+ \int_{t_{j-1}}^{t_j} C_2\phi_f(p, t_{j-1})\, dp\, \Sigma_f \int_{t_{j-1}}^{t_j} \phi_f'(r, t_{j-1})C_2'\, dr \\ &+ \int_{t_{j-1}}^{t_j} C_2 \int_{t_{j-1}}^{p} \phi_f(p, r)G_2G_2' \\ &\times \int_r^{t_j} \phi_f(l, r)C_2'\, dl\, dr\, dp + R_j,\end{aligned} \tag{66}$$

$$\begin{aligned}S_1(j) = &\Bigg[\phi_s(t_j, t_{j-1})\Sigma_s(t_{j-1}) \int_{t_{j-1}}^{t_j} \phi_s'(r, t_{j-1})C_1'\, dr \\ &+ \int_{t_{j-1}}^{t_j} \phi_s(t_j, p)G_1G_1' \int_p^{t_j} \phi_s'(r, p)C_1'\, dr\, dp\Bigg]\hat{R}_j^{-1},\end{aligned} \tag{67}$$

$$\dot{\phi}_s(t, t_j) = A_1\phi_s(t, t_j), \quad \phi_s(t_j, t_j) = I,$$
$$t \in [t_j, t_{j+1}), \quad j \in \theta, \tag{68}$$

$$\epsilon\phi_f(t, t_j) = A_2\phi_f(t, t_j), \quad \phi_f(t_j, t_j) = I,$$
$$t \in [t_j, t_{j+1}), \quad j \in \theta, \tag{69}$$

$$A_2\Sigma_f + \Sigma_f A_2' + G_2G_2' = 0, \tag{70}$$

$$u_f(t) = -B_2'K_2\Psi_2(t, t_j)\hat{z}_f(t_j),$$
$$t \in [t_j, t_{j+1}), \quad j \in \theta, \tag{71}$$

$$A_2'K_2 + K_2A_2 + Q_2 - K_2B_2B_2'K_2 = 0, \tag{72}$$

$$\epsilon\dot{\Psi}_2(t, t_j) = \left(A_2 - B_2B_2'K_2\right)\Psi_2(t, t_j), \quad \Psi_2(t_j, t_j) = I,$$
$$t \in [t_j, t_{j+1}), \quad j \in \theta, \tag{73}$$

$$\epsilon\dot{\hat{z}}_f(t) = A_2\hat{z}_f(t) + B_2u_f(t), \quad \hat{z}_f(0) = E[z(0)],$$
$$t \in [t_{j-1}, t_j), \quad j = 1, 2, \ldots, N,$$
$$\hat{z}_f(t_j) = \hat{z}_f\left(t_j^-\right) + S_2(j)$$
$$\times \left[y(j) - \int_{t_{j-1}}^{t_j} \left[C_1\hat{x}_s(r) + C_2\hat{z}_f(r) - C_2A_2^{-1}B_2u_s(r)\right] dr\right], \tag{74}$$

$$S_2(j) = \left[\phi_f(t_j, t_{j-1})\Sigma_f \int_{t_{j-1}}^{t_j} \phi_f'(r, t_{j-1})C_2' \, dr + \int_{t_{j-1}}^{t_j} \phi_f(t_j, p)G_2G_2' \int_p^{t_j} \phi_f'(r, p)C_2' \, dr \, dp\right]\hat{R}_j^{-1}. \tag{75}$$

If u^* is the optimal solution to the problem defined by (40), (41), (59), then it can be shown that

$$\lim_{\epsilon \to 0} u^* = u_0, \quad 0 < t < T,$$
$$\lim_{\epsilon \to 0}\left(J(u^*) - J(u_0)\right) = 0. \tag{76}$$

We should point out that the near-optimality of the composite control u_0 in both Cases 1 and 2 is valid only in the open interval (0, T) because the boundary layer terms have been neglected.

An important distinction between the above formulations involving discrete observations and the earlier formulation involving continuous observations is that, in the discrete observations cases, there is no need to scale the measurement noise and it is not necessary to have a separate observation channel for the fast variables. This is because the sampling interval is fixed and independent of ϵ, and hence there is no interaction between the dynamics of the observation process and the input noise process.

Now that we understand the subtleties involved in the modeling and control of stochastic singularly perturbed systems under various observation patterns, the next step is to study multiagent decision problems. But before we do this, we shall introduce, in the next section, the important concept of multimodeling of large-scale systems within the framework of time scales and singular perturbations. This concept plays a crucial role in the near-optimal design of multiagent decision policies for stochastic singularly perturbed systems.

III. MULTIMODELING BY SINGULAR PERTURBATIONS

The need for model simplification with a reduction (or distribution) of computational effort is particularly acute for large-scale systems involving hundreds or thousands of state variables, often at different geographical locations. Some form of decentralized modeling and control which exploits the weak interactions between subsystems is then required. While there are a number of approaches to the study of large-scale systems [1], the success of any proposed decentralized scheme critically depends upon the choice of subsystems [11].

A fundamental relationship between time scales and weak coupling has been developed for power systems, Markov chains, and other classes of large-scale networks [12-15]. If the interactions of N "local" subsystems are treated as $O(\epsilon)$, and if each subsystem has an equilibrium manifold (null space), then the local subsystems are decoupled in the fast time scale. However, they strongly interact in a slow time scale and form an aggregate model whose dimension is equal to the number (N) of the local subsystems. The system is thus decomposed into N + 1 subsystems (N in the fast and one in the slow time scale).

To elucidate this relationship, consider the following class of interconnected subsystems:

$$\frac{d\overline{x}_i}{dt} = \frac{1}{\epsilon_i} A_{ii}\overline{x}_i + \sum_{\substack{j=1 \\ j\neq i}}^{N} A_{ij}\overline{x}_j, \quad i = 1, 2, \ldots, N, \tag{77}$$

where $\epsilon_i > 0$ and A_{ii} is a stable matrix with one zero eigenvalue. Assuming that $\overline{x}_i(0)$ is not in the null space of A_{ii}, the first term dominates the second term on the right-hand side of (1), and therefore the interconnections can be neglected initially. As the fast transients draw $\bar{x}_i(t)$ toward the equilibrium manifold (the null space of A_{ii}), the two terms on the right-hand side of (77) become the same order of magnitude, and therefore from this time onward the interconnections can no longer be neglected. Hence, the dynamic behavior of (77) can be characterized by two separate motions: an initial fast transient within each isolated subsystem, followed by a slow motion around the equilibrium manifold obtained on neglecting the interconnections. Therefore, in the short term the subsystems can be treated in isolation, while in the longer term they become strongly coupled.

We now introduce a transformation to make the slow and fast parts of $\bar{x}_i(t)$ explicit. Let

$$\frac{d}{dt}\begin{bmatrix}\bar{x}_1\\ \bar{x}_2\\ \vdots\\ \bar{x}_N\end{bmatrix} = \begin{bmatrix}\epsilon_1 & & & 0\\ & \epsilon_2 & & \\ 0 & & \ddots & \\ & & & \epsilon_N\end{bmatrix}^{-1}\begin{bmatrix}A_{11} & & & 0\\ & A_{22} & & \\ 0 & & \ddots & \\ & & & A_{NN}\end{bmatrix}\begin{bmatrix}\bar{x}_1\\ \bar{x}_2\\ \vdots\\ \bar{x}_N\end{bmatrix}$$

$$+\begin{bmatrix}0 & A_{12} & \cdots & A_{1N}\\ A_{21} & 0 & \cdots & A_{2N}\\ \vdots & \vdots & \ddots & \vdots\\ A_{N1} & A_{N2} & \cdots & 0\end{bmatrix}\begin{bmatrix}\bar{x}_1\\ \bar{x}_2\\ \vdots\\ \bar{x}_N\end{bmatrix} \tag{78}$$

or

$$\dot{\bar{x}} = \left(\Omega^{-1}A_0 + A_1\right)\bar{x}. \tag{79}$$

Define the left and right eigenvectors of A_0 for the zero eigenvalue as

$$A_0T = 0, \quad VA_0 = 0, \quad VT = I_N$$

where

$$A_{ii}t_i = 0, \quad v_iA_{ii} = 0, \quad v_it_i = 1, \quad i = 1, 2, \ldots, N,$$
$$T = \text{block diag}[t_1, t_2, \ldots, t_N],$$
$$V = \text{block diag}[v_1, v_2, \ldots, v_N]. \tag{80}$$

We also define block-diagonal matrices W and S as

$$WT = 0, \quad VS = 0, \quad WS = I_{n-N}. \tag{81}$$

Now, using the transformation

$$x = V\overline{x}, \quad x \in R^N; \quad z = W\overline{x}, \quad z \in R^{n-N} \tag{82a}$$

and its inverse

$$\overline{x} = Tx + Sz, \tag{82b}$$

the interconnected system (79) can be transformed into

$$\begin{aligned} \dot{x} &= VA_1Tx + VA_1Sz, \\ \Omega\dot{z} &= \Omega WA_1Tx + W(A_0 + \Omega A_1)Sz. \end{aligned} \tag{83}$$

For sufficiently small ϵ_i, (83) can be approximated by the model

$$\dot{x} = VA_1Tx + \sum_{j=1}^{N} \hat{A}_jz_j,$$
$$\epsilon_i\dot{z}_i = w_iA_{ii}s_iz_i, \quad i = 1, 2, \ldots, N, \tag{84}$$

where

$$\hat{A}_j = \begin{bmatrix} v_1A_{1j} \\ v_2A_{2j} \\ \vdots \\ v_NA_{Nj} \end{bmatrix} s_j.$$

Notice that the fast transients within the subsystems are decoupled, and they interact only through the slow core. A long-term aggregate model is obtained by letting $\epsilon_i \to 0$, and is given by

$$\dot{x}_s = VA_1Tx_s. \tag{85}$$

The previous analysis has shown that for a wide class of large-scale systems, the notions of subsystems, their coupling and time scales are interrelated and lead to a multiparameter singularly perturbed model with a strongly coupled slow "core" representing the long-term system-wide behavior, and weakly coupled fast subsystems representing the short-term local behavior.

With the presence of control and stochastic disturbance inputs, a generalization of (84) can be obtained as

$$dx = A_{00}x\ dt + \sum_{j=1}^{N} (A_{0j}z_j\ dt + B_{0j}u_j\ dt + G_{0i}\ dw_i), \tag{86a}$$

$$\epsilon_i\ dz_i = \left(A_{i0}x + A_{ii}z_i + \sum_{\substack{j=1 \\ j\neq i}}^{N} \epsilon_{ij}A_{ij}z_j + B_{ii}u_i\right) dt + \sqrt{\epsilon_i}G_{ii}\ dw_i, \quad i = 1, 2, \ldots, N, \tag{86b}$$

where $\{u_i(t),\ i = 1, 2, \ldots, N\}$ are the control inputs, and $\{w_i(t),\ i = 1, 2, \ldots, N\}$ are standard Wiener processes independent of each other. Each fast subsystem has its own singular perturbation parameter ϵ_i, and is weakly coupled to other fast subsystems through ϵ_{ij}. The fast subsystem i is affected by its own control input $u_i(t)$ and disturbance input $w_i(t)$. The slow subsystem, being the common "core," is affected, in general, by all the subsystem controls and disturbances.

In a situation like this, it is rational for a subsystem controller to neglect all other fast subsystems and to concentrate on its own subsystem, plus, of course, the slow interaction with others through the "core." For the i-th controller "to neglect all other subsystems" simply means to set all

ϵ parameters equal to zero, except for ϵ_i, which is to be kept at its true value. The i-th controller's simplified model is then

$$dx^i = A_i x^i \, dt + A_{0i} z_i \, dt + B_{0i} u_i \, dt + \sum_{\substack{j=1 \\ j \neq i}}^{N} (B_{ij} u_j \, dt + G_{0i} \, dw_i), \tag{87a}$$

$$\epsilon_i \, dz_i = A_{i0} x^i \, dt + A_{ii} z_i \, dt + B_{ii} u_i \, dt + \sqrt{\epsilon_i} G_{ii} \, dw_i \tag{87b}$$

where

$$A_i = A_{00} - \sum_{j \neq i} A_{0j} A_{jj}^{-1} A_{j0}, \quad B_{ij} = B_{0j} - A_{0j} A_{jj}^{-1} B_{jj}.$$

We denote x^i with a superscript rather than a subscript to stress the fact that x^i is not a component of x, but the i-th controller's view of x. In reality, the model (87) is often all that i-th controller knows about the whole system. The k-th controller, on the other hand, has a different model of the same large-scale system. This situation, called multimodeling, was first formulated and investigated in [2] in a deterministic setup (with no disturbance inputs).

In the next section we shall study the impact of multimodel assumptions on the design of multiagent control strategies in the presence of disturbance inputs and noisy observations.

IV. MULTIAGENT DECISION PROBLEMS

We shall restrict our discussion in this section to the case of two decision makers, as this will keep the notation simple and ease the exposition of the principle ideas. All the results that we shall present here extend to the case of more than two agents in a fairly straightforward fashion. Furthermore, we shall present and discuss only the main results; the proofs of the various propositions shall be omitted, but they can be found in the references cited.

It is well known that a system of the form (86) can be transformed into a system with purely slow and fast variables [2]. Hence, without loss of generality, we shall consider multiparameter singularly perturbed systems of the form

$$dz_0 = A_{00}z_0 \, dt + \sum_{j=1}^{2} (B_{0j}u_j \, dt + G_{0i} \, dw_i), \tag{88a}$$

$$\epsilon_i \, dz_i = (A_{ii}z_i + \epsilon_{ij}A_{ij}z_j + B_{ii}u_i) \, dt + \sqrt{\epsilon_i}G_{ii} \, dw_i, \quad i, j = 1, 2, \quad i \neq j \tag{88b}$$

with $\dim z_i = n_i$, $i = 0, 1, 2$, and $\dim u_i = m_i$, $i = 1, 2$. The initial conditions are assumed to be Gaussian with

$$E[z_i(0) = \bar{z}_{i0}, \quad E\left[z_i(0)z_j'(0)\right] = N_{ij}, \quad i, j = 0, 1, 2. \tag{89}$$

Furthermore, we shall restrict ourselves to the case $\{\mathrm{Re}\,\lambda(A_{ii}) < 0,\ i = 1, 2\}$.

In a multimodel situation, decision maker i models only z_0 and z_i, but neglects z_j. Also, his observations are functions of z_0 and z_i alone. This situation with decentralized observations leads to problems involving nonclassical information patterns, for which no finite-dimensional solution exists in general. In order to obtain finite-dimensional solutions which can be implemented in practice, one needs to modify the information structure. In this section we shall study three problems with quasi-classical information patterns. The first problem is a Nash problem with continuous measurements, where the information available to the decision makers is restricted to the state of a finite-dimensional compensator of a specified structure. The next two problems are team problems with sampled measurements, where the decision makers exchange information with a delay of one sample period. The two types of sampled measurements are those that we have considered in Section II.

A. *NASH GAME WITH CONTINUOUS MEASUREMENTS*

The decision makers make decentralized continuous measurements which are given by

$$dy_{0i} = C_{0i}z_0 \, dt + dv_{0i},$$

$$dy_{ii} = C_{ii}z_i \, dt + \sqrt{\epsilon_i} \, dv_{ii}, \quad i = 1, 2, \tag{90}$$

where dim $y_{0i} = p_{0i}$ and dim $y_{ii} = p_{ii}$. The processes $v_{0i}(t)$ and $v_{ii}(t)$ are standard Wiener processes, independent of each other and of the process noise $w_i(t)$. Defining $x' = [z_0' \; z_1' \; z_2']$, $y_i' = [y_{0i}' \; 1/\sqrt{\epsilon_i} \; y_{ii}']$, $v_i' = [v_{0i}' \; v_{ii}']$, and $w' = [w_1' \; w_2']$. The system of equations (88)-(90) can be written in a composite form as

$$dx = \left(A(\epsilon)x + \sum_{i=1}^{2} B_i(\epsilon)u_i \right) dt + G(\epsilon) \, dw, \tag{91}$$

$$dy_i = C_i(\epsilon)x \, dt + dv_i, \quad i = 1, 2, \tag{92}$$

$$E[x(0)] = \bar{x}_0, \quad E[x(0)x'(0)] = N \tag{93}$$

where dim $x = n = n_0 + n_1 + n_2$ and dim $y_i = p_i = p_{0i} + p_{ii}$. The matrices $A(\epsilon)$, $B_i(\epsilon)$, $G(\epsilon)$, $C_i(\epsilon)$, and N are appropriately defined.

The information available to decision maker i at time t is given by

$$\alpha_i(t) = \left\{\hat{x}_i(t),\ \bar{x}_0,\ N\right\} \tag{94}$$

where $\hat{x}_i(t)$ is the state of the n-dimensional compensator

$$d\hat{x}_i = \left(F_i\hat{x}_i + H_iu_i\right) dt + L_i\left[dy_i - C_i\hat{x}_i\ dt\right]. \tag{95}$$

Let $\sigma_i(t)$ denote the sigma-algebra generated by the information set $\alpha_i(t)$. Further, let H_i denote the class of second-order stochastic processes $\{u_i(t),\ t \geq 0\}$ which are $\sigma_i(t)$-measurable. Then, a permissible strategy for decision maker i is a mapping ν_i: $[0, T] \times \mathbb{R}^n \to \mathbb{R}^{m_i}$, such that $\nu_i(\cdot, \alpha_i) \in H_i$. Denote the class of all such strategies for decision maker i by Γ_i.

For each $\{\nu_i \in \Gamma_i,\ i = 1, 2\}$, the cost functionals for the two decision makers are given by

$$\begin{aligned} J_i(\nu_1, \nu_2) &= E\left\{z_0'(T)\Gamma_{0i}z_0(T) + \epsilon_i z_i'(T)\Gamma_{ii}z_i(T)\right. \\ &\quad + \int_0^T \left(z_0'Q_{0i}z_0 + z_i'Q_{ii}z_i + u_i'u_i\right) dt \,|\, u_j(t) \\ &\quad \left. = \nu_j(t, \alpha_j),\quad j = 1, 2\right\},\quad i = 1, 2 \end{aligned} \tag{96a}$$

or, equivalently

$$\begin{aligned} J_i(\nu_1, \nu_2) &= E\left\{x'(T)\Gamma_i(\epsilon)x(T)\right. \\ &\quad + \int_0^T \left(x'Q_ix + u_i'u_i\right) dt \,|\, u_j(t) \\ &\quad \left. = \nu_j(t, \alpha_j),\quad j = 1, 2\right\},\quad i = 1, 2 \end{aligned} \tag{96b}$$

where the expectation is taken over the underlying statistics.

The decision makers are required to select the matrices F_i^*, H_i^*, L_i^*; the initial conditions $\hat{x}_i^*(0)$ and strategies

$\nu_i^*[t, x_i(t)]$ such that

$$J_i\left(\nu_i^*, \nu_j^*\right) \leq J_i\left(\nu_i, \nu_j^*\right) \quad \forall \nu_i \in \Gamma_i,$$
$$i, j = 1, 2, \quad i \neq j. \tag{97}$$

The pair of inequalities above defines the *Nash equilibrium point*.

The optimal solution to the problem defined by (88)-(97) is obtained by extending the results of [16] to the nonzero-sum case, and is given by

$$\nu_i^* = -B_i'K_i\hat{x}_i, \quad i = 1, 2, \tag{98a}$$

$$F_i^* = A - B_jB_j'K_j\left[I + (M_{j0} - M_{ji})(M_{00} - M_{0i})^{-1}\right],$$
$$i, j = 1, 2, \quad i \neq j, \tag{98b}$$

$$L_i^* = M_{ii}C_i', \quad i = 1, 2, \tag{98c}$$

$$H_i^* = B_i, \quad i = 1, 2, \tag{98d}$$

$$\hat{x}_i^*(0) = \bar{x}_0, \quad i = 1, 2, \tag{98e}$$

where K_i satisfies the coupled set of Riccati equations

$$\dot{K}_i = -K_iA - A'K_i - Q_i + K_iS_iK_i + K_iS_jK_j$$
$$+ K_jS_jK_i, \quad K_i(T) = \Gamma_i, \quad S_i = B_iB_i',$$
$$i, j = 1, 2, \quad i \neq j. \tag{99}$$

$M(t)$ is a symmetric nonnegative definite matrix satisfying the Lyapunov equation

$$\dot{M} = FM + FM' + BB', \quad M_{ij}(0) = \begin{cases} \bar{x}_0\bar{x}_0' + N, & i = j = 0, \\ N, & \text{otherwise}, \end{cases} \tag{100a}$$

where

$$F = \begin{bmatrix} A - S_1K_1 - S_2K_2 & S_1K_1 & S_2K_2 \\ A - F_1^* - S_2K_2 & F_1^* - L_1^*C_1 & S_2K_2 \\ A - F_2^* - S_1K_1 & S_1K_1 & F_2^* - L_2^*C_2 \end{bmatrix} \tag{100b}$$

$$B = \begin{bmatrix} -G & 0 & 0 \\ -G & L_1^* & 0 \\ -G & 0 & L_2^* \end{bmatrix}.$$

The compensators are unbiased, in the sense that for all $t \in [0, T)$,

$$E\left\{x(t) \,|\, \hat{x}_i(t)\right\} = \hat{x}_i(t), \qquad i = 1, 2. \tag{101}$$

Furthermore

$$E\left\{\left[x(t) - \hat{x}_i(t)\right]\hat{x}_i'(t)\right\} = 0, \qquad i = 1, 2. \tag{102}$$

Thus, each component of the error $x(t) - \hat{x}_i(t)$ is orthogonal to each component of $\hat{x}_i(t)$, and $\hat{x}_i(t)$ may be regarded in some sense an estimate of $x(t)$. Notice that the solution exhibits a unidirectional separation in estimation and control. Although the control gains are obtained independently, the optimal filter matrices and covariance $M(t)$ depend on the control gains, resulting in a "dual effect" [17].

The optimal costs are given by

$$J_i^* = \overline{x}_0'K_i(0)\overline{x}_0 + \mathrm{tr}\left\{M_{ii}(0)K_i(0) + \int_0^T (K_iS_iK_iM_{ii} + K_iS_jK_jM_{j0} + K_jS_jK_iM_{0j})\, dt\right\},$$

$$i, j = 1, 2, \quad i \neq j. \tag{103}$$

The linear strategy (98a) is the unique Nash strategy for this problem. Since the finite-dimensional estimators (95) are not Kalman filters, it is not clear, at the outset, what their limiting structure (as the small parameters go to zero) looks like. Does the full-order estimator decompose into a number of decoupled low-order estimators? Is it possible to obtain a near-equilibrium solution from low-order subproblems?

It will be shown that, in the limit as the small parameters go to zero, the full-order estimator (95) decomposes into an n_0-dimensional estimator in the slow time scale which has a similar structure, and two n_1- and n_2-dimensional Kalman filters in the fast time scale. Furthermore, the near-equilibrium solution is in fact the multimodel solution, i.e., the solution obtained when decision maker i neglects z_j, and models only z_0 and z_i. The multimodel assumption leads to the formulation of three low-order subproblems: two independent stochastic control problems, one for each decision maker, in the fast time scale, and a stochastic Nash game in the slow time scale.

The slow subproblem is obtained by neglecting all the small parameters in (88), and is given by

$$dz_{0s} = \left(A_{00} z_{0s} + \sum_{i=1}^{2} B_{0i} u_{is} \right) dt + \sum_{i=1}^{2} G_{0i}\, dw_i, \qquad (104)$$

$$dy_{is} = \begin{bmatrix} C_{0i} \\ 0 \end{bmatrix} z_{0s}\, dt + \begin{bmatrix} 0 \\ -(1/\sqrt{\epsilon_i}) C_{ii} A_{ii}^{-1} B_{ii} \end{bmatrix} u_{is}\, dt + \begin{bmatrix} dv_{0i} \\ dv_{ii} - C_{ii} A_{ii}^{-1} G_{ii}\, dw_i \end{bmatrix}$$

$$= (C_{is} z_{0s} + D_{is} u_{is})\, dt + dv_{is}, \qquad i = 1, 2, \quad (105)$$

$$E[z_{0s}(0)] = \bar{z}_{00}, \quad E\left[z_{0s}(0) z_{0s}'(0)\right] = N_{00}. \qquad (106)$$

Each decision maker is constrained to use only an n_0-dimensional compensator of the form

$$d\hat{z}_{is} = \left(F_{is}\hat{z}_{is} + H_{is}u_{is}\right) dt + L_{is}\left[dy_{is} - C_{is}\hat{z}_{is}\, dt - D_{is}u_{is}\, dt\right], \quad i = 1, 2. \tag{107}$$

Let

$$\alpha_{is}(t) = \left\{\hat{z}_{is}(t), \bar{z}_{00}, N_{00}\right\} \tag{108}$$

and $\sigma_{is}(t)$ denote the sigma-algebra generated by the information set $\alpha_{is}(t)$. Further, let H_{is} denote the class of second-order stochastic processes $\{u_{is}(t), t \geq 0\}$ which are $\sigma_{is}(t)$-measurable. Define the slow strategy ν_{is} as the mapping $\nu_{is}: [0, T] \times \mathbb{R}^{n_0} \to \mathbb{R}^{m_i}$, such that $\nu_{is}(\cdot, \alpha_{is}) \in H_{is}$. Denote the class of all such slow strategies for decision maker i by Γ_{is}.

For each $\{\nu_{is} \in \Gamma_{is}, i = 1, 2\}$, the slow cost functionals for the decision makers are given by

$$J_{is}(\nu_{1s}, \nu_{2s}) = E\left\{z'_{0s}(T)\Gamma_{0i}z_{0s}(T) + \int_0^T \left(z'_{0s}Q_{0i}z_{0s} + u'_{is}R_{is}u_{is}\right) dt \,\middle|\, u_{js}(t) = \nu_j(t, \alpha_{js}), \quad j = 1, 2\right\}, \quad i = 1, 2, \tag{109}$$

where

$$R_{is} = I + \left(A_{ii}^{-1}B_{ii}\right)'Q_i\left(A_{ii}^{-1}B_{ii}\right).$$

The decision makers are required to select the matrices F^*_{is}, H^*_{is}, L^*_{is}, the initial conditions $\hat{z}^*_{is}(0)$, and strategies $\nu^*_{is}\left[t, z_{is}(t)\right]$ such that

$$J_i\left(\nu^*_{is}, \nu^*_{js}\right) \leq J_i\left(\nu_{is}, \nu^*_{js}\right) \quad \forall \nu_{is} \in \Gamma_{is}, \quad i, j = 1, 2, \quad i \neq j. \tag{110}$$

The optimal solution to the slow subproblem defined by (104)-(110) is given by

$$\nu_{is}^{*} = -R_{is}^{-1}B_{0i}'K_{is}\hat{z}_{is}, \quad i = 1, 2, \tag{111a}$$

$$\begin{aligned} F_{is}^{*} &= A_{00} - B_{0j}R_{js}^{-1}B_{0j}'K_{js} \\ &\quad \times \left[I + \left(\overline{M}_{j0} - \overline{M}_{ji}\right)\left(\overline{M}_{00} - \overline{M}_{0i}\right)^{-1}\right], \\ &\qquad i, j = 1, 2, \quad i \neq j, \end{aligned} \tag{111b}$$

$$\begin{aligned} L_{is}^{*} &= \left[\overline{M}_{ii}C_{0i}' \;\middle|\; G_{0i}\left(C_{ii}A_{ii}^{-1}G_{ii}\right)' \right. \\ &\quad \left. \times \left\{I + \left(C_{ii}A_{ii}^{-1}G_{ii}\right)\left(C_{ii}A_{ii}^{-1}G_{ii}\right)'\right\}^{-1}\right], \\ &\qquad i = 1, 2, \end{aligned} \tag{111c}$$

$$H_{is}^{*} = B_{0i}, \quad i = 1, 2, \tag{111d}$$

$$\hat{z}_{is}^{*}(0) = \overline{z}_{00}, \quad i = 1, 2, \tag{111e}$$

where K_{is} is the solution of the coupled set of Riccati equations

$$\begin{aligned} \dot{K}_{is} &= -K_{is}A_{00} - A_{00}'K_{is} - Q_{0i} \\ &\quad + K_{is}S_{is}K_{is} + K_{is}S_{js}K_{js} + K_{js}S_{js}K_{is}, \end{aligned} \tag{112}$$

$$K_{is}(T) = \Gamma_{0i}, \quad S_{is} = B_{0i}R_{is}^{-1}B_{0i}', \quad i, j = 1, 2, \quad i \neq j.$$

$\overline{M}(t)$ is a symmetric nonnegative definite matrix satisfying the Lyapunov equation

$$\dot{\overline{M}} = F_s\overline{M} + \overline{M}F_s' + B_sB_s', \quad \overline{M}_{ij}(0) = \begin{cases} \overline{z}_{00}\overline{z}_{00}' + N_{00}, & i = j = 0, \\ N_{00}, & \text{otherwise}, \end{cases} \tag{113a}$$

where

$$F_s = \begin{bmatrix} A_{00} - S_{1s}K_{1s} - S_{2s}K_{2s} & S_{1s}K_{1s} & S_{2s}L_{2s} \\ A_{00} - F^*_{1s} - S_{2s}K_{2s} & F^*_{1s} - L^*_{1s}C_{1s} & S_{2s}K_{2s} \\ A_{00} - F^*_{2s} - S_{1s}K_{1s} & S_{1s}K_{1s} & F^*_{2s} - L^*_{2s}C_{2s} \end{bmatrix},$$

$$B_s = \begin{bmatrix} -G_0 & 0 & 0 \\ -G_0 - L^*_{1s}P_1 & L^*_{1s} & 0 \\ -G_0 - L^*_{2s}P_2 & 0 & L^*_{2s} \end{bmatrix},$$

$$G_0 = [G_{01} \quad G_{02}],$$

$$P_i = \begin{bmatrix} 0 & 0 \\ C_{ii}A^{-1}G_{ii} & 0 \end{bmatrix}, \quad i = 1, 2. \tag{113b}$$

The optimal costs are given by

$$J^*_{is} = \bar{z}'_{00}K_{is}(0)\bar{z}_{00} + \mathrm{tr}\Big\{\bar{M}_{ii}(0)K_{is}(0) + \int_0^T \Big(K_{is}S_{is}K_{is}\bar{M}_{ii} + K_{is}S_{js}K_{js}\bar{M}_{j0} + K_{js}S_{js}K_{is}\bar{M}_{0j}\Big)\,dt\Big\}, \quad i, j = 1, 2, \quad i \neq j. \tag{114}$$

The fast subproblems, on the other hand, are formulated "locally" at the subsystem level. These are stochastic control problems because the decision makers do not interact in the fast time scale:

$$\epsilon_i\, dz_{if} = (A_{ii}z_{if} + B_{ii}u_{if})\, dt + \sqrt{\epsilon_i}G_{ii}\, dw_i, \tag{115}$$

$$dy_{if} = C_{ii}z_{if}\, dt + \sqrt{\epsilon_i}\, d\nu_{ii}, \tag{116}$$

$$E[z_{if}(0)] = \bar{z}_{i0}, \quad E\big[z_{if}(0) \quad z'_{if}(0)\big] = N_{ii}, \tag{117}$$

$$J_{if} = E\Big\{\epsilon_i z'_{if}(T)\Gamma_{ii}z_{if}(T) + \int_0^T \big(z'_{if}Q_{ii}z_{if} + u'_{if}u_{if}\big)\, dt\Big\}. \tag{118}$$

Notice that this fast subproblem is exactly the one we studied in detail in Section II. Its solution, as $\epsilon_i \to 0$, is given by

$$u_{if}^* = -B_{ii}'K_{if}\hat{z}_{if} \tag{119}$$

where K_{if} satisfies the Riccati equation

$$K_{if}A_{ii} + A_{ii}'K_{if} + Q_{ii} - K_{if}B_{ii}B_{ii}'K_{if} = 0 \tag{120}$$

and $\hat{z}_{if}$ is the state of the Kalman filter

$$\epsilon_i \, d\hat{z}_{if} = \left(A_{ii}\hat{z}_{if} + B_{ii}u_{if}^*\right) dt + P_{if}C_{ii}' \times \left[dy_{if} - C_{ii}\hat{z}_{if}\, dt\right], \quad \hat{z}_{if}(0) = \bar{z}_{i0}, \tag{121}$$

P_{if} is the error covariance of $\hat{z}_{if}$ satisfying

$$P_{if}A_{ii}' + A_{ii}P_{if} + G_{ii}G_{ii}' - P_{if}C_{ii}'C_{ii}P_{if} = 0, \tag{122}$$

and the optimal cost is given by

$$J_{if}^* = T \operatorname{tr}\left\{P_{if}Q_{ii} + C_{ii}P_{if}K_{if}P_{if}C_{ii}'\right\}. \tag{123}$$

The following proposition establishes the connection between the solutions of the slow and fast subproblems and the full-order problem. Its proof may be found in [7].

Proposition 1

(a) $\nu_i^*\left(t, \hat{x}_i(t)\right) = \nu_{is}^*\left(t, \hat{z}_{is}(t)\right) + u_{if}^*\left(\hat{z}_{if}(t)\right) + O(\|\epsilon\|), \quad t \in (0, T),$

(b) $J_i^* = J_{is}^* + J_{if}^* + T \operatorname{tr}\{Q_{ii}W_i\} + O(\|\epsilon\|), \quad i = 1, 2$

where

$$\epsilon = [\epsilon_1 \quad \epsilon_2 \quad \epsilon_{12} \quad \epsilon_{21}]$$

and W_i is the nonnegative definite solution of the Lyapunov equation

$$A_{ii}W_i + W_iA_{ii}' + G_{ii}G_{ii}' = 0, \quad i = 1, 2. \quad \square \tag{124}$$

Since the multimodel strategies need only decentralized "state estimates," each decision maker needs to construct only two filters of dimensions n_0 and n_i, respectively, instead of constructing one filter of dimension $n_0 + n_1 + n_2$ as required by the optimal solution. This would result in lower implementation costs.

B. *TEAM PROBLEMS WITH SAMPLED MEASUREMENTS*

We shall now consider problems wherein the measurement processes of the decision makers are not continuous on the entire time interval [0, T], but consist of sampled values observed at time instants $t_0, t_1, \ldots, t_{N-1}$, where $0 = t_0 < t_1 < \cdots < t_{N-1} < t_N = T$. Let θ denote the index set $\{0, 1, \ldots, N - 1\}$, and $y_i(j)$ denote the p_i-dimensional observations made by decision maker -i at time instant t_j, $j \in \theta$. Thus the only measurement of decision maker -i in the subinterval $[t_j, t_{j+1})$ is $y_i(j)$.

The quasiclassical information pattern that we shall consider here is the so-called "one-step-delay observation sharing pattern," wherein the decision makers exchange their independent sampled observations with a delay of one sampling interval. Hence, the information available to decision maker -i in the time interval $[t_j, t_{j+1})$ is

$$\alpha_i^j = \{y_i(j), \delta_{j-1}\} \tag{125a}$$

where δ_{j-1} denotes the common information available to the decision makers in the same interval, i.e.,

$$\delta_{j-1} = \{y_1(j - 1), y_2(j - 1), \ldots, y_1(0), y_2(0)\}. \tag{125b}$$

Let σ_i^j denote the sigma-algebra generated by the information set α_i^j, and H_i^N denote the class of stochastic processes $\{u_i(t), t \geq 0\}$ whose restriction to the interval $[t_j, t_{j+1})$ is

σ_i^j-measurable for all $j \in \theta$. Then a permissible strategy for decision maker -i is a mapping ν_i: $[0, T] \times \mathbb{R}^{(p_1+p_2)N} \to \mathbb{R}^{m_i}$, such that $\nu_i(\cdot, \alpha_i) \in H_i^N$. Denote the class of all such strategies for decision maker -i by Γ_i^N. For each $\left\{\nu_i \in \Gamma_i^N, i = 1, 2\right\}$, we define the quadratic strictly convex cost function as

$$J(\nu_1, \nu_2) = E\left\{z_0'(T)\Gamma_0 z_0(T) + \sum_{i=1}^{2} \epsilon_i z_i'(T)\Gamma_i z_i'(T) + \int_0^T \left(z_0'Q_0 z_0 + \sum_{i=1}^{2}\left(z_i'Q_i z_i + u_i'u_i\right)\right) dt \,\middle|\, u_j(t) = \nu_j(t, \alpha_j),\quad j = 1, 2\right\} \tag{126a}$$

where $\{\Gamma_i \geq 0, Q_i \geq 0, i = 0, 1, 2\}$, and the expectation operation is taken over the underlying statistics.

Equivalently, in terms of the composite state vector $x(t)$ of (91), the cost function can be written as

$$J(\nu_1, \nu_2) = E\left\{x'(T)\Gamma(\epsilon)x(T) + \int_0^T \left(x'Qx + u_1'u_1 + u_2'u_2\right) dt \,\middle|\, u_j(t) = \nu_j(t, \alpha_j),\quad j = 1, 2\right\} \tag{126b}$$

where $\Gamma(\epsilon)$ and Q are appropriately defined in terms of the matrices appearing in (126a).

A *team optimal solution* is a pair $\left\{\nu_i^* \in \Gamma_i^N, i = 1, 2\right\}$ which satisfies

$$J\left(\nu_1^*, \nu_2^*\right) = \inf_{\Gamma_1^N} \inf_{\Gamma_2^N} J(\nu_1, \nu_2). \tag{127}$$

Here optimal and near-optimal strategies will be obtained for two cases of sampled observations, as delineated below.

Case 1. Noisy Measurements of Sampled Values of State. At sampled time instant t_j, $j \in \theta$, the decision makers observe

$$y_i(j) = C_{i0}z_0(t_j) + C_{ii}z_i(t_j) + v_i(j)$$
$$\equiv C_i x(t_j) + v_i(j), \quad i = 1, 2. \tag{128}$$

The random vectors $\{v_i(j), j \in \theta, i = 1, 2\}$ are assumed to have independent Gaussian statistics $\{v_i(j) \sim N(0, V_{ij}), V_{ij} > 0, j \in \theta, i = 1, 2\}$. Their statistics are also assumed to be independent of the Wiener processes $\{v_i(t), i = 1, 2\}$ and the initial state vector $x(0)$.

The optimal team solution to the problem defined by (91), (93), and (125)-(128) has been derived in [18], and is given by

$$\nu_i^*(t, \alpha_i) = P_i(t)\Big[y_i(j) - C_i\hat{\xi}(j)\Big] - B_i'S(t)\psi(t, t_j)\hat{\xi}(j),$$
$$i = 1, 2, \quad t \in [t_j, t_{j+1}), \quad j \in \theta \tag{129a}$$

where $P_1(t)$, $P_2(t)$ are piecewise continuous functions on $[0, T]$ and satisfy the coupled set of linear integral equations

$$P_i(t) = B_i'S_i(t)\int_{t_j}^{t} \psi_{ij}(t, \tau)B_iB_i'L_{ij}(\tau)\, d\tau - B_i'L_{ij}(t),$$
$$i = 1, 2, \quad t \in [t_j, t_{j+1}), \quad j \in \theta \tag{129b}$$

where

$$L_{ij}(t) = S_i(t)\left[\phi(t, t_j) + \int_{t_j}^{t} \phi(t, \tau)B_kP_k(\tau)\, d\tau\, C_k\right]\Sigma_i(j)$$
$$+ K_{ij}(t), \quad i, k = 1, 2, \quad i \neq k,$$
$$t \in [t_j, t_{j+1}), \quad j \in \theta, \tag{129c}$$

$$\dot{K}_{ij}(t) = -\big(A - B_iB_i'S_i(t)\big)'K_{ij}(t) - S_i(t)B_kP_k(t)C_k\Sigma_{ij},$$
$$i, k = 1, 2, \quad i \neq k, \quad K_{ij}(t_{j+1}) = 0,$$
$$t \in [t_j, t_{j+1}], \quad j \in \theta, \tag{129d}$$

$S(t)$ and $S_i(t)$ satisfy the Riccati equations

$$\dot{S} = -A'S - SA - Q + S\left[B_1B_1' + B_2B_2'\right]S, \quad S(T) = \Gamma, \tag{129e}$$

$$\dot{S}_i = -A'S_i - S_iA - Q + S_iB_iB_i'S_i, \quad S_i(t_j) = S(t_j),$$
$$t \in (t_{j-1}, t_j], \quad i = 1, 2, \quad j = N, \ldots, 1, \tag{129f}$$

$\psi(t, \tau)$ is the state transition matrix satisfying

$$\dot{\psi}(t, \tau) = \left(A - B_1B_1'S - B_2B_2'S\right)\psi(t, \tau),$$
$$\psi(\tau, \tau) = I, \tag{130a}$$

$\psi_{ij}(t, \tau)$ is the state transition matrix satisfying

$$\dot{\psi}_{ij}(t, \tau) = \left(A - B_iB_i'S_i\right)\psi_{ij}(t, \tau), \quad \psi_{ij}(\tau, \tau) = I,$$
$$t \in [t_j, t_{j+1}), \quad i = 1, 2, \quad j \in \theta. \tag{130b}$$

$\phi(t, \tau)$ is the state transition matrix satisfying

$$\dot{\phi}(t, \tau) = A\phi(t, \tau), \quad \phi(\tau, \tau) = I. \tag{130c}$$

$\hat{\xi}(j) = \eta\left(t_j^-\right) = E[x(t_j) | \delta_{j-1}]$ and $\eta(t)$ satisfies

$$\dot{\eta} = A\eta + \sum_{i=1}^{2} B_i\nu_i^*(t, \alpha_i), \quad \eta(0) = \bar{x}_0,$$
$$t \in [t_{j-1}, t_j), \quad j = 1, \ldots, N, \tag{131}$$

$$\eta(t_j) = \eta\left(t_j^-\right) + M(j)\left[y(j) - C\eta\left(t_j^-\right)\right],$$

$$\Sigma_i(j) = \Sigma(t_j)C_i'\left[C_i\Sigma(t_j)C_i' + V_{ij}\right]^{-1},$$
$$i = 1, 2, \quad j \in \theta \tag{132}$$

where $\Sigma\left(t_j^-\right) = E\left[\left(x(t_j) - \eta\left(t_j^-\right)\right)\left(x(t_j) - \eta\left(t_j^-\right)\right)'\right]$ and $\Sigma(t)$ satisfies

$$\dot{\Sigma} = A\Sigma + \Sigma A' + GG', \quad \Sigma(0) = N,$$
$$t \in [t_{j-1}, t_j), \quad j = 1, \ldots, N, \tag{133}$$

$$\Sigma(t_j) = \Sigma\left(t_j^-\right) - M(j)C\Sigma\left(t_j^-\right),$$

and

$$M(j) = \Sigma\left(t_j^-\right)C'\left[C\Sigma\left(t_j^-\right)C' + V_j\right]^{-1}, \tag{134a}$$

$$V_j = \mathrm{diag}(V_{1j}, V_{2j}), \tag{134b}$$

$$y(j) = \left[y_1'(j) \quad y_2'(j)\right]', \tag{134c}$$

$$C = \left[C_1' \quad C_2'\right]'. \tag{134d}$$

Due to the presence of widely separated eigenvalues, the integrodifferential equations (129)-(134) involved for computing the optimal solutions are numerically stiff. This renders the optimal solution computationally infeasible, especially when the order of the system is very large. Furthermore, when the small perturbation parameters are unknown, or when one decision maker does not have a knowledge of the fast dynamics of the other decision maker, it is not even possible to compute the optimal solution. Hence, there is a need to look for suboptimal solutions. The multimodel solution proposed below exploits the special structure of the system to yield a solution which does not require a knowledge of the small parameters, and allows the decision makers to model only their own fast dynamics. More importantly, as in the problem with continuous measurements, the multimodel solution is well posed in the sense that it is the limit of the optimal solution as the small parameters go to zero.

The multimodel solution is obtained on solving three low-order problems: a slow team problem under the one-step-delay observation sharing pattern, and two fast stochastic control problems, one for each decision maker.

The system model for *the slow subproblem* is given by (104), (106), and the observations by

$$y_{is}(j) = C_{i0}z_{0s}(t_j) + v_i(j)$$
$$\equiv y_i(j) - C_{ii}z_{is}(t_j), \quad j \in \theta, \quad i = 1, 2. \tag{135}$$

The cost function is given by

$$J_s(\nu_{1s}, \nu_{2s}) = E\left\{z'_{0s}(T)\Gamma_0 z_{0s}(T) + \int_0^T \left(z'_{0s}Q_0 z_{0s} + \sum_{i=1}^{2} u'_{is}R_{is}u_{is}\right) dt \,\middle|\, u_{js}(t) = \nu_{js}(t, \alpha_j), \quad j = 1, 2\right\} \tag{136}$$

where

$$R_{is} = I + \left(A_{ii}^{-1}B_{ii}\right)' Q_i\left(A_{ii}^{-1}B_{ii}\right).$$

The optimal solution to the slow team problem defined by (104), (106), (135), and (136) is given by

$$\nu^*_{is}(t, \alpha_i) = P_{is}(t)\left[y_{is}(j) - C_{i0}\hat{\xi}_s(j)\right] - R_{is}^{-1}B'_{0i}S_s\psi_s(t, t_j)\hat{\xi}_s(j), \quad i = 1, 2,$$
$$t \in [t_j, t_{j+1}), \quad j \in \theta \tag{137a}$$

where $P_{1s}(t)$, $P_{2s}(t)$ satisfy the coupled set of linear integral equations

$$P_{is}(t) = R_{is}^{-1}B'_{0i}S_{is}(t)\int_{t_j}^{t} \psi_{ijs}(t, \tau)B_{0i}R_{is}^{-1}B'_{0i}L_{ijs}(\tau)\, d\tau - R_{is}^{-1}B'_{0i}L_{ijs}(t), \quad i = 1, 2,$$
$$t \in [t_j, t_{j+1}), \quad j \in \theta \tag{137b}$$

where

$$L_{ijs}(t) = S_{is}(t)\left[\phi_s(t, t_j) + \int_{t_j}^{t} \phi_s(t, \tau)B_{0k}R_{ks}^{-1}P_{ks}(\tau)\ d\tau\ C_{k0}\right]\Sigma_{is}(j) + K_{ijs}(t), \quad i, k = 1, 2, \quad i \neq k, \quad t \in [t_j, t_{j+1}), \quad j \in \theta, \tag{137c}$$

$$\begin{aligned} \dot{K}_{ijs}(t) &= -\left(A_{00} - B_{0i}R_{is}^{-1}B_{0i}'S_{is}(t)\right)' K_{ijs}(t) - S_{is}(t)B_{0k}R_{ks}^{-1}P_{ks}(t)C_{k0}\Sigma_{is}(j), \\ K_{ijs}(t_{j+1}) &= 0, \quad i, k = 1, 2, \quad i \neq k, \quad t \in [t_j, t_{j+1}), \quad j \in \theta, \end{aligned} \tag{137d}$$

$S_s(t)$ and $S_{is}(t)$ satisfy the Riccati equations

$$\begin{aligned} \dot{S}_s &= -A_{00}'S_s - S_sA_{00} - Q_0 + S_s\left[B_{01}R_{1s}^{-1}B_{01}' + B_{02}R_{2s}^{-1}B_{02}'\right]S_s, \\ S_s(T) &= \Gamma_0, \end{aligned} \tag{137e}$$

$$\begin{aligned} \dot{S}_{is} &= -A_{00}'S_{is} - S_{is}A_{01} - Q_0 + S_{is}B_{0i}R_{is}^{-1}B_{0i}'S_{is}', \\ S_{is}(t_j) &= S_s(t_j), \quad t \in (t_{j-1}, t_j], \quad i = 1, 2, \quad j = N, \ldots, 1, \end{aligned} \tag{137f}$$

$\psi_s(t, \tau)$ is the state transition matrix satisfying

$$\begin{aligned} \dot{\psi}_s(t, \tau) &= \left(A_{00} - B_{01}R_{1s}^{-1}B_{01}'S_s - B_{02}R_{2s}^{-1}B_{02}'S_s\right)\psi_s(t, \tau), \\ \psi_s(\tau, \tau) &= I, \end{aligned} \tag{138a}$$

$\psi_{ijs}(t, \tau)$ is the state transition matrix satisfying

$$\begin{aligned} \dot{\psi}_{ijs}(t, \tau) &= \left(A_{00} - B_{0i}R_{is}^{-1}B_{0i}'S_{is}\right)\psi_{ijs}(t, \tau), \\ \psi_{ijs}(\tau, \tau) &= I, \quad t \in [t_j, t_{j+1}), \quad i = 1, 2, \quad j \in \theta, \end{aligned} \tag{138b}$$

$\phi_s(t, \tau)$ is the state transition matrix satisfying

$$\dot{\phi}_s(t, \tau) = A_{00}\phi_s(t, \tau), \quad \phi_s(\tau, \tau) = I, \tag{138c}$$

$\hat{\xi}_s(j) = \eta_s\left(t_j^-\right) = E[z_{0s}(t_j) \mid \delta_{j-1}]$ and $\eta_s(t)$ satisfies

$$\dot{\eta}_s = A_{00}\eta_s + \sum_{i=1}^{2} B_{0i}\nu_{is}^*(t, \alpha_i),$$

$$\eta_s(0) = \bar{z}_{00}, \quad t \in [t_{j-1}, t_j), \quad j = 1, \ldots, N, \tag{139}$$

$$\eta_s(t_j) = \eta_s\left(t_j^-\right) + M_s(j)\left[y_s(j) - C_0\eta_s\left(t_j^-\right)\right],$$

$$\Sigma_{is}(j) = \Sigma_s(t_j)C_{i0}'\left[C_{i0}\Sigma_s(t_j)C_{i0}' + C_{ii}W_iC_{ii}' + V_{ij}\right]^{-1}.$$

$$i = 1, 2, \quad j \in \theta \tag{140}$$

where W_i satisfies (124).

$\Sigma_s\left(t_j^-\right) = E\left[\left(z_{0s}(t_j) - \eta_s\left(t_j^-\right)\right)\left(z_{0s}(t_j) - \eta_s\left(t_j^-\right)\right)'\right]$ and $\Sigma_s(t)$ satisfies

$$\dot{\Sigma}_s = A_{00}\Sigma_s + \Sigma_s A_{00}' + \sum_{i=1}^{2} G_{0i}G_{0i}',$$

$$\Sigma_s(0) = N_{00}, \quad t \in [t_{j-1}, t_j), \quad j = 1, \ldots, N,$$

$$\Sigma_s(t_j) = \Sigma_s\left(t_j^-\right) - M_s(j)C_0\Sigma_s\left(t_j^-\right)$$

and

$$M_s(j) = \Sigma_s\left(t_j^-\right)C_0'\left[C_0\Sigma_s\left(t_j^-\right)C_0' + \sum_{i=1}^{2} \bar{C}_{ii}W_i\bar{C}_{ii} + V_j\right]^{-1}, \tag{142a}$$

$$y_s(j) = \left[y_{1s}'(j) \quad y_{2s}'(j)\right]', \tag{142b}$$

$$C_0 = \left[C_{10}' \quad C_{20}'\right]', \tag{142c}$$

$$\bar{C}_{11} = \left[C_{11}' \quad 0\right]', \tag{142d}$$

$$\bar{C}_{22} = \left[0 \quad C_{22}'\right]'. \tag{142e}$$

The fast subproblem for decision maker -i is defined by the system equations (115), (117), the observations

$$y_{if}(j) = C_{ii}z_{if}(t_j) + v_i(j)$$
$$\equiv y_i(j) - C_{i0}z_{0s}(t_j) - C_{ii}z_{is}(t_j), \quad j \in \theta, \tag{143}$$

and the cost function

$$J_{if} = E\left\{\epsilon_i z_{if}'(T)\Gamma_i z_{if}(T) + \int_0^T \left(z_{if}'Q_i z_{if} + u_{if}'u_{if}\right) dt\right\}. \tag{144}$$

Notice that we have studied this stochastic control problem earlier in Section II. Its solution, as $\epsilon_i \to 0$, is given by

$$u_{if}^* = -B_{ii}'K_{if}\psi_{if}(t, t_j)\hat{z}_{ij}(t_j),$$
$$t \in [t_j, t_{j+1}), \quad j \in \theta \tag{145}$$

where K_{if} satisfies the Riccati equation

$$A_{ii}'K_{if} + K_{if}A_{ii} + Q_i - K_{if}B_{ii}B_{ii}'K_{if} = 0, \tag{146}$$

$\psi_{if}(t, t_j)$ is the state transition matrix satisfying

$$\epsilon_i\dot{\psi}_{if}(t, t_j) = \left(A_{ii} - B_{ii}B_{ii}'K_{if}\right)\psi_{if}(t, t_j),$$
$$\psi_{if}(t_j, t_j) = I, \quad t \in [t_j, t_{j+1}), \quad j \in \theta, \tag{147}$$

$\hat{z}_{if}$ is the output of the filter

$$\epsilon_i\dot{\hat{z}}_{if} = A_{ii}\hat{z}_{if} + B_{ii}u_{if}^*, \quad t \in [t_{j-1}, t_j),$$
$$j = 1, 2, \ldots, N,$$
$$\hat{z}_{if}(0) = \overline{z}_{i0}, \tag{148}$$
$$\hat{z}_{if}(t_j) = \hat{z}_{if}\left(t_j^-\right) + M_{if}(j)\left[y_{if}(j) - C_{ii}\hat{z}_{if}\left(t_j^-\right)\right],$$

and

$$M_{if}(j) = W_iC_{ii}'\left[C_{i0}\Sigma_s\left(t_j^-\right)C_{i0}' + C_{ii}W_iC_{ii}' + V_{ij}\right]^{-1}. \tag{149}$$

The following proposition establishes the near-optimality of the multimodel solution. Its proof may be found in [19].

Proposition 2

(a) $\nu_i^*(t, \alpha_i) = \nu_{is}^*(t, \alpha_i) + u_{if}^*(t) + O(\|\epsilon\|),$

$$\forall t \in (0, T), \quad i = 1, 2,$$

(b) $$J\left(\nu_1^*, \nu_2^*\right) = J_s\left(\nu_{1s}^*, \nu_{2s}^*\right) + \sum_{i=1}^{2}\left[J_{if}\left(u_{if}^*\right) + T\ \mathrm{tr}(Q_i W_i)\right] + O(\|\epsilon\|). \quad \square$$

Case 2. Sampled Values of Continuous Noisy Measurements. At sampled time instant t_j, $j \in \theta - \{0\}$, the decision makers observe

$$y_i(j) = \int_0^{t_j} [C_{i0}z(\tau) + C_{ii}z_i(\tau)]\, d\tau + q_i(t_j)$$

$$= \int_0^{t_j} C_i x(\tau)\, d\tau + q_i(t_j), \quad i = 1, 2. \tag{150}$$

Note that in the time interval $[t_0, t_1)$ no observations are made and the decision makers have access only to the prior statistics of the random quantities involved. Here, $\{q_i(t);\ i = 1, 2\}$ are standard Wiener processes independent of each other. Furthermore, their statistics are also assumed to be independent of the Wiener processes $\{v_i(t),\ i = 1, 2\}$ and the initial state vector $x(0)$.

Let

$$\bar{y}_i(j) = y_i(j) - y_i(j-1)$$

$$= \int_{t_{j-1}}^{t_j} C_i x(\tau)\, d\tau + v_i(j), \quad i = 1, 2 \tag{151}$$

where $v_i(j) = q_i(t_j) - q_i(t_{j-1})$ is a discrete-time Gaussian white noise process with zero mean and variance $V_{ij} = (t_j - t_{j-1})I$.

Let $\bar{\alpha}_j^i$ be given by (125) with $y_i(j)$ replaced by $\bar{y}_i(j)$, and let $\bar{\sigma}_i^j$ denote the sigma-algebra generated by $\bar{\alpha}_i^j$. Then clearly, σ_i^j and $\bar{\sigma}_i^j$ are equivalent.

The optimal team solution to the problem defined by (91), (93), (125)-(127), and (151) can be obtained in a manner analogous to Case 1, and is given by [20]

$$\nu_i^*(t, \bar{\alpha}_i) = P_i(t)\left[\bar{y}_i(j) - \int_{t_{j-1}}^{t_j} C_i\eta(\tau)\, d\tau\right] - B_i'S(t)\psi(t, t_j)\hat{\xi}(j), \quad i = 1, 2, \quad t \in [t_j, t_{j+1}), \quad j \in \theta \tag{152a}$$

where $P_1(t)$, $P_2(t)$ satisfy the coupled set of linear integral equations

$$P_i(t) = B_i'S_i(t)\int_{t_j}^{t} \psi_{ij}(t, \tau)B_iB_i'L_{ij}(\tau)\, d\tau - B_i'L_{ij}(t), \quad i = 1, 2, \quad t \in [t_j, t_{j+1}), \quad j \in \theta \tag{152b}$$

where

$$L_{ij}(t) = S_i(t)\phi(t, t_j)\Sigma_i(j) + S_i(t)\int_{t_j}^{t} \phi(t, \tau)B_kP_k(\tau)\, d\tau\, \Delta_i(j) + K_{ij}(t), \quad i, k = 1, 2, \quad i \neq k, \quad t \in [t_j, t_{j+1}), \quad j \in \theta, \tag{152c}$$

$$\dot{K}_{ij}(t) = -\left(A - B_iB_i'S_i(t)\right)'K_{ij}(t) - S_i(t)B_kP_k(t)\,\Delta_i(j),$$
$$K_{ij}(t_{j+1}) = 0, \quad i, k = 1, 2, \quad i \neq k, \quad t \in (t_j, t_{j+1}], \quad j \in \theta. \tag{152d}$$

$S(t)$ and $S_i(t)$ satisfy the Riccati equations (129e) and (129f), respectively. The state transition matrices $\psi(t, \tau)$, $\psi_{ij}(t, \tau)$, and $\phi(t, \tau)$ satisfy Eqs. (130).

$\hat{\xi}(j) = \eta\left(t_j^-\right) = E\left[x(t_j) \mid \overline{\delta}_{j-1}\right]$ and $\eta(t)$ satisfies

$$\dot{\eta} = A\eta + \sum_{i=1}^{2} B_i \nu_i^*\left(t, \overline{\alpha}_i\right), \quad \eta(0) = \overline{x}_0,$$

$$t \in [t_{j-1}, t_j), \quad j = 1, \ldots, N, \tag{153}$$

$$\eta(t_j) = \eta\left(t_j^-\right) + M(j)\left[\overline{y}(j) - \int_{t_{j-1}}^{t_j} C\eta(\tau)\, d\tau\right].$$

$\Sigma_i(j)$ and $\Delta_i(j)$ are appropriate-dimensional matrices defined by

$$\Sigma_i(j) = \left[\phi(t_j, t_{j-1})\Sigma(t_{j-1}) \int_{t_{j-1}}^{t_j} \phi'(t, t_{j-1})C_i'\, dt \right.$$
$$\left. + \int_{t_{j-1}}^{t_j} \phi(t_j, r)GG' \int_r^{t_j} \phi'(\tau, r)C_i'\, d\tau\, dr\right]\hat{V}_{ij}^{-1},$$
$$i = 1, 2, \quad j \in \theta, \tag{154a}$$

$$\Delta_i(j) = \left[\int_{t_{j-1}}^{t_j} C_k\phi(t, t_{j-1})\, dt\, \Sigma(t_{j-1}) \int_{t_{j-1}}^{t_j} \phi'(t, t_{j-1})C_i'\, dt \right.$$
$$\left. + \int_{t_{j-1}}^{t_j} C_k\phi(t_j, r)GG' \int_r^{t_j} \phi(\tau, r)C_i'\, d\tau\, dr\right]\hat{V}_{ij}^{-1},$$
$$i, k = 1, 2, \quad i \neq k, \quad j \in \theta \tag{154b}$$

where

$$\hat{V}_{ij} = \int_{t_{j-1}}^{t_j} C_i\phi(t, t_{j-1})\, dt\, \Sigma(t_{j-1}) \int_{t_{j-1}}^{t_j} \phi'(t, t_{j-1})C_i'\, dt + V_i$$
$$+ \int_{t_{j-1}}^{t_j} C_i \int_{t_{j-1}}^{r} \phi(\tau, r)GG' \int_{\tau}^{t_j} \phi'(l, \tau)C_i'\, dl\, d\tau\, dr,$$
$$i = 1, 2, \quad j \in \theta, \tag{154c}$$

$\Sigma\left(t_j^-\right) = E\left[\left(x(t_j) - \eta\left(t_j^-\right)\right)\left(x(t_j) - \eta\left(t_j^-\right)\right)'\right]$ and $\Sigma(t)$ satisfies

$$\dot{\Sigma} = A\Sigma + \Sigma A' + GG',$$

$$\Sigma(0) = N, \quad t \in [t_{j-1}, t_j), \quad j = 1, \ldots, N,$$

$$\Sigma(t_j) = \Sigma\left(t_j^-\right) - M(j)\left[\int_{t_{j-1}}^{t_j} C\phi(r, t_{j-1})\, dr\, \Sigma(t_{j-1})\phi'(t_j, t_{j-1}) + \int_{t_{j-1}}^{t_j}\int_r^{t_j} C\phi(r, \tau)GG'\phi'(t_j, \tau)\, d\tau\, dr\right]. \tag{155}$$

$M(j)$ is given by

$$M(j) = \left[\phi(t_j, t_{j-1})\Sigma(t_{j-1})\int_{t_{j-1}}^{t_j}\phi'(r, t_{j-1})C'\, dr + \int_{t_{j-1}}^{t_j}\phi(t_j, \tau)GG'\int_\tau^{t_j}\phi'(r, \tau)C'\, dr\, d\tau\right]\hat{V}_j^{-1}, \quad j \in \theta \tag{156a}$$

where

$$\hat{V}_j = \int_{t_{j-1}}^{t_j} C\phi(\tau, t_{j-1})\, d\tau\, \Sigma(t_{j-1})\int_{t_{j-1}}^{t_j}\phi'(r, t_{j-1})C'\, dr + V_j + \int_{t_{j-1}}^{t_j} C\int_{t_{j-1}}^{r}\phi(\tau, r)GG'\int_\tau^{t_j}\phi'(l, \tau)C'\, dl\, d\tau\, dr, \quad j \in \theta, \tag{156b}$$

$$V_j = \operatorname{diag}(V_{1j}, V_{2j}), \tag{157a}$$

$$\bar{y}(j) = \left[\bar{y}_1'(j) \quad \bar{y}_2'(j)\right]', \tag{157b}$$

$$C = \left[C_1' \quad C_2'\right]'. \tag{157c}$$

As in Case 1, the optimal team strategies are unique and linear in the information available to the decision makers, but the expressions involved are more complicated. Hence, the computational problem worsens, making the need for suboptimal solutions more acute. Again the appealing structure of the multimodel solution makes it an attractive alternative.

As in earlier problems, the multimodel solution is obtained on solving a lower-order team problem in the slow time scale and two low-order decentralized control problems in the fast time scale. The system model for *the slow subproblem* is given by (104), (106), the cost function by (136), and the observations by

$$\overline{y}_{is}(j) = \int_{t_{j-1}}^{t_j} C_{i0} z_{0s}(\tau)\, d\tau + v_i(j)$$

$$\equiv \overline{y}_i(j) - \int_{t_{j-1}}^{t_j} C_{ii} z_{is}(\tau)\, d\tau,$$

$$i = 1, 2, \quad j \in \theta - \{0\}. \tag{158}$$

The optimal team solution to this slow subproblem is given by

$$\nu_{is}^*\left(t, \overline{\alpha}_i\right) = P_{is}(t)\left[\overline{y}_{is}(j) - \int_{t_{j-1}}^{t_j} C_{i0} \eta_s(\tau)\, d\tau\right]$$

$$- R_{is}^{-1} B_{0i}' S_s \psi_s(t, t_j) \hat{\xi}_s(j),$$

$$i = 1, 2, \quad t \in [t_j, t_{j+1}),$$

$$j \in \theta, \tag{159a}$$

where $P_{1s}(t)$, $P_{2s}(t)$ satisfy the coupled set of linear integral equations

$$P_{is}(t) = R_{is}^{-1} B_{0i}' S_{is}(t) \int_{t_j}^{t} \psi_{ijs}(t, \tau) B_{0i} R_{is}^{-1} B_{0i}' L_{ijs}(\tau)\, d\tau$$

$$- R_{is}^{-1} B_{0i}' L_{ijs}(t), \quad i = 1, 2, \quad t \in [t_j, t_{j+1}),$$

$$j \in \theta, \tag{159b}$$

where

$$L_{ijs}(t) = S_{is}(t)\phi_s(t, t_j)\Sigma_{is}(j) + S_{is}(t)\int_{t_j}^{t} \phi_s(t, \tau)B_{0k}R_{ks}^{-1}P_{ks}(\tau)\, d\tau\, \Delta_{is}(j) + K_{ijs}(t), \quad i, k = 1, 2, \quad i \neq k, \quad t \in [t_j, t_{j+1}), \quad j \in \theta, \tag{159c}$$

$$\dot{K}_{ijs}(t) = -\left(A_{00} - B_{0i}R_{is}^{-1}B_{0i}'S_{is}(t)\right)'K_{ijs}(t) - S_{is}(t)B_{0k}R_{ks}^{-1}P_{ks}(t)\,\Delta_{is}(j),$$
$$K_{ijs}(t_{j+1}) = 0, \quad i, k = 1, 2, \quad i \neq k, \quad t \in [t_j, t_{j+1}), \quad j \in \theta, \tag{159d}$$

$S_s(t)$ and $S_{is}(t)$ satisfy the Riccati equations (137e) and (137f), respectively. The state transition matrices $\psi_s(t, \tau)$, $\psi_{ijs}(t, \tau)$, and $\phi_s(t, \tau)$ satisfy Eqs. (138). Furthermore, $\hat{\xi}_s(j) = \eta_s\left(t_j^-\right) = E\left[z_{0s}(t_j) \mid \overline{\delta}_{j-1}\right]$ and $\eta_s(t)$ satisfies

$$\dot{\eta}_s = A_{00}\eta_s + \sum_{i=1}^{2} B_{0i}\nu_{is}^{*}\left(t, \overline{\alpha}_i\right),$$
$$\eta_s(0) = \overline{z}_{00}, \quad t \in [t_{j-1}, t_j), \quad j = 1, \ldots, N, \tag{160}$$
$$\eta_s(t_j) = \eta_s\left(t_j^-\right) + M_s(j)\left[\overline{y}_s(j) - \int_{t_{j-1}}^{t_j} C_0\eta_s(\tau)\, d\tau\right],$$

$\Sigma_{is}(j)$ and $\Delta_{is}(j)$ are appropriate-dimensional matrices defined by

$$\Sigma_{is}(j) = \left[\phi_s(t_j, t_{j-1})\Sigma_s(t_{j-1})\int_{t_{j-1}}^{t_j} \phi_s'(t, t_{j-1})C_{i0}'\, dt + \int_{t_{j-1}}^{t_j} \phi_s(t_j, r)\sum_{i=1}^{2} G_{0i}G_{0i}'\int_{r}^{t_j} \phi_s'(\tau, r)C_{i0}'\, d\tau\, dr\right] \times \overline{V}_{ij}^{-1}, \quad i = 1, 2, \quad j \in \theta, \tag{161a}$$

$$\Delta_{is}(j) = \left[\int_{t_{j-1}}^{t_j} C_k\phi_s(t, t_{j-1})\, dt\, \Sigma_s(t_{j-1}) \times \int_{t_{j-1}}^{t_j} \phi'(t, t_{j-1})C_{i0}'\, dt + \int_{t_{j-1}}^{t_j} C_k\phi_s(t_j, r) \times \sum_{i=1}^{2} G_{0i}G_{0i}' \int_r^{t_j} \phi_s(\tau, r)C_{i0}'\, d\tau\, dr\right] \bar{V}_{ij}^{-1},$$

$$i, k = 1, 2, \quad i \neq k, \; j \in \theta, \tag{161b}$$

where

$$\bar{V}_{ij} = V_{ij} + \int_{t_{j-1}}^{t_j} C_{i0}\phi_s(t, t_{j-1})\, dt\, \Sigma_s(t_{j-1}) \times \int_{t_{j-1}}^{t_j} \phi_s'(t, t_{j-1})C_{i0}'\, dt + \int_{t_{j-1}}^{t_j} C_{ii}\phi_{if}(t, t_{j-1})\, dt\, W_i \int_{t_{j-1}}^{t_j} \phi_{if}'(t, t_{j-1})C_{ii}'\, dt + \int_{t_{j-1}}^{t_j}\int_{t_{j-1}}^{r} C_{i0}\phi_s(\tau, r) \sum_{i=1}^{2} G_{i0}G_{i0}' \times \int_\tau^{t_j} \phi_s'(l, \tau)C_{i0}'\, dl\, d\tau\, dr + \int_{t_{j-1}}^{t_j}\int_{t_{j-1}}^{r} C_{ii}\phi_{if}(\tau, r)G_{ii}G_{ii}' \times \int_\tau^{t_j} \phi_{if}'(l, \tau)C_{ii}'\, dl\, d\tau\, dr, \quad i = 1, 2,$$

$$j \in \theta, \tag{161c}$$

$\phi_{if}(t, t_j)$ is the state transition matrix satisfying

$$\epsilon_i \dot{\phi}_{if}(t, t_j) = A_{ii}\phi_{if}(t, t_j),$$

$$\phi_{if}(t_j, t_j) = I, \quad t \in [t_j, t_{j+1}), \quad i = 1, 2,$$

$$j \in \theta, \tag{161d}$$

and W_i satisfies (124). Now,

$$E\left[\left(z_{0s}(t_j) - \eta_s\left(t_j^-\right)\right)\left(z_{0s}(t_j) - \eta_s\left(t_j^-\right)\right)'\right] = \Sigma_s\left(t_j^-\right)$$

where $\Sigma_s(t)$ satisfies

$$\dot{\Sigma}_s = A_{00}\Sigma_s + \Sigma_s A_{00}' + \sum_{i=1}^{2} G_{0i}G_{0i}',$$

$$\Sigma_s(0) = N_{00}, \quad t \in [t_{j-1}, t_j), \quad j = 1, \ldots, N,$$

$$\begin{aligned} \Sigma_s(t_j) = \Sigma_s\left(t_j^-\right) - M_s(j) & \\ \times \Bigg[\int_{t_{j-1}}^{t_j} C_0\phi_s(r, t_{j-1})\, dr\, \Sigma_s(t_{j-1})\phi_s'(t_j, t_{j-1}) & \\ + \int_{t_{j-1}}^{t_j} \int_r^{t_j} C_0\phi_s(r, \tau) \sum_{i=1}^{2} G_{0i}G_{0i}'\phi_s'(t_j, \tau)\, d\tau\, dr\Bigg], & \end{aligned} \tag{162}$$

$M_s(j)$ is given by

$$\begin{aligned} M_s(j) = \Bigg[\phi_s(t_j, t_{j-1})\Sigma_s(t_{j-1}) \int_{t_{j-1}}^{t_j} \phi_s'(r, t_{j-1})C_0'\, dr & \\ + \int_{t_{j-1}}^{t_j} \phi_s(t_j, \tau) \sum_{i=1}^{2} G_{0i}G_{0i}' & \\ \times \int_\tau^{t_j} \phi_s'(r, \tau)C_0'\, dr\, d\tau\Bigg]\overline{V}_j^{-1}, \quad j \in \theta, & \end{aligned} \tag{163a}$$

where

$$\overline{V}_j = V_j + \int_{t_{j-1}}^{t_j} C_0\phi_s(t, t_{j-1})\, dt\, \Sigma_s(t_{j-1})$$

$$\times \int_{t_{j-1}}^{t_j} \phi_s'(t, t_{j-1})C_0'\, dt$$

$$+ \int_{t_{j-1}}^{t_j} \int_{t_{j-1}}^{r} C_0\phi_s(\tau, r) \sum_{i=1}^{2} G_{i0}G_{i0}'$$

$$\times \int_{\tau}^{t_j} \phi_s'(l, \tau)C_0'\, dl\, d\tau\, dr$$

$$+ \sum_{i=1}^{2}\Bigg[\int_{t_{j-1}}^{t_j} \overline{C}_{ii}\phi_{if}(t, t_{j-1})\, dt\, W_i \int_{t_{j-1}}^{t_j} \phi_{if}'(t, t_{j-1})\overline{C}_{ii}'\, dt$$

$$+ \int_{t_{j-1}}^{t_j} \int_{t_{j-1}}^{r} \overline{C}_{ii}\phi_{if}(\tau, r)G_{ii}G_{ii}'$$

$$\times \int_{\tau}^{t_j} \phi_{if}'(l, \tau)\overline{C}_{ii}'\, dl\, d\tau\, dr\Bigg], \quad j \in \theta, \tag{163b}$$

V_j is defined by (157a); C_0, $\overline{C}_{11}$, $\overline{C}_{22}$ are defined by (142c)-(142e), and

$$\overline{y}_s(j) = \left[\overline{y}_{1s}(j) \quad \overline{y}_{2s}(j)\right]'. \tag{164}$$

The fast subproblem for decision maker -i is defined by the system equations (115), (117), the cost function (144), and the observations

$$\overline{y}_{if}(j) = \int_{t_{j-1}}^{t_j} C_{ii}z_{if}(\tau)\, d\tau + v_i(j)$$

$$\equiv \overline{y}_i(j) - \int_{t_{j-1}}^{t_j} [C_{i0}z_{0s}(\tau) + C_{ii}z_{is}(\tau)]d\tau, \quad j \in \theta. \tag{165}$$

This control problem has been studied in Section II. Its solution, as $\epsilon_i \to 0$, is given by

$$u_{if}^* = -B_{ii}' K_{if} \psi_{if}(t, t_j) z_{if}(t_j),$$
$$t \in [t_j, t_{j+1}), \quad j \in \theta, \tag{166}$$

where K_{if} satisfies the Riccati equation (146) and $\psi_{if}(t, t_j)$ satisfies (147).

$\hat{z}_{if}$ is the output of the filter

$$\epsilon_i \dot{\hat{z}}_{if} = A_{ii} \hat{z}_{if} + B_{ii} u_{if}^*, \quad t \in [t_{j-1}, t_j),$$
$$j = 1, \ldots, N,$$
$$\hat{z}_{if}(0) = \bar{z}_{i0},$$
$$\hat{z}_{if}(t_j) = \hat{z}_{if}\left(t_j^-\right) + M_{if}(j)\left[\bar{y}_{if}(j) - \int_{t_{j-1}}^{t_j} C_{ii} \hat{z}_{if}(\tau)\, d\tau\right],$$

and

$$M_{if}(j) = \left[\phi_{if}(t_j, t_{j-1}) W_i \int_{t_{j-1}}^{t_j} \phi_{if}'(r, t_{j-1}) C_{ii}'\, dr\right.$$
$$+ \int_{t_{j-1}}^{t_j} \phi_{if}'(t_j, \tau) G_{ii} G_{ii}'$$
$$\left. \times \int_{\tau}^{t_j} \phi_{if}'(r, \tau) C_{ii}'\, dr\, d\tau\right] \bar{V}_{ij}^{-1}. \tag{168}$$

A near-optimality result, analogous to Proposition 2, can also be established in this case by following the same lines:

Proposition 3

(a) $\nu_i^*(t, \alpha_i) = \nu_{is}^*(t, \alpha_i) + u_{if}^* + O(\|\epsilon\|),$

$$\forall t \in (0, T), \quad i = 1, 2,$$

(b) $$J\left(\nu_1^*, \nu_2^*\right) = J_s\left(\nu_{1s}^*, \nu_{2s}^*\right) + \sum_{i=1}^{2}\left[J_{if}\left(u_{if}^*\right) + T\ \mathrm{tr}(Q_i, W_i)\right] + O(\|\epsilon\|). \quad \square$$

V. CONCLUSIONS

Through an informal discussion of a series of problems we have attempted to analyze the interaction between model simplification and strategy design in a multimodel context. The objective was to achieve a clear understanding of the interrelationships between the structural features of large-scale systems, like time scales and weak coupling, and strategy design under certain quasiclassical information patterns.

Weakly connected subsystems with continuous equilibria exhibit a two-time-scale behavior. The slow system-wide behavior is caused by the interconnections and is described by an aggregate "core" which appears as a slow subsystem in the singular perturbation form of the model. The fast phenomena which consist of "local" transients within each subsystem are weakly coupled. The control design problem for such systems can be approached via the multimodeling concept. Each decision maker's control can be divided into a slow part, which contributes to the control of the core, and a fast part controlling his own fast subsystem. Hence, the slow subproblem is a multiple decision-maker problem under the same solution concept (Nash, team, etc.) as the full problem, while the fast subproblems are decoupled stochastic control problems. Since each decision maker need not know the parameters associated with the fast subproblem of other decision makers, the multimodel solution is robust with respect to modeling errors; a very desirable feature in large-scale system design.

Our results serve to demonstrate the richness in the modeling structure with multiparameter singular perturbations in the context of multimodeling problems. In each case, the limit of seemingly complex integrodifferential equations associated with the optimal solution has a nice appealing structure when interpreted as a multimodel solution. Thus the multimodeling approach using singular perturbations is in some sense "robust" with respect to a class of solution concepts and information patterns.

REFERENCES

1. N. R. SANDELL, JR., P. VARAIYA, M. ATHANS, and M. G. SAFANOV, "Survey of Decentralized Control Methods for Large Scale Systems," *IEEE Trans. Automatic Control AC-23*, 108-128 (1978).

2. H. K. KHALIL and P. V. KOKOTOVIC, "Control Strategies for Decision Makers using Different Models of the Same System," *IEEE Trans. Automatic Control AC-23*, 289-298 (1978).

3. J. R. WINKELMAN, J. H. CHOW, B. C. BOWLER, B. AVRAMOVIC, and P. V. KOKOTOVIC, "An Analysis of Interarea Dynamics of Multimachine Systems," *IEEE Trans. Power Appl. and Systems 100*, 754-763 (1981).

4. P. V. KOKOTOVIC, R. E. O'MALLEY, JR., and P. SANNUTI, "Singular Perturbations and Order Reduction in Control Theory — An Overview," *Automatica 12*, 123-132 (1976).

5. A. H. HADDAD, "Linear Filtering of Singularly Perturbed Systems," *IEEE Trans. Automatic Control AC-31*, 515-519 (1976).

6. A. H. HADDAD and P. V. KOKOTOVIC, "Stochastic Control of Linear Singularly Perturbed Systems," *IEEE Trans. Automatic Control AC-22*, 815-821 (1977).

7. V. R. SAKSENA and J. B. CRUZ, JR., "A Multimodel Approach to Stochastic Nash Games," *Automatica 18*, 295-305 (1982).

8. R. P. SINGH, "The Linear-Quadratic-Gaussian Problem for Singularly Perturbed Systems," *Int. J. System Science 13*, 93-100 (1982).

9. H. K. KHALIL, A. H. HADDAD, and G. BLANKENSHIP, "Parameter Scaling and Well-Posedness of Stochastic Singularly Perturbed Control Systems," *Proc. 12th Asilomar Conference on Circuits, Systems and Computers* (1978).

10. P. V. KOKOTOVIC, "A Riccati Equation for Block-Diagonalization of Ill-conditioned Systems," *IEEE Trans. Automatic Control AC-20*, 812-814 (1975).

11. P. V. KOKOTOVIC, "Subsystems, Time-Scales and Multimodeling," *Automatica 17*, 797-804 (1981).

12. P. V. KOKOTOVIC, B. AVRAMOVIC, J. H. CHOW, and J. R. WINKELMAN, "Coherency-Based Decomposition and Aggregation," *Automatica 17*, 47-56 (1982).

13. G. PEPONIDES, P. V. KOKOTOVIC, and J. H. CHOW, "Singular Perturbations and Time Scales in Nonlinear Models of Power Systems," *IEEE Trans. Circuits and Systems CAS-29*, 758-767 (1982).

14. F. DELEBECQUE and J. P. QUADRAT, "Optimal Control of Markov Chains Admitting Strong and Weak Interactions," *Automatica 17*, 281-296 (1981).

15. R. G. PHILLIPS and P. V. KOKOTOVIC, "A Singular Perturbation Approach to Modeling and Control of Markov Chains," *IEEE Trans. Automatic Control AC-26*, 1087-1094 (1981).

16. I. B. RHODES and D. G. LUENBERGER, "Stochastic Differential Games with Constrained State Estimators," *IEEE Trans. Automatic Control AC-14*, 476-481 (1969).

17. A. A. FELDBAUM, "Optimal Control Systems," Academic Press, New York, 1965.

18. A. BAGCHI and T. BAŞAR, "Team Decision Theory for Linear Continuous-Time Systems," *IEEE Trans. Automatic Control AC-25*, 1154-1161 (1980).

19. V. R. SAKSENA and T. BAŞAR, "A Multimodel Approach to Stochastic Team Problems," *Automatica 18*, 713-720 (1982).

20. T. BAŞAR and D. H. CANSEVER, "Team-Optimal Strategies for LQG Continuous-Time Systems with Sampled Continuous Measurements," Internal Report, Marmara Research Institute, Gebze, Kocaeli, Turkey, 1980.

Resource Management of Time-Critical Data Processing Systems

LAWRENCE E. BERMAN
THOMAS J. HOLMES
KENNETH M. KESSLER
*Systems Control Technology, Inc.
Palo Alto, California*

I. INTRODUCTION

A. *SCOPE OF STUDY*

Distributed computing is playing an increasing role for defense systems applications in information processing. A variety of applications, particularly BMD (ballistic missile defense) and tactical C^3 (command, control, and communications) systems require very rapid processing of large quantities of data. The range of application of the methodology presented here is very broad and may include industrial process control systems as well as defense systems. The examples used to develop the methodology are specifically oriented toward BMD data processing systems.

The objective of a BMD system is the survival of defended land-based strategic missile systems under attack. The system operation can be broken into two parts: (i) the detection and identification of threatening objects and (ii) allocation of defense assets, e.g., interceptor missiles. Essential components of all BMD constructs include sensors, defensive weapons, data processors, and communication links.

The extent to which a BMD system can fulfill its function is fundamentally resource-limited. Given finite interceptor resources, data processing plays a major role in BMD systems. It is critical that threatening objects be accurately identified, and that interceptor allocation be performed as efficiently as possible.

Given the importance of data processing systems to the successful performance of BMD, it is essential that these systems perform reliably. If all data processing functions are concentrated within a single processor, the loss of that processor would constitute a catastrophic system failure. Accordingly, technology necessary to permit the development of efficient distributed BMD data processing systems is being pursued. In order to achieve the advantages of enhanced system reliability inherent in distributed data processing, the allocation and control of BMD (data processing) resources should also be decentralized.

Although distributed systems offer inherent reliability advantages over centralized (single-processor) systems, efficiency losses occur due to the need for communication and data transfer between separate processors. The developed data processing control strategies must address these costs.

BMD systems, like all time-critical systems, must respond to rapidly changing conditions. Data that are processed too slowly lose value for decision-making purposes. This issue must also be addressed by the developed control strategies.

B. STRUCTURE OF DECENTRALIZED HIERARCHICAL SYSTEM

An example of a hierarchical control structure is shown in Fig. 1. In this example, commands flow down from the global controller to a sequence of lower-level controllers. The global controller may be centrally organized or may be distributed, allowing calculations to be decentralized.

The global or high-level control sends control information (b_1, b_2) to lower-level controllers. Global control calculations may be performed in a separate, third processor or may be in either or both of processors 1 and 2. The diagram illustrates the organization of the control system and information flows. The local controllers, which are located in separate

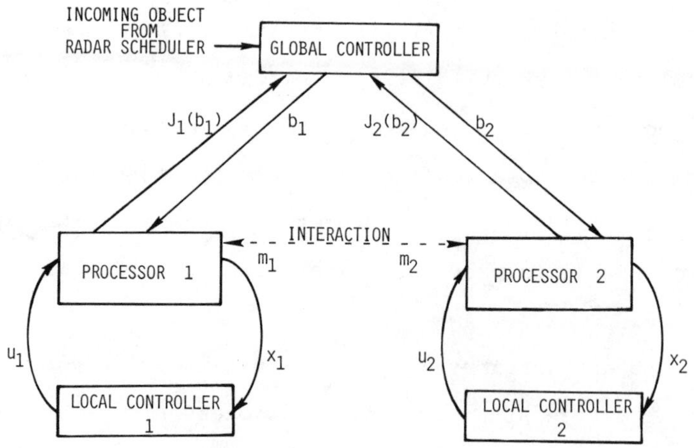

Fig. 1. Hierarchical control structure.

processors, send up performance information (J_1, J_2) which serves as the basis for global coordination. The global controllers also monitor local state information (x_1, x_2) and generate controls (u_1, u_2). The dashed line indicates that data transfer between processors may occur as a result of directives from the global controller.

High-level control is based on aggregated information and, accordingly, uses low-order system models. The use of low-order models and aggregated information serves to reduce interprocessor communication and provides for faster calculation of controls. At the lower level, local controllers can respond to local conditions, incorporating global control directives, without full knowledge of the global state. For these reasons, a hierarchical/decentralized control system is more responsive to time-critical requirements than a single-level global control structure.

Within the context of BMD, there is a natural separation between local and global control functions. At the local or individual processor level is the problem of throughput capacity allocation; namely, the determination of the fraction of processor time spent on each data processing task. This problem can be resolved internally within a processor without any global control directives. At the global level, the control system can respond to system overloads by reallocating objects between processors. This requires aggregate measures of processor loading and performance, although not at the same level of detail required to do throughput capacity allocation within a single processor.

C. OVERVIEW OF TECHNICAL APPROACH AND ORGANIZATION OF THE CHAPTER

The focus of the work reported here is on the development of adaptive global data processing control strategies. Detailed procedures for low-level control algorithms are not developed here. The intent of this research is to develop high-level control strategies that can be incorporated within a distributed computer operating system. However, the approach taken is sufficiently generic so as not to depend on characteristics of particular operating systems and is suitable for a wide range of applications.

Key issues in the formulation of global control strategies include:

(a) structure of the time-critical data processing system;

(b) establishment of control objectives;

(c) identification and separation of global and local control functions; and

(d) determination of informational requirements, models, and algorithms for global control.

The basic structure assumed here for a time-critical system is a collection of identical processors, each performing identical data processing functions, although on different object data. Two degrees of freedom for control exist within this structure: (i) allocation of resources within a processor and (ii) transfer of data between processors. Other degrees of freedom may exist, e.g., in the initial assignment of object data to processors; these are not considered here.

The primary concern of the high-level controller is the overall distribution of load across processors. Its function is to maintain an optimal load distribution at all times so as to minimize the likelihood of a severe overload within a single processor. In order to assess the costs and benefits of object data transfer, it is necessary that the global controller have information on processor loading at an appropriate level of detail. Accordingly, it is necessary that the global controller have a model for how local controllers use their information, and how the local control systems will respond to global directives.

An essential feature of the technical approach used here is the development of resource allocation procedures for throughput capacity allocation within a single processor. These procedures establish, at an aggregate level, how the local controller would optimally time-slice data processing functions in response to varying loading conditions. These single-processor aggregate resource allocation procedures can themselves form the basis for design of detailed local control procedures. They constitute the link between the global controller and the operating system. An essential step in formulating single-processor resource allocation procedures is to model the dynamics of the flow of object data through a processor, and to formulate appropriate control objectives and algorithms.

The overall technical approach can be summarized as follows. First, the dynamics of data flow through a single processor are modeled using an aggregate model of time-critical data processing functions. These models are presented in Section II. Next, a number of candidate control objectives are formulated in Section III. These include process time, transit time, and others. In Section IV, candidate algorithms suitable for real-time resource allocation within a single processor are developed. These procedures are evaluated in Section V using a simulation of a single-processor system representative of a generic BMD system.

Given the procedures developed and tested in Sections II-V, it is then possible to formulate explicit global control strategies for redistributing the data processing load globally. This procedure, called object reallocation, is developed in Section VI, consistent with the framework and control objectives developed in the previous sections. Finally, the results of the entire study are summarized in Section VII.

II. SINGLE-PROCESSOR LOAD DYNAMICS

This section presents a model for the flow of data through a sequence of computing stations. Since communication costs are not treated in this section, the analysis is most applicable to a single processor, e.g., a BMD tactical function processor. For the model here, we assume data can enter through the processor through a single entry point (node). In the global controller development (Section VI), multiple entry points are permitted and interprocessor communication time delays are considered.

Section A formulates the issues involved in the dynamics of load flow through the processor. In Section B, the dynamics of a single-node system are modeled. Stochastic queueing theory is, in principle, most directly applicable to the description of such processes. However, the complexity of such models can still be too great to be of practical value for real-time control. A modeling approach that leads to simple suboptimal algorithms that are robust under system operating conditions is preferable to a more exact approach that leads to computationally intense solutions. The approach used here for modeling and control is based on a theory developed by Agnew [1] for congestion-prone systems. We refer to this approach as "certain equivalent" queueing theory, since the stochastic effects are not explicitly modeled; the time dynamics are representative of expected loading. This theory may be viewed as an extension of deterministic queueing theories developed by earlier researchers, e.g., Gazis [2], for traffic control. The earlier deterministic models are strictly representative only of saturated systems, i.e., systems so heavily loaded that throughput is independent of the input rate. The certain equivalent model is representative of saturated systems, i.e., systems so heavily loaded that throughput is independent of the input rate. The certain equivalent model is representative of saturated and unsaturated system behavior, yet the analytic simplicity of the less sophisticated models is retained. The control strategies based on this model are correspondingly simple and have both practical and pedagogic value.

In Section C, the single-server model developed in Section B is extended to accommodate a pipeline or tandem network of servers. An important characteristic of some systems is that there may be severe timing constraints on how long data on a particular object can remain in a queue without being processed. The object data may lose value for decision-making purposes or, for example, in the case of BMD, slow processing could result in the loss of the object by the tracking system. In such cases where the object data become useless, it will be purged (we assume) by the operating system. In Section D, the pipeline model is extended to account for object data purged as a result of system overloading.

A. MODELING ISSUES

There may be multiple types of data input to time-critical systems. For BMD systems, such data may consist of trajectory information or physical characteristics of potentially threatening objects under observation; these can be high-quality decoys or other nonthreatening objects, as well as armed reentry vehicles (RVs).

At an aggregate level, within a single processor, a time-critical system is assumed to consist of a fixed sequence of computing stations or nodes (Fig. 2). Objects (actually object data) move from node to node through the system. After processing at a node is completed for a particular object, a decision is made to pass the object data to the next node or drop them from further processing. The decision to drop can occur for two reasons: (i) no further processing is required, e.g., if the object is classified as nonthreatening; or (ii) the data have become useless due to slow processing. In the context of BMD, threatening objects that are dropped are referred to as "leakers."

The data processing system is assumed to have an aggregate throughput capacity T^0 measured in machine language instructions per second (MLI) or other suitable unit. A key assumption used

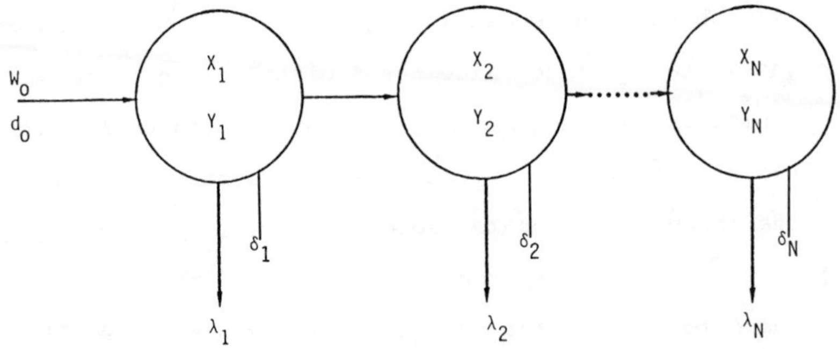

Fig. 2. Pipeline flow model.

here is that throughput capacity can be allocated to each of the data processing nodes in real time. Let N be the number of computing stations (nodes). Let T_K, K = 1, ..., N, be the throughput capacity allocated to the K-th node. Then the summed throughput capacities over nodes cannot exceed total system capacity. Thus

$$\sum_{K=1}^{N} T_K \leq T^0. \tag{1}$$

In this chapter, time-critical system functions within a single processor are assumed to be organized as a tandem queueing network. The service time at a node is inversely related to the throughput capacity allocated to that node. The following assumptions about the service mechanism are used in the remainder of this chapter.

(a) Objects wait for service in a single input queue at each node and incur a delay while waiting for service.

(b) Each server contains a fixed set of machine language instruction that must be executed for each object.

(c) Once an object completes service at a node, it is either dropped from further processing, or is passed to the subsequent nodes input queue without delay.

(d) Objects are served at each node according to a first-in/first-out discipline.

These assumptions ignore the presence of output queues and the possible use of priority based or other service disciplines. Such issues are of concern for the design of actual systems; however, at an aggregate level assumptions (a)-(d) are adequate for formulating resource allocation strategies.

In the next section, the issues presented here are developed formally for a single-node system.

B. SINGLE-NODE LOAD DYNAMICS

Consider a data processing system consisting of a single node or server. Although the dynamics of such a system are most appropriately represented in discrete-time, a continuous-time model provides a more compact representation and is valid on average over an interval greater than the discrete processing time. Using a continuous-time model, the following conservation differential equation relates the load (queue length) to the input flow rate (objects/second) and throughput:

$$\dot{S} = -\mu + \rho. \qquad (2)$$

In Eq. (2), S is the number of objects waiting for service; μ, the processing rate in objects per second; and ρ, the input rate. The time derivative of S, $\dot{S}$, is the throughput or output rate of the server. The maximum throughput is independent of the load and input rates and is given by

$$\mu_0 = T/\alpha. \qquad (3)$$

In Eq. (3), T is the throughput capacity of the server and α is the number of machine language instructions required to process an object. The constant μ_0 is the maximum throughput (objects/second) and is attained only when the system is saturated, namely, when S is large.

In general, the average throughput at a server is dependent on the average load. The particular functional form which characterizes this dependence is closely tied to particular system characteristics, and as Agnew [1] has indicated, the choice of function is not completely open. At the very least, the function $\mu(S)$ must be strictly concave in S. A particular functional form we use for purposes of formulating resource allocation strategies is

$$\mu(S) = \frac{T}{\alpha} \frac{\gamma S}{1 + \gamma S}. \tag{4}$$

In Eq. (4), γ is a positive parameter that is characteristic of the particular system in question. For actual systems, γ values should be obtainable from simulation or analysis of system design or requirements can be established for γ for performance objectives. The functional form used in Eq. (4) has the property that throughput varies linearly with load for small-load values, but saturates at the level μ_0 as S becomes large. A typical throughput-load curve is depicted in Fig. 3.

The model developed here can be extended to account for the flow of multiple object types. Suppose there are two object types: (i) threatening objects (e.g., reentry vehicles); and (ii) nonthreatening objects (e.g., high-quality decoys). Let X represent the number of threatening objects at the node and let Y represent the number of nonthreatening objects at the node. Similarly, let w represent the input rate for the threatening objects and let d be the input rate for the nonthreatening objects. Then the following identities hold:

$$X + Y = S, \quad w + d = \rho. \tag{5}$$

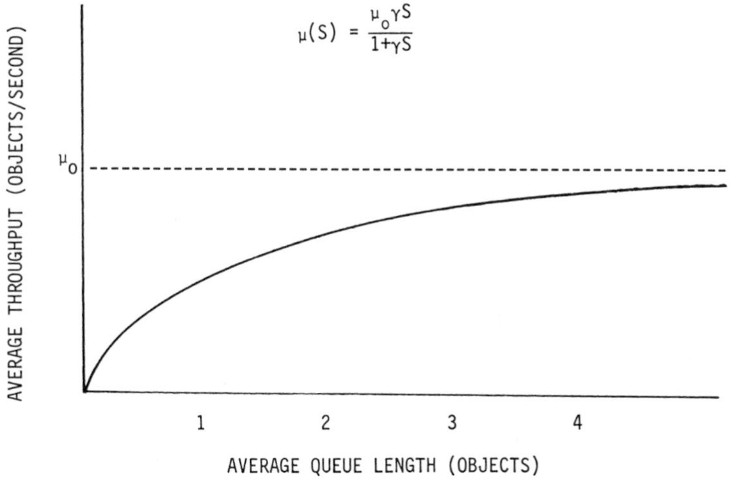

Fig. 3. Throughput-load curve for single-node system.

Assuming that threatening and nonthreatening objects are uniformly distributed throughout the input stream and in the queue, we obtain the system dynamics

$$\dot{X} = -\frac{X}{X+Y}\mu(X+Y) + w, \qquad \dot{Y} = -\frac{Y}{X+Y}\mu(X+Y) + d. \qquad (6)$$

Although only two object types are considered here, the above structure is easily extendable to systems with more categories, e.g., C^3 systems.

In the next section the model presented in this section is extended to a pipeline of servers.

C. PIPELINE FLOW MODEL

The pipeline model developed here can be used to represent information flow through a single serial processor, or through multiple processors when communication time delays are negligible. An important feature of time-critical systems is that object information may be dropped at a node if processing is too slow. Modeling of object loss (leakage) is considered in detail in the next section. However, lost objects must be accounted for in the pipeline system flow dynamics. We define the following variables:

N Number of data processing functions or nodes

$X_K(t)$ Number of threatening objects in node K at time t, $K = 1, \ldots, N$

$Y_K(t)$ Number of nonthreatening objects in node K at time t, $K = 1, \ldots, N$

$S_K(t)$ Total number of objects at node K at time t

$w_0(t)$ Rate at which threatening objects enter the processor (threatening objects/second) at time t

$d_0(t)$ Rate at which nonthreatening objects enter the processor (nonthreatening objects/second) at time t

$w_K(t)$ Threatening objects input rate (threatening objects/second) at node K + 1, $K = 1, \ldots, N - 1$

$d_K(t)$ Nonthreatening objects input rate (nonthreatening objects/second) at node K + 1, $K = 1, \ldots, N - 1$

$\mu_K(t)$ Function which relates output rate at node K to the load (objects/second)

$\delta_K(t)$ Rate at which nonthreatening objects are dropped (objects/second) at node K at time t

$\lambda_K(t)$ Leakage rate from node K (threatening objects/second) at time t, $K = 1, \ldots, N$

Continuous-time differential equations which characterize the load dynamics at each node K, $K = 1, \ldots, N$, are

$$\begin{aligned} \dot{X}_K(t) &= -\left(\frac{X_K(t)}{X_K(t) + Y_K(t)}\right)\mu_K(S_K(t)) + w_{K-1}(t), \\ \dot{Y}_K(t) &= -\left(\frac{X_K(t)}{X_K(t) + Y_K(t)}\right)\mu_K(S_K(t)) + d_{K-1}(t), \end{aligned} \tag{7}$$

where

$$S_K(t) = X_K(t) + Y_K(t). \tag{8}$$

The input rates w_{K-1}, d_{K-1} are simply the system input rates w_0, d_0 in the case $K = 1$. In the case $K > 1$, w_{K-1}, d_{K-1} are related to the output rate at node $K - 1$ by the equations

$$w_{K-1}(t) = \left(\frac{X_{K-1}(t)}{X_{K-1}(t) + Y_{K-1}(t)}\right)\mu_{K-1}(S_{K-1}(t)) - \lambda_{K-1}(t), \tag{9}$$

$$d_{K-1}(t) = \left(\frac{Y_{K-1}(t)}{X_{K-1}(t) + Y_{K-1}(t)}\right)\mu_{K-1}(S_{K-1}(t)) - \delta_{K-1}(t). \tag{10}$$

In Eq. (9), the rate of threatening objects is simply the output rate of the preceeding node minus the leakage rate. A similar relationship must hold for nonthreatening objects, Eq. (10).

D. LEAKAGE MODELING

Long time delays in processing object information, even on the order of milliseconds for BMD system applications, can significantly reduce the value of the information. In this section, we present a model for predicting the number of objects that are dropped from the system due to congestion and slow processing. A basic assumption is that object loss is a random event, and the probability that an object will be purged is an increasing dunction of time spent at a node. For BMD systems, such an assumption is approapriate in the case of target tracking. Objects that are tracked too slowly will be lost, resulting in the purging of the object data file, regardless of whether the object is threatening or not.

Let t_K^d be the time delay incurred by an object in node K. A simple candidate functional form is assumed here for modeling the dependence of P_K^w (the probability that an object's data is passed to the next node, given that it is threatening) on the time delay at the server. The main modeling requirements for such a functional form are that P_K^w be equal to one or nearly one when the delay is small, and that the probability decreases monotonically as the delay increases. A functional form used here for the purpose of illustration is

$$P_K^w = \begin{cases} 1 - \left(t_K^{d^2} \big/ \tau_K^2\right), & t_K^d \le \tau_K, \\ 0, & t_K^d > \tau_K. \end{cases} \tag{11}$$

In the above, τ_K is the maximum allowable processing time delay at node K. Delays longer than this result in the assured leakage of threatening objects. We note that, in general, leakage can result as the outcome of two types of events: (i) a threatening object is purged as a result of slow processing; or (ii) a threatening object is processed in a timely manner, but is incorrectly classified as nonthreatening and purged from the system. The functional form specified by Eq. (11) is strictly suitable only for characterizing leakage of the first type. For systems in which improper classification is an issue, it may be necessary to modify the functional form to accommodate that effect.

The selection of the particular function form (11) does not place a severe limitation on the methodology developed here. If feedback control is suitably implemented to mitigate against long wait times, it may not be necessary to model performance accurately with long wait times. It would then be sufficient to model performance accurately only for a narrow range of values around the optimum. The simple models presented here may be adequate for this purpose.

Also modeled here is the probability P_K^d, i.e., the probability an object is passed given that it is nonthreatening. As is the case with P_K^w, a number of functional forms are possible. In the case of a BMD system, it is reasonable to assume that a properly functioning system will purge most nonthreatening objects from the system. Thus, P_K^d will be small even when the time delay is small. Let $\overline{\delta}_K$ be a constant that represents the probability a nonthreatening object is dropped when there is zero delay at node K. Then a functional form which represents the probability of passing a nonthreatening object is

$$P_K^d = \begin{cases} \left(1 - \overline{\delta}_K\right)\left(1 - \left(t_K^{d^2} \big/ \tau_K^2\right)\right), & t_K^d < \tau_K, \\ 0, & t_K^d < \tau_K. \end{cases} \qquad (12)$$

A remaining issue here is the evaluation of the delay time for an object awaiting service, t_K^d. The delay must be directly proportional to the load at the node and inversely proportional to the throughput. Both load and throughput are dynamic quantities, and it is difficult, within the context of the model, to specify the actual delay time for an individual object. In lieu of this, we use the dimensionally correct expression, which represents the average delay time experienced by objects at node K:

$$t_K^d = S_K/\mu_K. \qquad (13)$$

The above expression correctly estimates the delay time for an object to pass through node K, given that both S_K and μ_K are time-invariant.

Using formulas (11)-(13), we can write expressions for the leakage rates for λ_K, threatening objects, and for δ_K, the rate at which nonthreatening objects are dropped. For example, leakage is given by

$$\lambda_K(t) = \frac{X_K(t)}{X_K(t) + Y_K(t)} \mu_K(t)\left(1 - P_K^w(t)\right)$$

$$= \frac{\alpha_K X_K(t)[1 + \gamma_K(X_K(t) + Y_K(t))]}{T_K \tau_K^2 \gamma_K}. \tag{14}$$

In the above, γ_K is a dimensionless constant which characterizes the functional dependence of output rate on load at node K [γ for a single-node system was introduced in Eq. (4)]. The constant α_K is the number of machine language instructions required to process an object at node K and T_K is the throughput capacity allocated to the node.

III. PERFORMANCE MEASURES

An important step in the development and evaluation of resource allocation strategies is the formulation of suitable measures of system performance. Four such criteria are formulated here:

(a) process time,

(b) transit (or port-to-port) time,

(c) system leakage,

(d) capacity utilization.

The suitability of a performance measure for a particular application depends on the objectives of the particular data processing system and on the availability of information to the local controller required to effect a specific allocation.

A. *PROCESS TIME*

Process time t^p is the simplest measure of system performance to formulate. In an uncongested system an object entering node K will complete service at that node in α_K/T_K seconds where

α_K is the number of machine language instructions required to process an object and T_K is the throughput allocated to that node. The total process time through the sequence of N servers is given by

$$t^P = \sum_{k=1}^{N} \frac{\alpha_K}{T_K}. \quad (15)$$

The above performance measure is most approapriate for systems in which congestion is not present. In general the process time considerably underestimates the actual time for an object to complete all N data processing functions. However, it may be of value for systems in which estimates of (X_K, Y_K, S_K) are difficult to obtain. Process time is a measure of system performance that is independent of the system state.

B. TRANSIT TIME

The time available to make a decision to intercept or ignore a potentially threatening object is a critical factor in the design of BMD systems. From the time an object is initially detected to the time a commit decision is made, the object data must pass through the entire sequence of data processing functions. Hence, a useful performance measure for the data processing system is the port-to-port time for an object to complete the entire sequence of functions. The process time index, developed in A, is a measure of port-to-port time only for an uncongested system. The transit time index developed here is also an approximate measure, but is sensitive to system loading.

In Section II.D, we have used the variable t_K^d to denote the time delay incurred by an individual object in passing through node K. Formally, the port-to-port time t^S for an object to pass through all N nodes is given by

$$t^S = \sum_{K=1}^{N} t_K^d. \tag{16}$$

Let t_K^S represent the clock time at which an object entering the processor (node 1) at time t_0 would pass through the K-th node. The quantities t_K^S are given recursively by

$$\begin{aligned} t_1^S &= t_0 + t_1^d, \\ t_2^S &= t_1^S + t_2^d, \\ &\vdots \\ t^S = t_N^S &= t_{N-1}^S + t_N^d. \end{aligned} \tag{17}$$

The time delays t_K^d are dependent on the distribution of the load and, since the load is evolving dynamically, the time delays themselves change with time. It is evident from Eq. (17) that in order to predict the actual port-to-port time t^S for an object entering node 1 at time t, it is necessary (at a minimum) to solve the system dynamic equations (7) forward in time.

A simple technique for estimating t^S in real time is based on the following. Assume that the current loads are constant at all future times, i.e.,

$$S_K(t) \cong S_K(t_0); \quad K = 1, \ldots, N, \quad t > t_0. \tag{18}$$

Then at time t_0, t^S is estimated by

$$t^S = \sum_{K=1}^{N} \frac{\alpha_K(1 + \gamma_K S_K(t_0))}{\gamma_K T_K}. \tag{19}$$

This formula is obtained using Eqs. (13) and (4) and summing over nodes. Equation (19) is an estimator of the time for an object to complete all N data processing functions given that it enters the system at time t_0. The instantaneous performance measure may be integrated over a time interval $[t_i, t_f]$ to yield the aggregate transit time for all objects over the control interval

$$\Lambda^S = \int_{t_i}^{t_f} \sum_{K=1}^{N} \frac{\alpha_K(1 + \gamma_K S_K(t))}{\gamma_K T_K(t_0)} \, dt. \tag{20}$$

The above measure is cumulative over a time window and is sensitive to system dynamics.

C. LEAKAGE INDEX

For time-critical systems subject to leakage, a natural performance measure is the total number of threatening objects that are inadvertently purged from the system due to overloading. Integrating Eq. (14) and summing over all nodes in the pipeline yields accumulated leakage over a time window:

$$\Lambda^L = \int_{t_i}^{t_f} \sum_{K=1}^{N} \frac{\alpha_K X_K(1 + \gamma_K S_K(t))}{\tau_K^2 T_K(t_0)} \, dt. \tag{21}$$

The above measure directly addresses performance of BMD systems where leakage minimization is critical.

D. CAPACITY UTILIZATION

Another useful index of system efficiency is the fraction of computing capacity that is idle during the operating period. Idle capacity at a node is calculated as the difference between the saturated throughput [see Eq. (3)] at a node and the unsaturated throughput [see Eq. (4)]. Idle capacity normalized by total throughput capacity $I_K(t)$ at node K at time t is given by

$$I_K(t) = \frac{1}{1 + \gamma_K S_K(t)}. \tag{22}$$

Aggregate idle capacity I(t) for the entire system is

$$I(t) = \frac{1}{T^0} \sum_{K=1}^{N} \frac{T_K}{1 + \gamma_K S_K(t)}. \quad (23)$$

While minimization of idle capacity is not by itself a primary performance objective for any time-critical system performance. The idle capacity index I(t) can serve as the basis for a simple local control strategy. This is pursued further in the next section.

IV. CONTROL STRATEGIES

This section presents strategies for resource management within a single processor based on the performance measures developed in the previous section. The emphasis is on developing control algorithms that can be implemented in real time. The remainder of this section is organized as follows. Section A presents additional constraints which are incorporated into the optimization methods. These constraints provide upper and lower limits on the throughput capacity allocated to each server. Section B presents methods for allocating throughput based on the objectives of minimum process time, minimum transit time, and minimum leakage. In Section C an algorithm is presented which is applicable to time-critical systems with long transport delays between nodes. Formulation of this algorithm requires a modification of the leakage model developed in Section II. In Section D, a linear programming procedure is discussed which minimizes system idle capacity. The initial algorithm formulations require full state information (X, Y, S). An algorithm is presented in Section E that uses only partial state information together with a priori state information. In general, only incomplete information (S only) on the system state is available; this is especially true for BMD systems, where long transport delays in data processing preclude accurate state observations. In the remainder of this chapter, we suppress the explicit time dependence of the system states and performance measures for notational convenience.

A. *OPTIMIZATION CONSTRAINTS*

In addition to the capacity constraint specified by Eq. (1), a number of constraints may be incorporated into resource management strategies. The first type to be discussed is a constraint on the minimum throughput capacity allocated to a node. The second type of constraint is appropriate for time-critical systems in which all objects must incur some minimum time delay at a node, independent of the throughput capacity allocation, e.g., BMD systems.

1. *Minimum Throughput Constraint*

There are at least two reasons for assigning minimum throughput to nodes. One is to ensure that the system will achieve a minimum prespecified performance level, and another, which is of particular concern for systems with leakage, is that the leakage probability model may be accurate only over a limited range of load values (see Section II.D). In particular, the model may be valid only for small to moderate loads. A minimum throughput constraint per node is a hedge against unanticipated or unmodeled large leakage levels.

The throughput constraint is implemented as follows. Let $t_K^{d^*}$ be the desired maximum delay time for an object to complete service at node K. Then the minimum throughput constraint $\underline{T}_K$

is given by

$$T_K \geq \underline{T}_K = \frac{\alpha_K(1 + \gamma_K S_K)}{\gamma_K t_K^{d^*}}. \tag{24}$$

In the case that it is desired not to exceed a maximum allowable leakage probability per node, PC, the maximum time delay is calculated as

$$t_K^{d^*} = \tau_K \sqrt{1 - PC}. \tag{25}$$

This formula for t^{d^*} is obtained using the quadratic leakage function, Eq. (11). The process for selecting the maximum desirable time delay is depicted in Fig. 4.

If the system becomes severely overloaded it may not be possible to maintain the leakage probabilities above the prespecified level. In such cases a candidate strategy for throughput capacity allocation is to allocate equal leakage probabilities to each node. The purpose of this strategy is to maintain the performance of each node as closely as possible to the prespecified cutoff level. The associated resource allocations

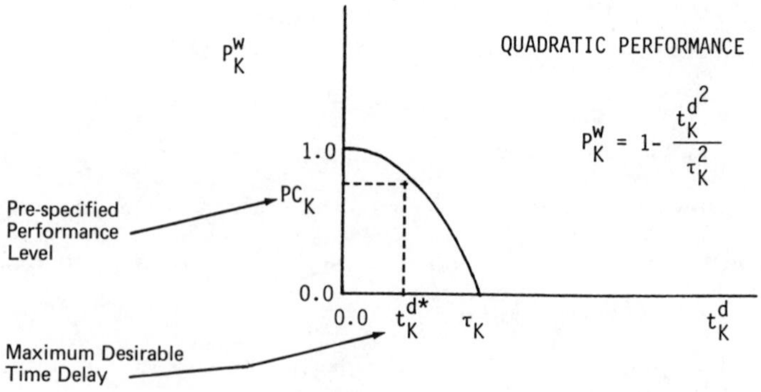

Fig. 4. Selection of maximum desirable average time delay.

are calculated as

$$T_K = F_K T^0 \Bigg/ \left(\tau_K \sum_{j=1}^{N} \frac{F_j}{j} \right). \tag{26}$$

In the above F_j is given by

$$F_j = \frac{\alpha_j (1 + \gamma_j S_j)}{\gamma_j}. \tag{27}$$

2. Transport Delay Constraints

In certain time-critical systems objects may incur minimum service delays at a node independent of the throughput capacity allocated to that node. For example, if objects are being tracked at an externally set prespecified pulse rate there is no benefit to assigning additional throughput capacity to a node than is required to match the pulse rate of the tracking system; any additional capacity is unused. To fully address this issue it is necessary to impose a state-dependent maximum throughput constraint at each node. For such systems, it is also necessary to modify the leakage probability model to incorporate the additional transport delay.

Let t_K^0 be the minimum delay time for an object passing through the K-th server. Then a candidate functional form which represents the probability that a threatening object is passed as a function of the total delay time is given by

$$P_K^W = \begin{cases} 1, & 0 \le t_K \le t_K^0, \\ 1 - \left(\left(t_K - t_K^0 \right)^2 \Big/ \tau_K^2 \right), & t_K^0 \le t_K \le \tau_K + t_K^0, \\ 0, & t_K \ge \tau_K + t_K^0. \end{cases} \tag{28}$$

The above model, depicted in Fig. 5, is an extension of the quadratic performance function specified by Eq. (11). For such systems, performance degrades only if the actual time delay is

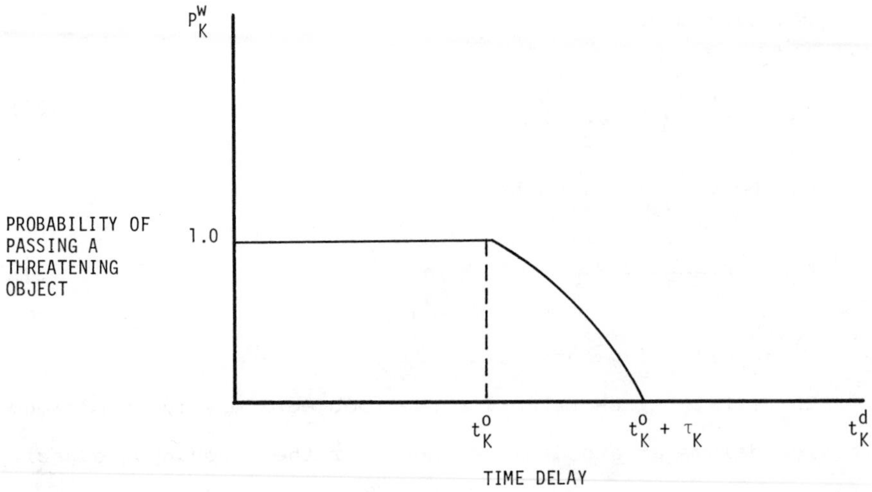

Fig. 5. Performance degradation of congested system with minimum transport delay.

greater than some minimum acceptable level. Additionally, the following optimization constraint is imposed to ensure that excess throughput capacity is not allocated:

$$T_K \leq \overline{T}_K = \alpha_K(1 + \gamma_K S_K)/\gamma_K t_K^0. \tag{29}$$

In principle the transport delays discussed here can be incorporated directly into the system dynamics; however, the resulting model is considerably less tractable than the one used here. The upper bound throughput constraint at a node (29) imposes a rate constraint on object flow [in addition to the rate constraint imposed by Eq. (1)]. The transport delay dynamics model incorporating rate constraints is intermediate in complexity between a nontransport delayed system $\left(t_K^0 = 0\right)$ and a true discrete event delayed system. In a discrete event system, there is a minimum transport delay for each object regardless of the rate constraint for groups of each object.

B. SOME SIMPLE FEEDBACK LAWS

This section presents some simple open-loop feedback control laws suitable for systems in which leakage is characterized by the quadratic probability function (11). It is assumed that lower bounds on throughput capacity allocations of the type specified by Eq. (24) are required. No upper bound constraints or minimum transport delays are assumed.

Using the quadratic probability function (11) each of the performance measures, process time, transit time, and leakage can be expressed using the same general form:

$$\Lambda = \int_{t_i}^{t_f} \frac{G_K}{T_K}\, dt. \tag{30}$$

In the above, Λ is the performance criterion. The time interval $[t_i, t_f]$ is the time interval in which control is implemented. The T_K are the throughput capacity allocations for the N data processing functions. For the process time criterion, G_K is given by

$$G_K = \alpha_K. \tag{31}$$

For the transit time criterion with quadratic probability function (11),

$$G_K = \alpha_K(1 + \gamma_K S_K)/\gamma_K. \tag{32}$$

For the leakage criterion with quadratic performance degradation,

$$G_K = \alpha_K X_K(1 + \gamma_K S_K)/\tau_K^2. \tag{33}$$

The optimal control problem for obtaining dynamic resource allocation strategies for a pipeline of nodes is

$$\min_{T_1(t),\ldots,T_N(t)} \Lambda, \qquad t \in [t_i, t_f]. \tag{34}$$

The optimization is subject to the capacity constraint (1), the minimum throughput constraint (24), and the pipeline flow dynamics (7). The optimization may also be subject to a maximum throughput constraint, e.g., Eq. (29), although further consideration of such constraints is postponed until Section C.

An open-loop feedback solution to Eq. (34) is available in closed form. This solution is optimal instantaneously (i.e., as $t_f - t_i \to 0$), and is obtained by minimizing the integrand in Eq. (30). First, ignore the upper and lower bound constraints on throughput capacity. Then the closed-form solution assuming only the capacity constraint (1) is

$$T_K = \left(\sqrt{G_K} \bigg/ \sum_{J=1}^{N} \sqrt{G_J}\right) T^0. \tag{35}$$

Equation (35) can serve as the basis for a four-step procedure for calculating throughput capacity allocations that satisfy the lower bound and capacity constraints. We denote this Procedure I; it is presented in detail in the Appendix.

The basic structure of Procedure I can be summarized as follows. First, determine if there is sufficient capacity to meet all lower-bound constraints. If not, the constraints are relaxed. If there is sufficient capacity, calculate controls that minimize the instantaneous performance subject to the capacity constraint. If the resulting allocations do not satisfy the lower-bound constraints, then increase any infeasible allocations to the constraint values, and reiterate the procedure until a feasible allocation is obtained.

C. A LEAKAGE-MINIMIZING ALGORITHM FOR SYSTEMS WITH MINIMUM TRANSPORT DELAYS

The algorithms discussed in the previous section are most suitable for systems in which the time delay between nodes is determined solely by the throughput capacity allocated to each node. Some nodes, e.g., in BMD systems, may have built-in transport delays that are independent of the throughput capacity for a range of values. Specifically, let S be the load at a node. Let α, T, γ be the previously defined parameters, machine language instructions per node, throughput capacity, and throughput-load parameter. Then, if t^0 is a minimum delay time for the node, the delay time t^d as a function of the system parameters is given by

$$t^d = \max\left\{t^0, \frac{\alpha}{T}\,\frac{(1+\gamma S)}{\gamma}\right\}. \tag{36}$$

The above dependence of delay on load is depicted in Fig. 6. The time delay is independent of throughput and load until the load reaches a critical level. Beyond that level, the time delay increases linearly. Note that for loads beyond the critical level, the time delay is affected by the throughput capacity T.

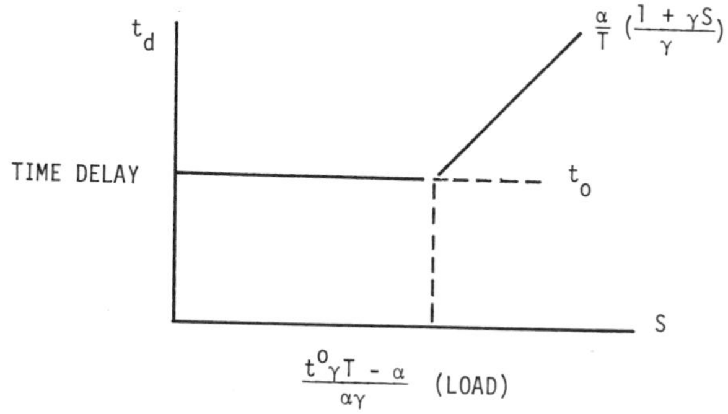

Fig. 6. Time delay versus load for transport delay system.

For the systems considered here, the probability of leakage is specified by the modified performance function [Eq. (28)]. The total system leakage rate Λ^D for the time delay system is given by

$$\Lambda^D = \sum_{K=1}^{N} \frac{X_K}{S_K} \mu_K(S_K)\left(1 - P_K^W(S_K)\right)$$

$$= \sum_{K=1}^{N} \frac{X_K \mu_K(S_K)}{S_K}\left(\frac{\max\left\{\frac{\alpha_K}{T_K}\frac{1 + \gamma_K S_K}{\gamma_K} - t_K^0,\ 0\right\}}{\tau_K}\right)^2. \tag{37}$$

In the above, t_K^0 is the minimum transport delay through node K. Equation (37) can be rewritten as

$$\Lambda^D = \sum_{K=1}^{N} \max\left\{\frac{A_K}{T_K} + B_K + C_K T_K^2,\ 0\right\}. \tag{38}$$

where

$$A_K = \frac{X_K}{\tau_K^2}\frac{(1 + \gamma_K S_K)}{\gamma_K},$$

$$B_K = -\frac{X_K t_K^0}{\tau_K^2}, \tag{39}$$

$$C_K = \frac{2t_K^{0^2} X_K}{\tau_K^2}\frac{\gamma_K}{\alpha_K(1 + \gamma_K S_K)}.$$

The instantaneous leakage minimizing problem is to find controls $T_1, \ldots, T_N$ which minimize Λ^D subject to the capacity constraint (1) and minimum throughput constraint (24). It is also apparent that there is a maximum throughput constraint implicit at each node; throughput allocation at a node beyond the level that yields zero leakage is redundant. The maximum level at each node $\overline{T}_K$ is given by Eq. (29).

As in the previous section, a solution approach for minimizing (38) is to neglect the lower-bound constraints and solve for an allocation that satisfies the system capacity constraint (1). The lower-bound constraints can then be satisfied using a procedure analogous to Procedure I (see the Appendix). Unfortunately for all nodes but the first, there is no simple analytic solution to the capacity-constrained problem. However, an efficient iterative search procedure has been developed and is discussed here.

Now we consider the problem of minimizing leakage (38) subject to the capacity constraint (1). A useful insight in solving this problem is that the cost function Λ^D can be replaced by the modified cost function $\Lambda^{D'}$:

$$\Lambda^{D'} = \sum_{K=1}^{N} \frac{A_K}{T_K} + B_K + C_K T_K^2. \tag{40}$$

The quadratic term in the function $\Lambda^{D'}$ acts as a penalty on the implicit constraint $T_K \leq \overline{T}_K$ in (38); hence, the max operator can be dropped.

The Lagrangian L, corresponding to $\Lambda^{D'}$, and the constraint (1) are given by

$$L = \sum_{K=1}^{N} \frac{A_K}{T_K} + B_K + C_K T_K^2 + \eta\left(\sum_{K=1}^{N} T_K - T^0\right). \tag{41}$$

In the above, η is a Lagrange multiplier for the capacity constraint. The Lagrange multiplier η is the solution of the equation

$$\sum_{K=1}^{N} \sqrt{\frac{A_K}{\eta + C_K}} = T^0. \tag{42}$$

This equation can be solved very efficiently using Newton's method for finding roots. First, we define the function

$g(\eta)$ by

$$g(\eta) = \left(\sum_{k=1}^{N} \sqrt{\frac{A_K}{\eta + C_K}} \right)^{-2} - (T^0)^{-2}. \tag{43}$$

Then an iterative procedure for finding η is given by

$$\eta_{j+1} = \eta_j - \left(g(\eta_j)/g'(\eta_j) \right). \tag{44}$$

In the above η_j is the j-th iterate of the procedure and $g'(\cdot)$ is the derivative of $g(\cdot)$. The purpose of using the particular functional form $g(\cdot)$ is that it is nearly linear in the vicinity of the solution. Thus, the Newton procedure results in very rapid convergence. This has been borne out by computational experience (Section V).

A natural initialization technique for the Newton procedure discussed here can also be specified. Note that the zero of the function $g(\eta)$ defined above must be greater than the largest pole of the function $h(\eta)$:

$$h(\eta) = \sum_{K=1}^{N} \sqrt{\frac{A_K}{\eta + C_K}}. \tag{45}$$

In practice, the initialization

$$\eta_0 = \max_K \{-C_K\} \tag{46}$$

is very close to the final solution.

A remaining issue in solving the transport delay system is developing a constraint relaxation procedure in the event that there is insufficient throughput capacity to meet the lower-bound throughput constraints. For the quadratic leakage model, the constraints are met by adjusting the parameter PC according to Eqs. (26) and (27). An analogous procedure for the transport delay system is to solve for a value PC such that

$$\sum_{K=1}^{N} \frac{\alpha_K(1 + \gamma_K S_K)}{\gamma_K\left(t_K^0 + \tau_K \sqrt{1 - PC}\right)} = T^0. \tag{47}$$

Solution of Eq. (47) requires an iterative procedure; again, Newton's method can be applied. The details are not specified here.

Procedure I', which extends Procedure I to accommodate the transport delay system, is described in the Appendix.

D. CAPACITY UTILIZATION ALGORITHM

As was indicated previously, although the minimization of system idle capacity is not by itself a performance goal for time-critical systems it can provide the basis for simple feedback resource allocation strategy, especially when both minimum and maximum throughput constraints are present.

When maximum throughput constraints are present, it is possible that the total throughput capacity exceeds the allocated throughput. In particular if we denote the upper limits on throughput capacity per node as $\overline{T}_1, \ldots, \overline{T}_N$ it is possible that

$$\sum_{K=1}^{N} \overline{T}_K < T^0. \tag{48}$$

Equation (48) indicates that at certain times there may be unallocated capacity. To account for this we include a slack node, denoted T_{N+1}. Using this slack variable aggregate idle capacity I is given by

$$I = \frac{1}{T^0} \sum_{K=1}^{N} \frac{T_K}{1 + \gamma_K S_K} + \frac{T_{N+1}}{T^0}. \tag{49}$$

The idle capacity minimization problem is to minimize the objective (49) subject to the capacity constraint

$$\sum_{K=1}^{N+1} T_K = T^0 \tag{50}$$

and upper and lower bounds

$$\underline{T}_K \leq T_K \leq \overline{T}_K, \quad K = 1, \ldots, N. \tag{51}$$

This problem is a linear programming problem with a very simple solution method. This solution method (Procedure II) is described in the Appendix.

The idea behind Procedure II is to allocate throughput capacity first to the node with the greatest marginal improvement. This is done until the node is at full capacity $\left(\overline{T}_K\right)$. Then the next node is treated similarly, etc. Any excess is allocated to the slack node, N + 1.

If there is insufficient capacity to meet the lower limits on throughput allocation, the lower-bound constraints can be relaxed by adjusting the parameter PC according to Eq. (47).

E. REDUCED INFORMATION ALGORITHM

Implementation of the algorithm developed in Section C for the transport delay system requires full knowledge of the system state. Within the context of BMD, this requires that the controller have available the number of threatening and non-threatening objects at each node. Typically, this type of information is not available. At best the controller receives information on the total number of objects at each node; their type is uncertain. A possible approach to remedy this is to combine the available measurements with knowledge of the system dynamics to estimate the system states. However, the long transport delays at each node render the system unobservable, at least on a time scale that is useful for feedback control.

Another possibility is to use prior information on the threat (system inputs) to perform real-time state estimation (and control). Such an approach is developed here. We assume that the ratio $r_0 = d_0/w_0$ of nonthreatening objects to threatening objects is known in advance, and that this ratio remains constant over time in the input stream. We also assume that at each node K, K = 1, ..., N, the number of objects S_K is known. Then the prior information r_0 can be incorporated into the algorithm described in Section IV.C. The idea is to estimate the states X_K and incorporate those estimates directly into the previously described algorithm. The estimates $\hat{X}_K$ are calculated as

$$\hat{X}_K = S_K \Bigg/ \left(1 + r_0 \prod_{j=1}^{K-1} 1 - \bar{\delta}_j\right). \tag{52}$$

In the above, $1 - \bar{\delta}_j$ is the maximum probability that nonthreatening objects are passed through node J. The state estimate $\hat{X}_K$ is substituted into the performance measure (38) and used to derive feedback controls.

V. BMD EXAMPLE

This section presents the results of simulation runs used to test the algorithms developed here. The model parameters have been selected to correspond to those of a generic ballistic missile defense (BMD) system. Two primary cases have been considered: (i) system performance is represented by the quadratic leakage function (12), and (ii) system performance is characterized by the transport delay leakage function (28).

Although the transport delay model is more representative of an actual system, the comparison here illustrates the response characteristics of the various systems.

Section A presents the model parameters used. Section B contains some algorithm comparisons for the quadratic leakage model. Results for the transport delay system are presented in Section C.

A. SIMULATION MODEL

A four-node model has been used to characterize a generic terminal BMD system. The choice of four is largely arbitrary; however, the particular four selected correspond to easily identifiable high-level sequential functions of a BMD data processing system: (i) search; (ii) track; (iii) discrimination; and (iv) intercept decision. Two types of objects enter the system: warheads and decoys. Objects are tracked for a brief period subsequent to detection. Active discrimination is performed to distinguish object types. Finally, interceptor resources are allocated. The parameters used here are for a generic system and are not necessarily representative of an actual BMD system.

Table 1 shows the values of three parameters, for each of the four nodes of an example BMD system. Column 1 shows the fraction of total machine language instructions for each of the four nodes.

In addition to the number of machine language instructions, the time delays τ_K, $K = 1, \ldots, 4$, are required as parameters in the quadratic node performance functions utilized by the controller. The values used in the simulation runs are shown in column 2 of Table 1.

Table 1. Parameters for BMD Example

Node	*Relative machine language instructions*	*Maximum service time delays τ_K (sec)*	*Decoy probabilities δ_K*
1	0.349	0.2	0.00
2	0.227	2.0	0.50
3	0.284	2.0	0.95
4	0.140	0.1	0.05

Another set of parameters used in the simulation are the $\overline{\delta}_K$, the maximum probabilities that a decoy is dropped at node K when there is no queue. The values assumed are shown in column 3 of Table 1.

For simulation purposes, a nominal threat was developed for analyzing the step response of the closed-loop systems. Three parameters characterize the threat: (i) r_0, the ratio of incoming nonthreatening objects to threatening objects; (ii) S_0, the total number of objects detected; and (iii) T_A, the duration of the attack. The nominal parameter values are listed in Table 2.

Another important parameter is γ_K, which measures the saturation characteristics of a node. A value of $\gamma_K = 10$, $K = 1, \ldots, 4$, is assumed at each node.

The parameter PC, which determines the values of lower bound throughput capacity constraints, is a very sensitive control design parameter. The importance of PC to algorithm performance is shown in the examples that follow.

Another important issue is algorithm performance sensitivity to the availability and quality of prior information. This

Table 2. Nominal Attack Parameter Values

Parameter	*Nominal value*
r_0	*8.0*
S_0	*40.0 objects*
T_A	*6.0 sec*

issue is explored for the reduced information algorithm (Section IV.e) in the simulation analysis (Section V.B).

B. QUADRATIC LEAKAGE MODEL

This section compares the performance of four resource allocations for the example BMD system with quadratic leakage. The four algorithms are (Q1) minimum process time, (Q2) minimum transit time, (Q3) minimum leakage rate, and (Q4) leakage equalizing algorithm. The quadratic leakage model may not be an adequate performance characterization of actual BMD systems since it ignores minimum transport delays. The results here are for comparison purposes only.

Algorithms Q1-Q3 are implemented using Procedure I of Section IV.B. These algorithms differ only in the specification of the variable G_K used to define the performance criterion. The leakage equalizing algorithm Q4 (also using Procedure I) has not been discussed previously. The leakage equalizing algorithm is defined by setting the value of the constraint parameter PC to unity. Setting PC = 1 causes Procedure I to attempt to allocate zero probability of leakage at each node. For a nontrivial system input, this must fail; hence, the procedure will allocate throughput capacity by uniformly relaxing the lower-bound constraint at each node according to Eqs. (26) and (27). This results in equal leakage probability.

Figure 7 shows the step response of the closed-loop system using the minimum leakage rate algorithm. The assumed threat is specified in Table 4. The constraint parameter PC was set at 0.05, and has no effect on the resource allocation. The upper left-hand graph shows the number of threatening objects $X_1, \ldots, X_4$ at each node as well as the input rate w_0 of warheads. The lower left-hand graph shows the decoys $Y_1, \ldots, Y_4$ at each node and the input rate d_0. Note that the X and Y values drop off rapidly after the attack ceases; time delays are short for this model. The upper right-hand graph shows the normalized throughput allocations at each node. The major portion of throughput capacity is shifted to intercept, node 4. The lower right-hand graph shows the probability that a threatening object is passed through each node. This probability is lowest for the search function (node 1) through most of the engagement, reflecting the relatively high number of objects processed at this node.

Table 3 shows algorithm performance for seven test cases. The first three cases show accumulated leakage for algorithms Q1, Q2, and Q3, using the value PC = 0.05. As would be expected, the minimum leakage rate algorithm Q3 showed the best performance with 43% leakage, although all algorithms yielded unsatisfactory performance for the selected parameters. The poor performance of the minimum process time algorithm Q1 can be attributed to its relative insensitivity to the system variables. This algorithm yields no state feedback unless the lower bound throughput constraint is violated. The next three runs compare the same three algorithms using PC = 0.95, a much tighter lower bound constraint. There is much less difference between the three algorithms; the lower-bound constraint is active through most of the engagement. Note that performance of the minimum

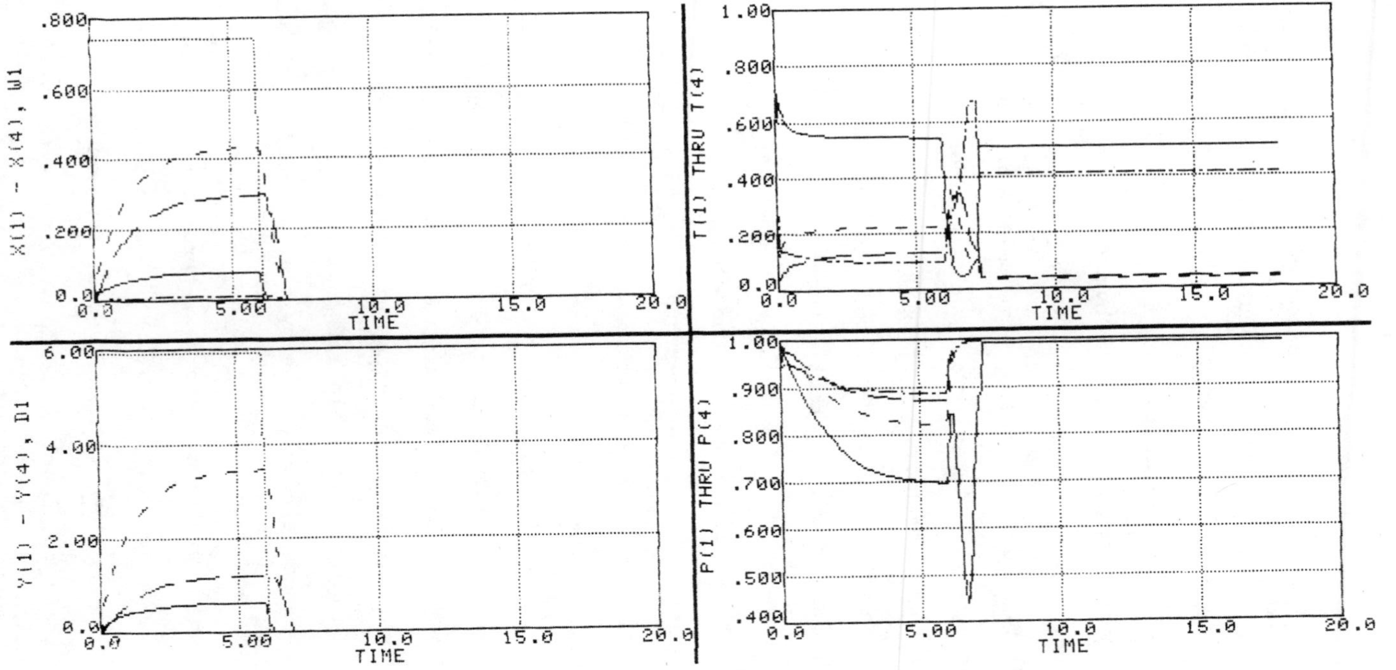

Fig. 7. Closed-loop step response with minimum leakage rate controller, quadratic model (Q3). Key: •••, threat; —, Node 1; ---, Node 2; — —, Node 3; •—•, Node 4.

Table 3. Algorithm Performance Comparison

Algorithm	*PC*	*Accumulated leakage*
Q1	*0.05*	*0.94*
Q2	*0.05*	*0.65*
Q3	*0.05*	*0.43*
Q1	*0.95*	*0.47*
Q2	*0.95*	*0.47*
Q3	*0.95*	*0.46*
Q4	*1.00*	*0.47*

leakage algorithm degrades slightly with the tighter constraint. Finally, the performance of the leakage equalizing algorithm Q4 is shown. There is little difference from the case PC = 0.95. The leakage equalizing algorithm has the advantage of being very simple computationally.

The apparent unsatisfactory performance of the algorithms is a consequence of using dynamic and leakage models, which do not include minimum transport delays. These models are discussed in the next section.

C. TRANSPORT DELAY SYSTEM

This section presents some algorithm comparisons for a BMD system with long minimum transport delays between nodes. For such systems, the leakage probability is given by the modified quadratic function (28). The assumed minimum time delays used for simulation purposes are shown in Table 4.

Three algorithms are compared here: (D1) minimum leakage rate algorithm; (D2) reduced information algorithm; and (D3) minimum idle capacity algorithm. Algorithm D1 is implemented using the iterative procedure discussed in Section IV.C. The

Table 4. Minimum Transport Delays t_K^0 *(sec)*

Node 1	*0.10*
Node 2	*1.00*
Node 3	*1.00*
Node 4	*0.05*

performance measure used is the leakage criterion (38). Implementation of this algorithm assumes perfect knowledge of the number of threatening and nonthreatening objects at each node. Algorithm D2 is similar to D1 except that it can be implemented using only information on the total number of objects at each node. At each time step, the state is estimated using a prior estimate r_0 of the ratio of nonthreatening to threatening objects. The estimation procedure is described in Section IV.C. The third algorithm tested, D3, is implemented using Procedure II, Section IV.D.

Figure 8 shows the step response of the closed-loop time delay system using algorithm D1 and the nominal threat. The lower-bound constraint parameter PC is set to 0.95. The main difference between this example and the examples of the previous section are the long time delays required to move objects from node to node. Although search processing ceases almost immediately after all incoming objects are detected, the remaining functions continue to process objects for several seconds; the discrimination load peaks after search has stopped.

Table 5 presents algorithm performance for the three algorithms discussed here. Algorithm D2 is implemented using a perfect prior estimate, $r_0 = 8.0$. Using the value PC = 0.95 in each case results in close identical performance for each method. The D3 algorithm performs slightly worse but has the

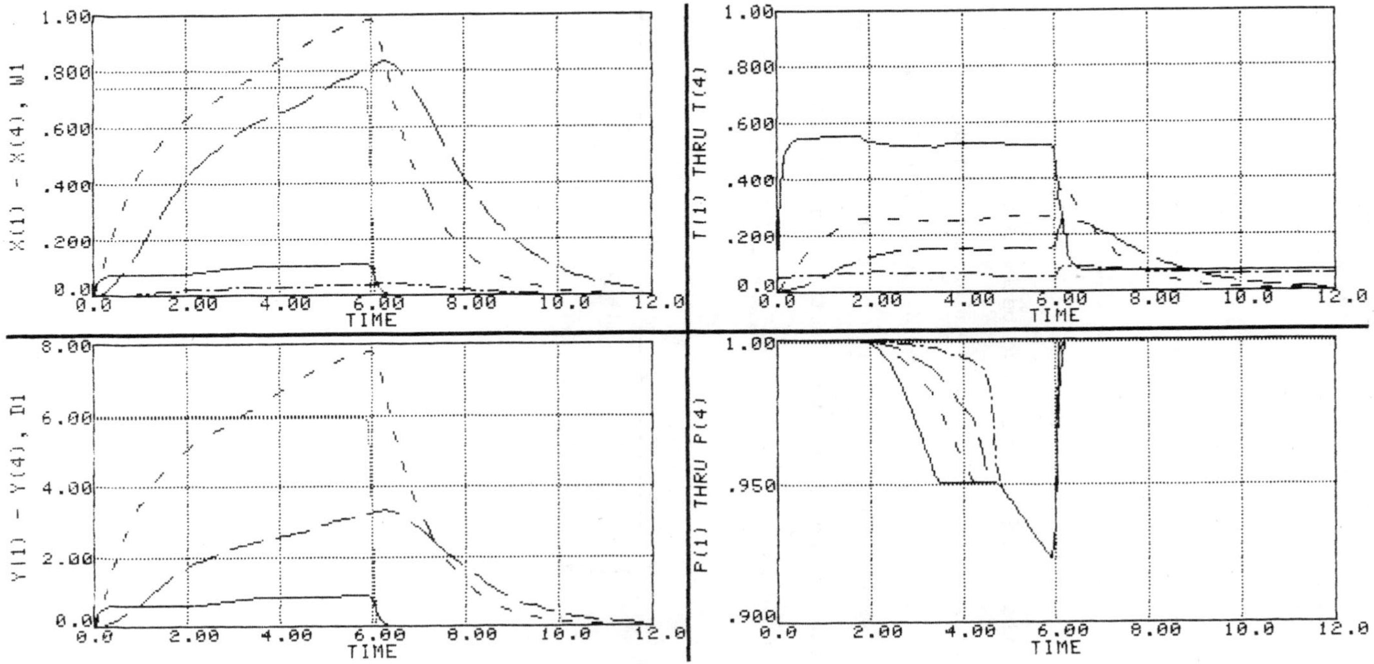

Fig. 8. Closed-loop step response with minimum leakage rate controller, transport delay system (D1). Key: •••, threat; —, Node 1; ---, Node 2; — —, Node 3; •—•, Node 4.

Table 5. Algorithm Performance Comparison

Algorithm	*PC*	*Accumulated leakage*
D1	*0.95*	*0.07*
D2	*0.95*	*0.07*
D3	*0.95*	*0.09*

advantage of fewer calculations per time step. This may prove useful for real-time applications. The CPU times required to implement these algorithms range between 0.001 (D3) and 0.003 (D1 and D2) seconds per control allocation on a VAX 11/780.

Also of interest is the time history of idle capacity at each node. Figure 9 shows this for algorithm D3. Idle capacity is greatest for the intercept function, which places the least demand on capacity in this example. Idle capacity is least for

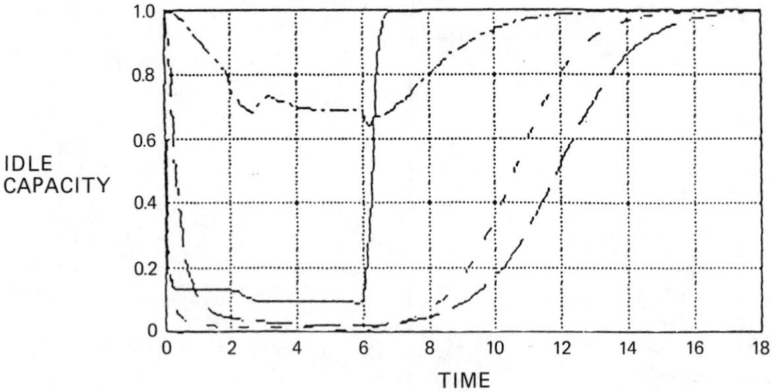

Fig. 9. Time history of idle capacity for minimum idle capacity algorithm (D3). Key: —, Node 1; ---, Node 2; — —, Node 3; •—•, Node 4.

track and discrimination, the functions with the longest transport delays. Aggregate idle capacity does not drop far below 10% in this example.

An important issue is the availability of high-quality prior information on the nature of the threat. In general, perfect state information is not available; the perfect information algorithm D1 is not applicable. Hence, it is necessary that any algorithm actually used either incorporate prior information or use state information directly observable during the engagement. If algorithm D2 is used, a valid concern is whether prior estimation error in r_0 will degrade algorithm performance relative to D1. Preliminary analysis (at least using the model parameters we have selected) indicates estimation error does not result in degradation of algorithm performance.

Table 6 presents the results of a sensitivity analysis used to investigate the effect of estimation error on performance of the reduced information algorithm. In each case, algorithm D2 uses the nominal estimate $r_0 = 8.0$. The actual value of r_0

Table 6. Algorithm Sensitivity to Prior Information

Estimation error (%)	*Algorithm*	*Leakage*
+60	D1	0.06
+60	D2	0.06
0	D1	0.07
0	D2	0.07
-60	D1	0.11
-60	D2	0.11

differs from the nominal estimate by the percentage shown in the left-hand column. Thus, the middle two rows show performance for D1 and D2 for the nominal case. For the other two cases, r_0 at 60% above nominal and r_0 at 60% below nominal, there is virtually no performance difference between the two methods.

VI. GLOBAL OBJECT REALLOCATION

The throughput capacity allocation algorithms have been developed to address the problem of load balancing within a single processor. In the previous section, it was shown that performance of an individual processor is highly sensitive to the internal loading. A natural way to address this sensitivity within a distributed system is to balance the load globally by shifting objects between processors.

A critical concern in transferring objects between processors is the communication time delay in performing object transfer. Even though it may be beneficial to remove an object from a heavily loaded processor, the receiving processor may have insufficient resources to meet the tight timing constraints resulting from long transfer delays. In this section, a procedure for global object allocation is presented, which accounts for the trade-offs involved in object transfer.

Section A contains a discussion of the issues involved, as well as the modeling assumptions used to formulate allocation strategies. In Section B, we extend the previously developed transport delay system to accommodate to processors with object transfer. The basic approach used is to augment the system state variable with additional states that account for transferred objects. Section C presents an algorithm for global object reallocations for a two-processor system. Section D presents the results of some simulation runs demonstrating the object transfer procedure for a two-processor system. Although most of the analysis presented here is strictly representative of a two-processor system, the procedures are easily extendable to the general case of a multiprocessor system.

A. MODELING ISSUES AND ASSUMPTIONS

The following assumptions are made here concerning the operation of a distributed time-critical data processing system:

(a) object data are transferred across a single bus;

(b) the transfer time per object is the same for all objects; and

(c) the time required to calculate resource allocations within an individual processor is much less than the time required to transfer an object between processors.

Assumption (a) is reasonable for a BMD terminal defense construct. Assumption (b) may not strictly be valid, but is a reasonable assumption for purposes of resource allocation if the variance of transfer time is small with respect to average transfer time. This assumption is very convenient for modeling purposes. Assumption (c) is also quite useful for modeling purposes; its validity depends to a great extent on the efficiency of the single-processor resource allocation algorithms. If the assumption is valid, then the decision to transfer can be performed on a single-object basis. That is, the global controller can evaluate the costs and benefits of transferring a single object between processors and then perform the transfer before considering further transfers. If the assumption is not valid, i.e., the transfer calculations are themselves very time-consuming, then it may be necessary to consider the effects of transferring multiple objects. This could add considerable complexity to the problem.

Consistent with the approach used in previous sections, we use global leakage rate minimization as the global control objective. This is not an overly restrictive approach, since the global controller formulated here can also be specified to address any of the other object functions considered in this report

B. AUGMENTED STATE MODEL

In this section, we present an extension of the tandem-queuing model developed in Sections I-V. This model extension accounts for communication time delays incurred in transferring objects between processors. For the sake of simplicity of presentation, only two processors are considered. The processors are assumed to perform identical functions, although on different objects. Within each processor, objects flow through a sequence of data processing functions. However, we include a global control function which can transfer an object from a node in one processor [say, the K-th node) to the (K + 1)-th node in the other processor]. The key to the modeling approach used here is the inclusion of additional state variables that account for transferred objects.

The augmented state model is most easily explained with the aid of Fig. 10. Let S_j^i represent the total number of objects at node j of processor i. In the figure, there are two processors and four nodes associated with each processor. The figure illustrates issues involved in modeling object transfer from node 1 of processor 1 to node 2 at processor 2. At node 2 of

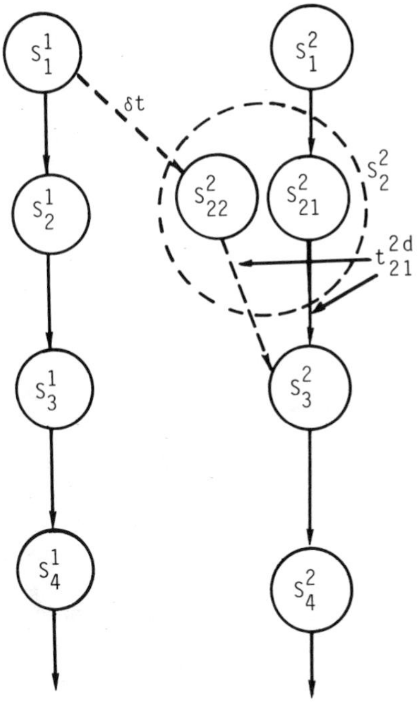

Fig. 10. Augmented state dynamics for a two-processor system.

processor 2, inputs are received from two sources. We use S_{22}^2 to represent the total number of objects at node 2 that are input from nodel of processor 2. We use S_{21}^2 to denote the total number of objects transferred from node 1 of processor 1. Thus, the total load S_2^2 at node 2 of processor 2 is given by

$$S_2^2 = S_{21}^2 + S_{22}^2. \tag{53}$$

The key variable used to calculate system performance is the total time delay across a node. For objects that originate within the receiving processor, the time delay t_{22}^{2d} through node 2 is given by

$$t_{22}^{2d} = S_2^2/\mu_2^2 \tag{54}$$

where μ_2^2 is the throughput (objects/second) at node 2 of processor 2. This throughput is strictly dependent on the throughput capacity at the node and the total load S_2^2 [see Eq. (4)]. For objects that have been transferred from processor 1, the time delay is

$$t_{21}^{2d} = \left(S_2^2/\mu_2^2\right) + \delta t \tag{55}$$

where δt is the transfer time. Thus, transferred objects incur a longer time delay than nontransferred objects, and correspondingly, there is a higher leakage probability for transferred threatening objects.

Another issue that must be addressed is accounting for threatening and nonthreatening objects that are transferred. In general, the type of the transferred object is unknown. Let ΔX_{21}^2 and ΔY_{21}^2 represent the number of threatening and nonthreatening objects, respectively, transferred from processor 1. Then we assume object types are transferred in the same proportions that existed in their previous node. Thus

$$\Delta X_{21}^2 = X_1^1/S_1^1, \quad \Delta Y_{21}^2 = Y_1^1/S_1^1. \tag{56}$$

When a single object is transferred from node 1 of processor 1 to node 2 of processor 2, the following conservation relationship is satisfied:

$$S_1^1 \leftarrow S_1^1 - 1, \quad X_2^2 \leftarrow X_{22}^2 + \Delta X_{21}^2, \quad X_{21}^2 \leftarrow Y_{21}^2 + \Delta Y_{21}^2. \tag{57}$$

In (57) the symbol $\leftarrow$ indicates the state transition due to object transfer. The state augmentation approach described above is extendable to accommodate transfer in either direction, i.e., to either processor, and for transfer between other nodes. For the remainder of this report, we assume transfers can be made only to the second nodes of each of the processors.

C. PROCEDURE FOR GLOBAL OBJECT TRANSFER

The augmented state model developed here permits the evaluation of processor performance, including performance loss due to transfer delays. This leads naturally to formulation of a procedure that uses global leakage rate minimization as its objective. For the two-processor system used here, let S^1, S^2 represent the total load at each processor, i.e.,

$$S^i = \sum_{K=1}^{N} S_K^i, \quad i = 1, 2. \tag{58}$$

Similarly, let $\lambda^1(S^1)$ and $\lambda^2(S^2)$ represent the total leakage rates (summed over nodes) at processors 1 and 2, respectively.

Then a four-step procedure for global object allocation that can be implemented either periodically or in an event-driven fashion (when a state transition occurs) is the following.

Step 1. Calculate loads S^1, S^2 and performance $\lambda^1(S^1)$, $\lambda^2(S^2)$.

Step 2. Calculate throughput allocations (using Procedure I', Section IV) for each processor assuming $S^1 \leftarrow S^1 - 1$, $S^2 \leftarrow S^1 + 1$. Calculate the predicted performance $\lambda^1(S^1 - 1) + \lambda^2(S^2 + 1)$.

Step 3. Calculate throughput allocations (using Procedure I', Section IV) for each processor assuming $S^1 \leftarrow S^1 + 1$, $S^2 \leftarrow S^2 - 1$. Calculate the predicted performance $\lambda^1(S^1 + 1)$, $\lambda^2(S^2 - 1)$.

Step 4. Reallocate a single object according to

$$\min\{\lambda^1(S^1) + \lambda^2(S^2),\ \lambda^1(S^1 - 1) + \lambda^2(S^2 + 1),\ \lambda^1(S^1 + 1) + \lambda^2(S^2 - 1)\}.$$

The first quantity in the minimization is the current cost. If this is the lowest, the best action is not to transfer; the transfer cost outweights any benefit to transfer. If this cost is not the lowest, an object is transferred to the processor with the best performance.

D. TWO-PROCESSOR EXAMPLE

The global object allocation methods presented in the previous section have been tested using a two-processor simulation. Figures 11 and 12 present state and control trajectories for two processors run in parallel without object transfer between processors. The model parameters for each processor are identical to those used in the Section V examples for the transport delay system. A leakage threshold of PC = 0.8 is used. The input threat trajectories are different for each processor, which results in different loading patterns in each processor. These variations in the load between the processors present opportunities for global load balancing by shifting the load between processors.

In processor 1 (Fig. 11), a high input level is sustained for the first four seconds of the attack. The number of input threat objects drops off considerably for the last two seconds. In the second processor (Fig. 12), objects enter in two main peaks; one from zero to two seconds, the next from four to six seconds, with a few objects entering in between. In both processors, the load trajectories follow the input peaks, although with a transport lag. Aggregate leakage for the two processors in parallel is 7.77%.

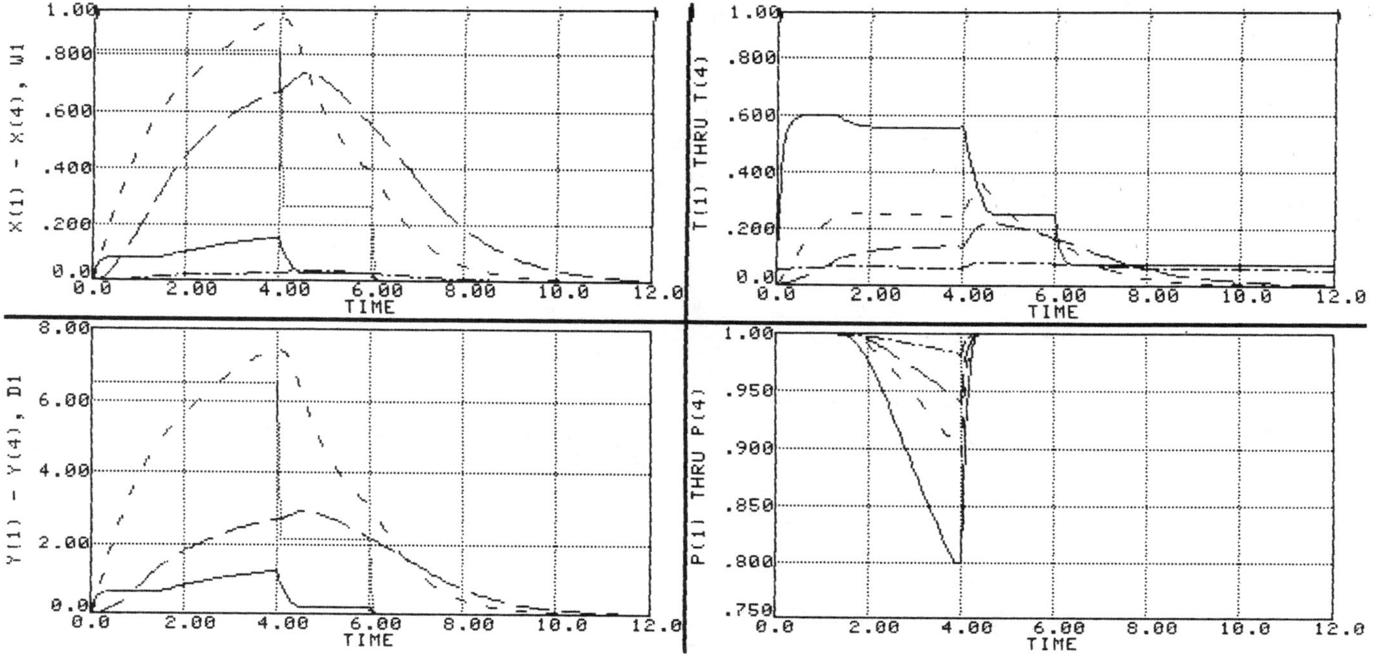

Fig. 11. Processor 1 state and control trajectories without object transfer. Key: •••, threat; —, Node 1; ---, Node 2; — —, Node 3; •—•, Node 4.

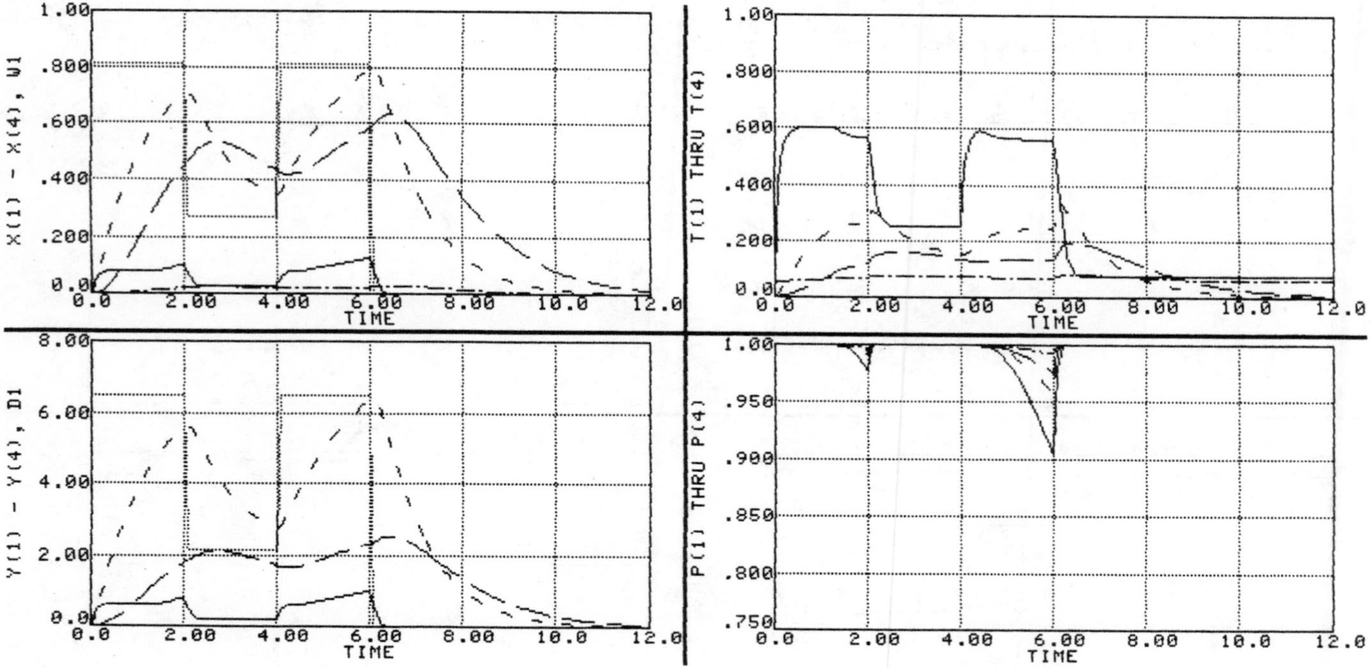

Fig. 12. Processor 2 state and control trajectories without object transfer. Key: •••, threat; —, Node 1; ---, Node 2; — —, Node 3; •—•, Node 4.

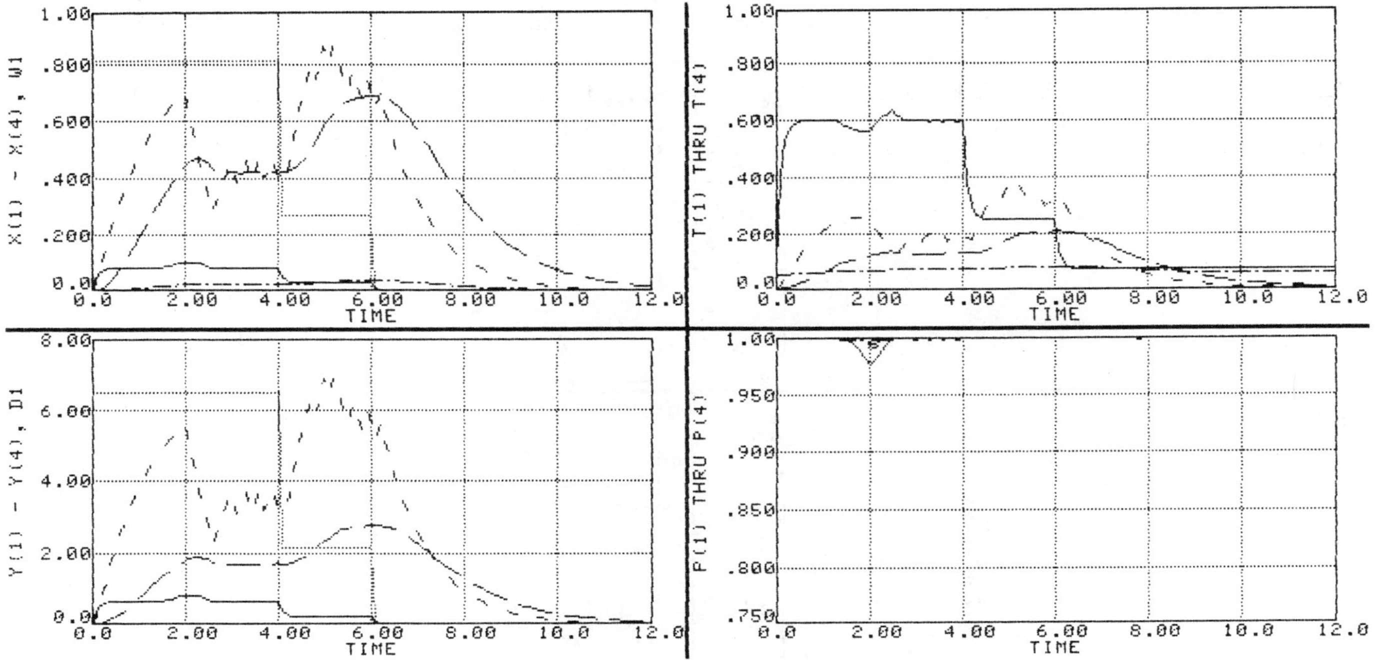

Fig. 13. Processor 1 state and control trajectories with object transfer. Key: •••, threat; —, Node 1; ---, Node 2; — —, Node 3; •—•, Node 4.

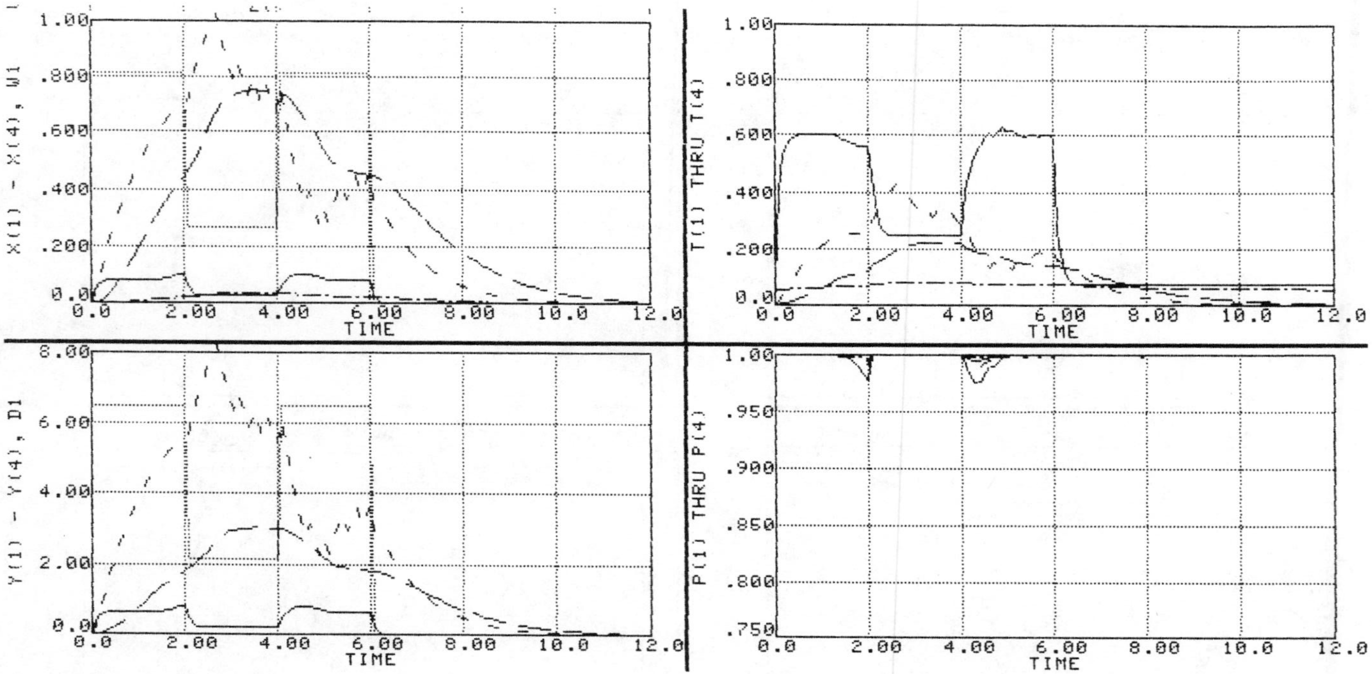

Fig. 14. Processor 2 state and control trajectories with object transfer. Key: •••, threat; —, Node 1; ---, Node 2; — —, Node 3; •—•, Node 4.

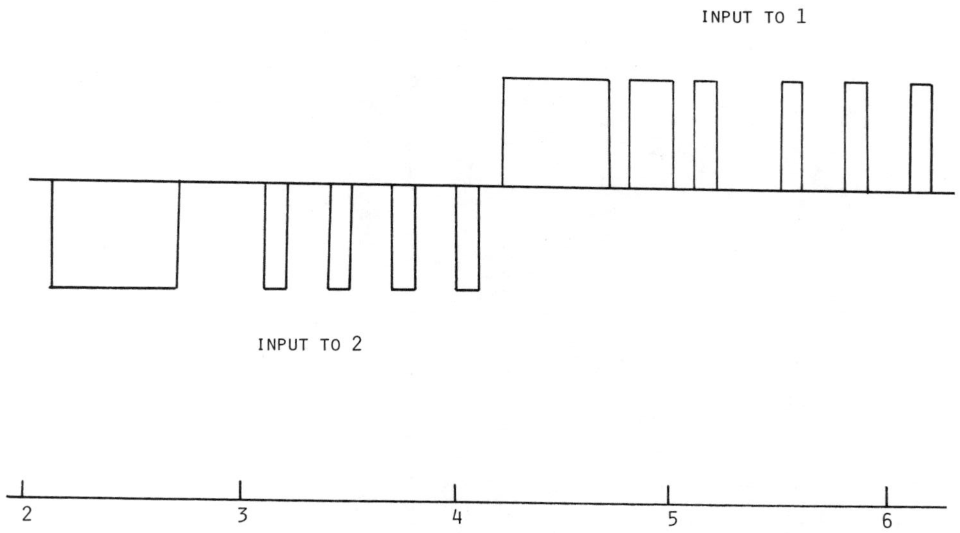

Fig. 15. Time history of object transfer (two-processor example).

In Figs. 13 and 14, state and control trajectories are presented for the same two processors, this time incorporating a global controller that transfers objects between processors using the allocation scheme presented in Section VI.B. Only transfers to node 2 (track) of each processor are permitted for this example case. A transfer time delay, $\delta t = 0.1$, is assumed for simulation purposes. Figure 15 shows the time history of object transfers between the two processors. For the first two seconds of the attack, both processors have identical input trajectories; without anticipation of future inputs, no object transfer occurs. After the first two seconds, the external input to processor 2 drops off, while the loading in processor 1 continues to build up. At this point, the global controller begins to transfer objects from processor 1 to processor 2. After two additional seconds, the input pattern reverses and the global controller shifts objects from processor 2 to processor 1. There is a considerable decrease in the leakage using the global object reallocation is less than 0.01%. These numerical results are summarized in Table 7, which shows cumulative leakage, measured in objects leaked, for each processor. These results clearly demonstrate the benefits of global object reallocation.

Table 7. Performance Summary for Oject Transfer Example

	Processor 1	*Processor 2*	*Total objects*
Leakage without transfer	*0.309*	*0.071*	*0.380 (7.77%)*
Leakage with transfer	*0.011*	*0.017*	*0.028 (0.01%)*

VII. SUMMARY AND CONCLUSION

Considerable progress has been made in the development of a decentralized/hierarchical control structure for a distributed time-critical data processing system. Two primary functions of the control system have been identified and developed in this study:

(a) throughput capacity allocation (single-processor load distribution); and

(b) object reallocation (global load distribution).

Control system design issues have been addressed within a unified framework. In particular, the load dynamics formulation and performance measures are used consistently in defining strategies for both the local (single-processor) and global (multiprocessor) control functions. The models developed are applicable to a general class of system constructs, but can be specialized for specific architectures.

A single-component processor of a distributed system is modeled here as a tandem-queuing system. The load flow dynamics have been formulated using a model for congestion-prone systems developed by Agnew [1] and incorporating a model for object "leakage." Leakage occurs when object data are processed too slowly to be of value for decision-making purposes, and the data are purged from the system. Also included in the model are parameters to represent transport delays that may be present in time-critical systems, e.g., BMD systems.

A variety of performance measures have been formulated in terms of the system variables. These include system leakage, transit time, process time, and system idle capacity. Various control algorithms have been developed to optimize throughput capacity allocation within a single processor. The algorithms use state feedback and therefore require estimates of numbers and types of objects distributed within processors. These algorithms have been tested using a simulation that implements the state space dynamics model developed here. Of the algorithms tested, the algorithm designed to minimize the system leakage rate yields the lowest cumulative leakage, although other algorithms yield comparable performance. The fastest algorithm, which minimizes system idle capacity, requires approximately 0.001 seconds (per allocation) in operation on a VAX 11/780, and is about a factor of 3 faster than the top-performing leakage-rate algorithm. Also developed is an algorithm that uses a priori information to estimate the system state variables on-line. This algorithm is most useful when long transport delays are present which render the states unobservable. Excellent results are obtained in this fashion, obviating the need for accurate on-line state estimates. Any of the developed algorithms are suitable for real-time application.

For data processing systems requiring multiple processors, one optimal procedure has been developed for transferring objects between processors in order to distribute the load globally. The costs of transferring objects between processors have been modeled using a time delay for object transfer, and by augmenting the system state variables specifically to account for transferred objects. This procedure, which achieves minimum global leakage rate, has been tested using a two-processor example. Substantial performance improvements can be obtained with this procedure.

The models developed here constitute a novel and promising approach for control of time-critical systems. Further study of these methods is recommended. In particular, it is desirable that the methods developed here be tested against more realistic discrete-event models. Also, there is a need for more investigation of the issues involved in the design of distributed operating systems that incorporate these resource management methods.

APPENDIX

This appendix presents formal specifications of Procedures I, I', and II discussed in Sections IV.B, IV.C, and IV.D, respectively.

Procedure I

Let $\mathcal{J}$ be the set of all indices of nodes that have not been allocated any throughput capacity. Initially, $\mathcal{J} = \{1, 2, \ldots, N\}$. Denote the elements of $\mathcal{J}$ by $J_1, \ldots, J_M$ where $M \le N$. Let T^{max} be the total unallocated throughput capacity, i.e.,

$$T^{max} = \sum_{j \in \mathcal{J}} T_J.$$

Initially, $T^{max} = T^0$. Then perform the following steps.

Step 1. Check if the following is true:

$$\sum_{k=1}^{N} \underline{T}_K > T^0.$$

If yes, there is insufficient capacity to meet the lower-bound constraints. Then relax the constraints and allocate throughput capacity according to Eqs. (26) and (27), and stop. If there is sufficient capacity to meet all lower-bound constraints, then go to Step 2.

Step 2. Solve for allocations T_K, $K \in \mathcal{J}$, using the formula

$$T_K = \left(\sqrt{G_K} \Big/ \sum_{J \in \mathcal{J}} \sqrt{G_J}\right) T^{max}.$$

The resulting allocation satisfies the capacity constraint (1).

Step 3. Check whether the allocations derived in Step 2 violate the lower-bound constraints, i.e., if

$$T_{J_K} < \underline{T}_{J_K}, \quad J_K \in \mathcal{J}.$$

If the constraint is violated, then fix the allocation

$$T_{J_K} = \underline{T}_{J_K}$$

and remove the index J_K from the set, i.e.,

$$\mathcal{J} \leftarrow \mathcal{J} \backslash \{J_K\}.$$

In the above $\backslash$ is the set difference operation.

Step. 4. If $\mathcal{J}$ is unchanged from Step 1, then stop. Otherwise, reset T^{max} using the formula

$$T^{max} = T^0 - \sum_{k \notin \mathcal{J}} T_K$$

and go to Step 2.

The above procedure must stop in a finite number of steps. Every time Step 3 is executed, at least one more node is allocated throughput or the procedure stops in Step 4.

Procedure I' (for the Transport Delay System)

Define $\mathcal{J}$ and T^{max} as in Procedure I.

Step 1. As in Procedure I, check if there is sufficient capacity to meet the lower-bound constraints. If not, then relax the constraints, solve for a value of PC that satisfies Eq. (47), and stop. If there is sufficient capacity to meet all lower-bound constraints, go to Step 2.

Step 2. Solve for allocations T_K, $K = 1, \ldots, N$, using the Newton procedure (44) with initialization (46). The resulting allocation satisfies the capacity constraint (1).

Step 3. This step is identical to Step 3 of Procedure I.

Step 4. This step is identical to Step 4 of Procedure I.

Procedure II (for the Capacity Utilization Algorithm)

Denote the coefficients of the objective (48) by $a_1, \ldots$ a_{N+1} where

$$a_K = \frac{1}{1 + \gamma_K S_K} \cdot \frac{1}{T^0}, \qquad 1 \leq K \leq N; \qquad a_{N+1} = \frac{1}{T^0}.$$

Let A_0 be the set consisting of the coefficients $a_1, \ldots a_{N+1}$. Then reorder the nodes in order of magnitude of the coefficients. Define $c_1, \ldots, c_{N+1}$ recursively by

$$c_1 = \min_{a_K \in A_0} a_K.$$

Define A_j, $j = 1, \ldots, N$, by

$$A_j = A_{j-1} \backslash \{c_j\}.$$

Then define c_j by

$$c_j = \min_{a_K \in A_j} A_j.$$

Note that $c_{N+1} = a_{N+1}$. Then assuming there is sufficient capacity to meet the lower-bound constraint at each node, the following two-step procedure solves the LP problem defined in this section.

Step 1. Set $T_K = \underline{T}_K$, $K = 1, \ldots, N$.

Step 2. If

$$T^0 - \sum_{K=1}^{N} T_K = 0$$

stop; or else set

$$T_1 = \max\left\{T^0 - \sum_{K=1}^{N} T_K,\ \overline{T}_1\right\}.$$

If

$$T^0 - \sum_{K=1}^{N} T_K = 0$$

stop; or else continue until at the k-th node

$$T_K = \max\left\{T^0 - \sum_{K=1}^{N} T_K,\ \overline{T}_K\right\}.$$

Finally, at the slack node,

$$T_{N+1} = \max\left\{T^0 - \sum_{K=1}^{N} T_K,\ 0\right\}.$$

ACKNOWLEDGMENTS

The authors gratefully acknowledge informative discussions with Carson E. Agnew. Programming for the examples presented here was performed by Robert Bullock of Systems Control Technology, Inc.

REFERENCES

1. C. AGNEW, "Dynamic Modeling and Control of Congestion-Prone Systems," *Operations Research 24* (1976).

2. D. GAZIS, "Optimal Control of a System of Oversaturated Intersections," *Operations Research 12*, 815-831 (1964).

Parametrical Optimization Approach for Decentralized Regulation of Discrete Systems*

J. C. GEROMEL

FEC/UNICAMP C.P.
Sao Paulo, Brazil

J. BERNUSSOU

LAAS/CNRS
Toulouse, France

I. INTRODUCTION

In practical situations and especially for large-scale systems, it is desirable not to use a centralized control strategy. The reasons for this are manifold; for instance, not all the state variables can be measured, the system is geographically

*This research has been developed with the financial support of CNPq, Brazil, under Grant 1.14.10.080-81, and CNRS, France.

widespread (interconnected systems), and/or, because of economic reasons, it is not worth carrying all of the state information for each local control.

For these reasons, in this chapter we deal with control strategies which do not require any information exchanges among subsystems controllers. This information structure and a performance criterion associated with some dynamic systems define the so-called *decentralized control problem*.

The main idea is to define the problem as the determination of a suboptimal control in an a priori given parametrized class of controls that satisfy the structural constraints (information structure). This determination can be accomplished, for instance, by solving a nonlinear programming problem, defined with respect to the parameters that characterize the given class.

One of the first papers which can be related to such an idea is the one by Levine and Athans [1] dealing with optimal output feedback. See also [2,3]; these papers provide necessary optimality conditions in terms of nonlinear matrix equations, the numerical solution of which is difficult and the convergence indefinite [4].

Here we present, in the discrete case, a gradient-type algorithm to solve the decentralized control problem, following the same steps given in [5] for continuous dynamic systems for which one is also referred to [6].

This chapter is divided into three sections. In Section II the parametrical nonlinear optimization problem is presented and a procedure is derived to compute the gradient matrix used in the proposed algorithm given in Section III, where sufficient conditions are provided to ascertain its convergence. Finally, in Section IV the stabilization problem under decentralized constraints is discussed.

II. MATHEMATICAL FORMULATION: THE GRADIENT MATRIX

Let us consider a discrete time-invariant interconnected system given by

$$x_i(t + 1) = A_i x_i(t) + B_i u_i(t) + \sum_{j \neq i}^{N} A_{ij} x_j(t),$$
$$x_i(0) = x_{i0}, \quad i = 1, \ldots, N, \tag{1}$$

where $x_i(\cdot) \in R^{n_i}$ are the state variables, and $u_i(\cdot) \in R^{m_i}$ are the control variables. The problem is to determine local feedback controls

$$u_i = -K_i x_i(t), \quad i = 1, \ldots, N, \tag{2}$$

so as to minimize the cost

$$J(K) = \sum_{i=1}^{N} \left(\sum_{t=0}^{T-1} \left\{ x_i(t)' Q_i x_i(t) + u_i(t)' R_i u_i(t) \right\} + x_i(T)' S_i X_i(T) \right). \tag{3}$$

For convenience, the preceding problem is written in a global matrix form,

$$\min_{K \in \Omega} \sum_{t=0}^{T-1} f(X(t), K) + g(X(T)),$$
$$X(t + 1) = F(X(t), K), \quad X(0) = X_0, \tag{4}$$

where for the linear quadratic problem stated above we have

$$f(X(t), K) = \mathrm{Tr}\{(Q + K'RK)X(t)\},$$
$$g(X(T)) = \mathrm{Tr}\{SX(T)\}, \tag{5}$$
$$F(X(t), K) = (A - BK)X(t)(A - BK)',$$

where $\mathrm{Tr}\{\cdot\}$ represents the trace function of $\{\cdot\}$; Q, S (symmetric nonnegative definite), R (symmetric positive definite), and B are block diagonal matrices with appropriate dimensions, the blocks of which consist of the subsystem matrices Q_i, R_i, S_i, and B_i. The overall state vector is $x(t)' = [x_1(t)', \ldots, x_N(t)']$ and $X(t) = x(t)x(t)'$. Finally Ω, called the *decentralization set*, defines the structural constraints to be imposed on the overall gain K; that is,

$$\Omega \triangleq \left\{K \in R^m \times R^n / K = \text{block diag}\{K_1, \ldots, K_N\}\right\}. \tag{6}$$

Problem (4)-(6) appears as a classical optimization problem with a quadratic cost criterion and linear constraints. In fact, the dynamic equations can also be viewed as a large algebraic system. The final purpose is to use a gradient-type algorithm to solve (4)-(6), so that we need the gradient matrix

$$dJ(K)/dK = \{\partial J(K)/\partial K_{ij},\ i = 1, \ldots, m,\ j = 1, \ldots, n\}; \tag{7}$$

we state the following theorem.

Theorem 1

Let the matrix discrete system be $X(t + 1) = F(X(t), K)$, with initial condition X_0 and a scalar-valued function

$$J(K) = \sum_{t=0}^{T-1} f(X(t), K) + g(X(T)). \tag{8}$$

Then, provided some differentiability assumptions, one has

$$\frac{dJ(K)}{dK} = \sum_{t=0}^{T-1} \frac{\partial H(X(t), P(t), K)}{\partial K} \tag{9}$$

where $H(\cdot)$ is the Hamiltonian function defined by

$$H(X(t), P(t), K) \triangleq f(X(t), K) + \mathrm{Tr}\{P(t)'F(X(t), K)\} \tag{10}$$

and $P(t)$ and $X(t)$, $t = 0, \ldots, T - 1$, are given by the stationary conditions

$$\begin{aligned} &\partial H/\partial X(t) - P(t - 1) = 0, \quad && P(T - 1) = \partial g/\partial X(T), \\ &\partial H/\partial P(t) - X(t + 1) = 0, && X(0) = X_0. \end{aligned} \tag{11}$$

Proof. Since f, g, and F are differentiable functions, we have

$$J(K + \epsilon\ \delta K) = J(K) + \epsilon \sum_{t=0}^{T-1} \{\mathrm{Tr}(\partial f'/\partial X\ \delta X(t)) + \mathrm{Tr}(\partial f'/\partial K\ \delta K)\} + \epsilon\ \mathrm{Tr}(\partial g'/\partial X(T)\ \delta X(T)) + O(\epsilon^2). \tag{12}$$

Clearly, we want to get the variation of $J(\cdot)$ only in terms of δK; in this sense we use the equality

$$\mathrm{Tr}\{\partial f'/\partial X\ \delta X(t)\} + \mathrm{Tr}\{\partial/\partial X\ \mathrm{Tr}(P'F(X, K))'\ \delta X(t)\} = \mathrm{Tr}\{P(t-1)'\ \delta X(t)\}. \tag{13}$$

On the other hand, with (11) we get

$$\sum_{t=0}^{T-1} \mathrm{Tr}\{P(t-1)'\ \delta X(t)\} = \sum_{t=0}^{T-1} \mathrm{Tr}\{P(t)'\ \delta X(t+1)\} - \mathrm{Tr}\{\partial g'/\partial X(T)\ \delta X(T)\}. \tag{14}$$

This equation turns out to be true because $\delta X(0) = 0$ and because of the adjoint matrix final condition (11). Now, expanding the dynamic equation and taking the first-order term in ϵ we obtain

$$\sum_{t=0}^{T-1} \mathrm{Tr}\{P(t)'\ \delta X(t+1)\} = \sum_{t=0}^{T-1} \mathrm{Tr}\left\{\frac{\partial}{\partial X}\ \mathrm{Tr}(P'F(X, K))'\ \delta X(t)\right\} + \mathrm{Tr}\left\{\frac{\partial}{\partial K}\ \mathrm{Tr}(P'F(X, K))'\ \delta K\right\}. \tag{15}$$

With (13)-(15) we have

$$\sum_{t=0}^{T-1} \mathrm{Tr}\left\{\frac{\partial f'}{\partial X}\ \delta X(t)\right\} + \mathrm{Tr}\left\{\frac{\partial g'}{\partial X(T)}\ \delta X(T)\right\} = \sum_{t=0}^{T-1} \mathrm{Tr}\left\{\frac{\partial}{\partial K}\ \mathrm{Tr}(P'F(X, K))'\ \delta K\right\}. \tag{16}$$

Finally, putting (16) in (12) and taking (10) into account it follows that

$$J(K + \epsilon\, \delta K) = J(K) + \epsilon \sum_{t=0}^{T-1} \mathrm{Tr}\left\{\frac{\partial H(X(t),\, P(t),\, K)'}{\partial K}\, \delta K\right\} + O(\epsilon^2). \tag{17}$$

Since $\lim_{\epsilon \to 0} O(\epsilon^2)/\epsilon = 0$ we can apply the result of Lemma 1 of [5] and we obtain (9) which proves the proposed theorem.

Returning to problem (4)-(5), and applying the results of the above theorem, we readily obtain

$$\frac{dJ(K)}{dK} = 2 \sum_{t=0}^{T-1} \{RK - B'P(t)(A - BK)\}X(t) \tag{18}$$

where $X(t)$ and $P(t)$ are given by

$$\begin{aligned} X(t + 1) &= (A - BK)X(t)(A - BK)', \quad X(0) = X_0, \\ P(t - 1) &= (A - BK)'P(t)(A - BK) + Q \\ &\quad + K'RK, \quad P(T - 1) = S. \end{aligned} \tag{19}$$

The gradient matrix (in the finite-time horizon case) requires the solution of two discrete recurrent equations; forward time for $X(t)$ and reverse time for the adjoint variable $P(t)$. Notice that with this matrix formulation, these two equations are decoupled.

Let us proceed to the infinite-time horizon case and let $T \to +\infty$ in (4). Then for the reverse-time solution we will have $P(t = \infty) = P$ so that

$$\frac{dJ(K)}{dK} = 2(RK - B'P(A - BK)) \sum_{t=0}^{\infty} X(t) \tag{20}$$

where $V = \Sigma_{t=0}^{\infty} X(t)$ is given by the solution of the Lyapunov equation

$$(A - BK)V(A - BK)' - V + X_0 = 0. \tag{21}$$

In addition, the stationary adjoint variable is given by

$$(A - BK)'P(A - BK) - P + Q + K'RK = 0. \tag{22}$$

Then, the required calculations reduce to two decoupled algebraic Lyapunov equations provided, of course, that $(A - BK)$ is asymptotically stable.

III. NUMERICAL ALGORITHM FOR THE DECENTRALIZED GAIN DETERMINATION

We propose a feasible direction algorithm with the following steps:

Step 1. Initialization with a feasible matrix gain $K^0 \in \Omega$. Set the iteration index $j = 0$.

Step 2. Determine the gradient matrix

$$\frac{dJ(K^j)}{dK} = \sum_{t=0}^{T-1} \frac{\partial H(X(t), P(t), K^j)}{\partial K} \tag{23}$$

where $H(\cdot)$ is the Hamiltonian function defined in Theorem 1.

Step 3. Determine the feasible direction

$$D^j \triangleq \underset{\Omega}{\text{Proj}}[dJ(K^j)/dK]. \tag{24}$$

Step 4. Optimality test: If $\|D^j\| < \epsilon$ (ϵ being a positive sufficiently small parameter), K^j is optimal; otherwise go to Step 5.

Step 5. Find a step size α^j so that $J(K^j - \alpha^j D^j) < J(K^j)$ and make $K^{j+1} \triangleq K^j - \alpha^j D^j$. Set $j = j + 1$ and return to Step 2.

Section II provides the calculations to be carried out for the determination of the gradient matrix of $J(K^j)$ with respect to K, which is a full matrix. The feasible direction D^j, i.e., a direction of decrease of the cost function $J(\cdot)$ satisfying the structural constraints (6), can be obtained by the orthogonal projection as stated in (24).

It can be shown [7] that in the case of decentralized control such a projection amounts to zeroing nondiagonal entries of the gradient matrix, i.e.,

$$D^j \triangleq \text{block diag}\{dJ(K)/dK^j\}. \tag{25}$$

Other cases of projections over sets defined by linear constraints can be found in [7].

Lemma 2

The projection direction given by (24) is such that

(a) If $\|D\| \neq 0$ so $\exists \bar{\alpha} > 0$ such that

$$J(K - \alpha D) < J(K), \quad \forall 0 < \alpha \leq \bar{\alpha}.$$

(b) If $\|D\| = 0$, the matrix K is optimal [i.e., it satisfies the Kuhn-Tucker conditions of problem (4)].

Proof. The proof is simple and turns out to be very similar to that corresponding to the continuous case given in [5].

This lemma gives the justification for Steps 3 and 4. It especially states the existence of a step size α^j such that the cost is decreased. For the determination of a numerical value for α^j, a one-dimensional optimization problem is possible for instance,

$$\min_{\alpha>0} J(K^j - \alpha D^j). \tag{26}$$

This, however, is a nontrivial problem which requires a lot of computations so that, in practical situations, the step size α^j is fixed in a heuristic adaptive manner, taking into account the results and information gained during the iterative procedure [8].

In the finite-time horizon case, the algorithm would converge to a feedback gain K^* satisfying the optimality condition $D^* = 0$. Now, the cost function J(K) is not generally convex with respect to K, so that K^* is only a local minimum and it depends on the initial gain K^0 considered in Step 1 of the algorithm.

In the infinite-time horizon case, we have to add another condition, that of the stability of (A - BK), at each step of the procedure. This condition is necessary for problem (4)-(5) to be defined.

Then, consider the set Φ defined as

$$\Phi \triangleq \{K \in \Omega,\ \Lambda(A - BK) \subset I\} \tag{27}$$

where $\Lambda(\cdot)$ denotes the set of eigenvalues of $(\cdot)$ and I represents the interior of the unit circle. First, the algorithm must be provided with an initial gain K^0 belonging to Φ. The problem of determining such a K^0 is not trivial, and it is discussed in Section IV.

Let us assume that a $K^0 \in \Phi$ has been found. The next theorem gives sufficient conditions to ensure that, at each iteration, the algorithm provides a matrix gain K belonging to Φ.

Theorem 3

Let $Q = C'C$. If the pair (A, C) is observable and $X_0 > 0$ (positive definite), then $K^0 \in \Phi$ implies that $K^j \in \Phi$, $\forall j > 0$.

Proof. In the infinite-time horizon case we have

$$J(K) = Tr\{H(K)X_0\}, \tag{28}$$

where H(K) is given by

$$H(K) = \sum_{t=0}^{\infty} (A - BK)'^t (Q + K'RK)(A - BK)^t. \tag{29}$$

Since (A, C) is observable, H(K) is definite positive and it is finite if and only if (A - BK) is asymptotically stable. However, $H(K) > 0$ and finite is equivalent to $Tr(H(K)) < \infty$ so that the stability can be proved by the finiteness of Tr(H(K)). With $X_0 > 0$ we have

$$Tr(H(K^{j+1})) \leq \lambda_{min}^{-1}(X_0)J(K^{j+1}) \leq \lambda_{min}^{-1}(X_0)J(K^j) < \infty \tag{30}$$

where $\lambda_{min}(\cdot)$ denotes the minimum eigenvalue of $(\cdot)$. Note that K^0 is found such that $K^0 \in \Phi$ implying that $J(K^0) < \infty$. So inequality (30) turns out to be true for any iteration index $j = 0, 1, \ldots, \infty$; then $K^j \in \Phi \; \forall j > 0$, and the theorem is proved.

Besides the dependence with respect to the initial gain K^0, the optimal gain K^* is also dependent on the initial-state condition X_0. To avoid the latter dependency several solutions have been proposed.

One of the most classical solutions is to consider the initial state $x_0 \in R^n$ as a random variable with zero mean and covariance matrix $X_0 > 0$. The problem, to minimize the mathematical expectation of the cost function with respect to K, has the same formulation as problem (4)-(5).

Another approach that gives good results with respect to the robustness properties of the controlled system is to use a worst case design. With $J(K, X_0)$ as the cost function, one can define the min-max problem the min-max problem

$$\underset{K\in\Omega}{\text{Min}}\ \underset{X_0}{\text{Max}}\left\{J(K,\ X_0)/\|X_0\|^2 \le 1\right\}. \qquad (31)$$

Theorem 4

Let $W(K):\ R^m \times R^n \to R$ be a matrix function defined as

$$W(K) \triangleq \underset{X_0}{\text{Max}}\left\{J(K,\ X_0)/\|X_0\|^2 \le 1\right\} \qquad (32)$$

where $J(K,\ X_0)$ is defined by (4)-(5). Then $W(K)$ is differentiable and its gradient matrix with respect to K is given by Theorem 1 where in (11) the initial state condition must be imposed to be

$$X_0 = P(-1)/\|P(-1)\|. \qquad (33)$$

Proof. The proof of this theorem is very close to that proposed for the continuous systems in [5]. It suffices to write the optimality conditions of problem (32) and note that

$$\partial J(K,\ X_0)/\partial X_0 = P(-1) \qquad (34)$$

where $P(-1)$ is the adjoint variable calculated at $t = -1$.

Since the min-max problem (31) can be rewritten as

$$\underset{K\in\Omega}{\text{Min}}\ W(K), \qquad (35)$$

the given algorithm can be used to solve (35) because Theorem 3 states that the objective function $W(\cdot)$ is differentiable with respect to K and its gradient matrix may be calculated with slight modifications of Theorem 1.

IV. DETERMINATION OF A STABILIZING INITIAL GAIN

As already stated, the present algorithm needs to be initialized with a feasible initial gain which stabilizes the closed-loop system, i.e., $K^0 \in \Phi$. In this section the problem of determining such a gain is discussed. For more details see [9].

Let us consider a special class of discrete dynamic systems for which it is possible to determine matrices L_{ij} such that

$$A_{ij} = B_i L_{ij}, \quad \forall i \neq j = 1, \ldots, N. \tag{36}$$

For the general case; that is, when (36) does not hold, see [10]. With (36), it is clear that we can rewrite the overall system matrix as

$$A = \tilde{A} + BL \tag{37}$$

where $\tilde{A} = \text{block diag}\{A_1, A_2, \ldots, A_N\}$.

Theorem 5

Suppose all pairs (A_i, B_i) are controllable. Then for the class of discrete linear discrete systems defined by (36),

$$\begin{aligned} K^0 &= (I + B'PB)^{-1}B'P\tilde{A}, \\ P &= \tilde{A}'P\tilde{A} - \tilde{A}'PB(I + B'PB)^{-1}B'P\tilde{A} + \beta I, \end{aligned} \tag{38}$$

$K^0 \in \Phi$ for all $\beta \in R^+$ such that

$$\beta I > L'(I + B'PB)L. \tag{39}$$

Proof. Since all matrices in (38) are block diagonals, $K^0 \in \Omega$ follows immediately and it remains to prove that the discrete linear system $x(t + 1) = (A - BK^0)x(t)$ is asymptotically stable. Let the Lyapunov function be

$$v(x(t)) = x(t)'Px(t). \tag{40}$$

Defining $V \triangleq (I + B'PB)$ and $G \triangleq L - V^{-1}B'P\tilde{A}$ we get

$$\Delta v(t + 1) \triangleq v(x(t + 1)) - v(x(t))$$
$$= x(t)'[(\tilde{A} + BG)'P(\tilde{A} + BG) - P]x(t) \quad (41)$$

which, with (38), gives

$$\Delta v(t + 1) = x(t)'[-\beta I + \tilde{A}'PBV^{-1}B'P\tilde{A} + G'B'P\tilde{A} + \tilde{A}'PBG + G'B'PBG]x(t). \quad (42)$$

Now, since $B'P\tilde{A} = V(L - G)$, from (42) we have

$$\Delta v(t + 1) = x(t)'[-\beta I + (L - G)'V(L - G) + G'V(L - G) + (L - G)'VG + G'B'PBG]x(t)$$
$$= x(t)'[-\beta I + L'VL - G'VG + G'B'PBG]x(t). \quad (43)$$

Finally, we get

$$\Delta v(t + 1) = -x(t)'[\beta I - L'VL] - x(t)'G'RGx(t)$$
$$\leq -x(t)'[\beta I - L'(I + B'PB)L]x(t). \quad (44)$$

With (39), we can conclude that $\Delta v(t + 1) < 0$, $\forall x(t) \neq 0$, implying that $K^0 \in \Phi$ which proves the theorem.

It is important to note that the Riccati equation (38) can be solved easily since it is in reality a set of N decoupled equations each one associated with a subsystem of the overall system under consideration.

On the other hand, the theorem does not provide the numerical value for the parameter $\beta \in R^+$. In [9] this problem has been studied and it has been proved that a $\beta > 0$ satisfying (39) can be obtained by means of a nonlinear recurrence

$$\beta_{l+1} = ||L||^2\left(1 + \lambda_{max}\left(B'P_l B\right)\right) \quad (45)$$

with the initial condition $\beta_0 = ||L||^2$, and P_l the solution of (38) for $\beta = \beta_l$.

Once more, the determination of the right-hand side of (45) is readily accomplished since only block diagonal matrices are involved in each iteration.

Finally, a sufficient condition for convergence is given by

$$\lambda_{max}\left(B'P_{\infty}B\right) < 1/||L||^2 \tag{46}$$

where $P_{\infty} = \lim_{\beta\to\infty} P/\beta$ which satisfies

$$P_{\infty} = \tilde{A}'P_{\infty}\tilde{A} - \tilde{A}'P_{\infty}B\left(B'P_{\infty}B\right)^{-1}B'P_{\infty}\tilde{A} + I. \tag{47}$$

In [9] some numerical experiments are provided for the determination of $K^0 \in \Phi$. One can see that the iterative procedure (45) converges quickly to a parameter β_* and then a K^0 is easily calculated by taking $\beta = \beta_* + \epsilon$, with ϵ a positive real number.

V. CONCLUSION

In this chapter, the problem of optimal decentralized control for an interconnected discrete system has been investigated. The approach used is called parameterical optimization which consists of defining a parametrized class of control and then using some nonlinear optimization algorithm in order to determine, in this class, an element which is, at least, locally optimum.

Starting from a linear quadratic dynamic optimization problem, the parametric optimization problem is first defined and witten in a matrix formulation. For that, a simple way to find the cost gradient matrix with respect to the feedback gain is derived. This is merely an extension to the discrete system case of that in [5] for the continuous case and, aside from a greater difficulty at the calculation level, there is nothing fundamentally different between the two cases. In Section II a gradient projection algorithm is proposed for the determination of the decentralized gain. The convergence toward a stabilizing decentralized gain in the infinite-time horizon is discussed and sufficient conditions are provided for that purpose.

A fundamental point in the infinite-time horizon case is the initialization of the iterative procedure by a stabilizing decentralized gain. In Section IV the problem of decentralized stabilization is discussed, in the frame work of linear quadratic design. For a special structure of the interconnection terms, it is shown that a stabilizing decentralized gain can be obtained by simply solving a recurrent decoupled Riccati-type equation.

REFERENCES

1. W. S. LEVINE and M. ATHANS, *IEEE Trans. Autom. Control AC-15*, 44 (1970).

2.

2. C. Y. CHONG and M. ATHANS, *IEEE Trans. Autom. Control AC-16*, 423 (1971).

3. T. L. JOHNSON and M. ATHANS, *IEEE Trans. Autom. Control AC-15*, 658 (1970).

4. B. D. O. ANDERSON and J. B. MORRE, "Linear Optimal Control," Prentice-Hall, Englewood Cliffs, New Jersey, 1971.

5. J. C. GEROMEL and J. BERNUSSOU, "Optimal Decentralized Control of Dynamic Systems," *Automatica 18*, 545 (1982).

6. G. COHEN, *R.A.I.R.O. J. 3* (1975).

7. J. C. GEROMEL, "Contribution à l'Etude des Systèmes Dynamiques Interconnectès: Aspects de Dècentralisation," Thèse de Doctorat d'Etat, Toulouse, 903 (1979).

8. J. C. GEROMEL and J. BERNUSSOU, *Automatica 14*, 489 (1979).

9. J. C. GEROMEL and A. YAMAKAMI, *Int. J. Control 63*, 429 (1982).

10. J. C. GEROMEL and E. P. MELO, *9th World Congress, IFAC, Budapest* (1984).

Decentralized Optimal Control for Large-Scale Interconnected Systems

KAZUNORI YASUDA

Faculty of Engineering
Kobe University
Kobe, Japan

I. INTRODUCTION

Reliability of control is an essential requirement in the design of dynamical systems, specifically large-scale systems. The reliability required in the design cannot be achieved merely by diligent application of standard design methods. For large-scale systems composed of a number of subsystems, it has been shown explicitly [1,2] that the decentralized strategy can be highly reliable to structural perturbations whereby subsystems are disconnected and again connected during operation. A decentralized control scheme is, however, more restrictive than a centralized one because of the control structure constraints. For this reason, there has been a considerable amount of research on the decentralized control for large-scale interconnected systems. Especially as concerns stabilization, a large number of results have been obtained providing conditions for decentralized stabilizability in terms of the structure of interconnections among subsystems [3-8].

In this chapter, we consider the linear-quadratic optimal control problem for large-scale systems by means of decentralized state feedback. The main objective is to establish a decentralized stabilizing control scheme being highly reliable against parameter perturbations in the subsystems as well as structural perturbations in the interconnections. To achieve this, we propose a decentralized optimal control, and at the same time provide the class of large-scale interconnected systems for which we can always find such a decentralized control law. We call these "decentrally optimizable large-scale systems." Although the optimal control for an arbitrarily chosen quadratic performance index is generally of a centralized form, we can achieve an optimal control in decentralized scheme by appropriately selecting quadratic weights in performance index. When the decentralized optimal control is applied, it is guaranteed that the resulting closed-loop system has robust and insensitive stability properties against variations in open-loop dynamics [9,10]. Furthermore, the optimality of the decentralized control law is preserved with respect to a modified performance index under perturbations in interconnections such that the strength of coupling does not increase. It is noted that the class of decentrally optimizable large-scale systems shown here is also a class of decentrally stabilizable large-scale systems which is larger than any class obtained so far.

The plan of this chapter is as follows. In Section II, after a system description, we briefly review the results concerning decentralized optimal control for large-scale systems which have motivated our work, and introduce the concept of decentral optimizability. In Section III, we consider the case of single-input subsystems, and show a condition for decentralized optimal control to be possible, which simultaneously provides the class of decentrally optimizable large-scale systems. In Section IV, we first show, using controllable canonical form, that a multi-input subsystem is reducible to a set of single-input subsystems and the result for the single-input case can be applied to the multi-input case in a straightforward manner. In Section V, an example is presented to illustrate the synthesis procedure for a decentralized optimal control law.

II. DECENTRALIZED OPTIMAL CONTROL PROBLEM

A. *SYSTEM DESCRIPTION*

Consider a large-scale system

$$S: \quad \dot{x}_i = A_i x_i + B_i u_i + \sum_{j=1}^{N} A_{ij} x_j, \quad i = 1, 2, \ldots, N, \tag{1}$$

composed of N linear time-invariant subsystems

$$S_i: \quad \dot{x}_i = A_i x_i + B_i u_i, \quad i = 1, 2, \ldots, N, \tag{2}$$

with the interconnections $\Sigma_{j=1}^{N} A_{ij} x_j$, where $x_i(t)$ is the n_i-dimensional state vector of S_i, $u_i(t)$ is the r_i-dimensional input vector, and A_i, B_i, and A_{ij} are constant matrices of appropriate dimensions. The overall system S can also be written as

$$S: \quad \dot{x} = (A_D + A_C)x + B_D u \tag{3}$$

where

$$x = \left[x_1^T, x_2^T, \ldots, x_N^T\right]^T, \qquad u = \left[u_1^T, u_2^T, \ldots, u_N^T\right]^T,$$

which have dimension $n \left(= \Sigma_{i=1}^N n_i\right)$ and dimension $r \left(= \Sigma_{i=1}^N r_i\right)$, respectively, and

$$A_D = \text{block diag}[A_1, A_2, \ldots, A_N],$$

$$A_C = \text{block matrix}[A_{ij}]_{N\times N},$$

$$B_D = \text{block diag}[B_1, B_2, \ldots, B_N].$$

B. PROBLEM STATEMENT

Let us first consider the ordinary linear-quadratic optimal control problem for the large-scale system S with respect to the performance index

$$J = \int_0^\infty (x^TQx + u^TRu)\ dt \tag{4}$$

where Q is an $n \times n$ symmetric nonnegative-definite matrix and R is an $r \times r$ symmetric positive-definite matrix. As is well know [11], the optimal control minimizing J can be obtained by a linear state feedback

$$u = -K^Tx, \qquad K^T = R^{-1}B_D^TP \tag{5}$$

where P is the $n \times n$ symmetric, positive-definite solution of the algebraic matrix Riccati equation

$$(A_D + A_C)^TP + P(A_D + A_C) - PB_DR^{-1}B_D^TP + Q = 0, \tag{6}$$

provided that the pair $(A_D + A_C, B_D)$ is stabilizable and that the pair $\left(A_D + A_C, C^T\right)$ is completely observable with a matrix C such that $Q = CC^T$. The optimal control law (5) is often referred to as the optimal regulator. It can be easily observed that to implement the optimal regulator (5), we generally need the entire state x to generate the input u_i of each subsystem S_i. Thus, the optimal regulator is not always decentralized; however, there are interconnected systems for which a decentralized optimal control law

$$u = -K_D^T x, \quad K_D = \text{block diag}[K_1, K_2, \ldots, K_N] \tag{7}$$

where K_i is an $r_i \times n_i$ matrix, exists; that is, compatible with the information structure imposed by the subsystems S_i [12-14]. Based on this fact, let us introduce the following definition.

Definition. We say that the large-scale interconnected system S described by Eq. (3) is decentrally optimizable if there exists a decentralized state feedback which is the optimal regulator for the system S with respect to some quadratic performance index.

Under this definition, the performance index J cannot be chosen arbitrarily to obtain such an optimal control law for decentrally optimizable interconnected systems. However, it is not altogether so disadvantageous, or is even meaningful, when we recognize the fact that, as far as control law is optimal, the resulting closed-loop system has robust stability properties against a wide range of variations in open-loop dynamics. That is, in case the matrix R is positive diagonal and Q is positive definite, the closed-loop system has an infinite gain margin, at least a 50% gain reduction tolerance, and at least a $\pm 60°$ phase margin in each input channel [10]. It can also be justified by the fact that for all practical purposes, the quadratic weights in performance index are seldom determined a priori, and are often tuned up in the design so as to achieve a desirable properties of the closed-loop system.

In the following sections, we consider the problem of finding the class of decentrally optimizable interconnected systems for which decentralized optimal control laws always exist.

III. SINGLE-INPUT SUBSYSTEMS

A. *MAIN RESULT*

We first consider the interconnected system constituted of single-input subsystems described by

$$S_i: \quad \dot{x}_i = A_i x_i + b_i u_i, \quad i = 1, 2, \ldots, N, \tag{8}$$

where b_i is an n_i-dimensional vector. We assume that the pair (A_i, b_i) is completely controllable and that the matrix A_i and b_i are given in the controllable canonical form

$$A_i = \begin{bmatrix} 0 & 1 & \cdots & 0 \\ 0 & 0 & \cdots & 0 \\ \hline 0 & 0 & \cdots & 1 \\ a_1^i & a_2^i & \cdots & a_{n_i}^i \end{bmatrix}, \quad b_i = \begin{bmatrix} 0 \\ 0 \\ \vdots \\ 0 \\ 1 \end{bmatrix}. \tag{9}$$

Under the assumption we can represent the interconnection matrix $A_{ij} = \left[a_{pq}^{ij}\right]$ in Eq. (1) as

$$A_{ij} = \hat{A}_{ij} + b_i f_{ij}^T \tag{10}$$

where $\hat{A}_{ij} = \left[\hat{a}_{pq}^{ij}\right]$ is the matrix obtained from A_{ij} replacing the bottom row with a zero row vector, and f_{ij}^T is the bottom row, that is,

$$\hat{a}^{ij}_{pq} = \begin{cases} a^{ij}_{pq}, & \text{if } p = 1, 2, \ldots, n_i - 1, \\ 0, & \text{if } p = n_i, \end{cases} \tag{11}$$

and

$$f^T_{ij} = \begin{bmatrix} a^{ij}_{n_i 1} & a^{ij}_{n_i 2} & \cdots & a^{ij}_{n_i n_j} \end{bmatrix}. \tag{12}$$

In Eq. (10), the vector f^T_{ij} can be regarded as describing the interconnection through the i-th subsystem input u_i, and the matrix $\hat{A}_{ij}$ represents the rest.

Now we introduce the number μ^{ij}_{pq} to characterize the structure of interconnection as

$$\mu^{ij}_{pq} = -[(p + \theta_i + 0.5)/\nu_i] + [(q + \theta_j - 0.5)/\nu_j] \tag{13}$$

with real numbers ν_i and θ_i, where $i, j = 1, 2, \ldots, N$, $p = 1, 2, \ldots, n_i$, and $q = 1, 2, \ldots, n_j$.

With these preliminaries, we are now in a position to state our main result.

Theorem 1

The interconnected system S is decentrally optimizable if there exist positive constants ν_i and constants θ_i, $i = 1, 2, \ldots, N$, such that for every quadruple (i, j; p, q),

$$\mu^{ij}_{pq} \geqq 0 \tag{14}$$

implies

$$\hat{a}^{ij}_{pq} = 0. \tag{15}$$

Theorem 1 provides the class of decentrally optimizable interconnected systems, which is characterized by the structure of interconnection matrix $\hat{A}_{ij}$. That is, the class is given independently of the coupling strength, the quadratic weights selection, and input interconnection matrix f_{ij}^T. We note that Theorem 1 includes the single-input case of [14], in which $\hat{A}_{ij} = 0$.

Let us illustrate two subclasses of the class of decentrally optimizable interconnected systems using the interconnection matrix A_{ij} (not $\hat{A}_{ij}$). In the following example we assume that the subsystems of Eq. (8) are in the controllable canonical form of Eq. (9) and that the dimension of these is $n_i \geqq n_j$ for $i < j$. The asterisks denote nonzero elements.

Example 1

The interconnected system S is decentrally optimizable when the interconnection matrix A_{ij} has the form illustrated in the following.

Case 1

$$A_{ij} = \overbrace{\begin{bmatrix} * & & \bigcirc \\ \vdots & \ddots & \\ * & \cdots & * \\ * & \cdots & * \\ \vdots & & \vdots \\ * & \cdots & * \\ * & \cdots & * \end{bmatrix}}^{n_j} \begin{matrix} \left.\vphantom{\begin{matrix} * \\ \vdots \\ * \end{matrix}}\right\} n_j \\ \left.\vphantom{\begin{matrix} * \\ \vdots \\ * \end{matrix}}\right\} n_i - n_j - 1 \\ \} \, 1 \end{matrix} \qquad (i < j),$$

$$A_{ij} = \begin{bmatrix} * & & \bigcirc \\ \vdots & \ddots & \\ * & \cdots & * \end{bmatrix} \Bigg\} \, n_i \; (=n_j) \qquad (i = j),$$

$$A_{ij} = \begin{bmatrix} * & * & & & & & \\ \vdots & \ddots & \ddots & & & \bigcirc & \\ * & \cdots & * & * & 0 & \cdots & 0 \\ * & \cdots & * & * & * & \cdots & * \end{bmatrix} \begin{matrix} \left.\vphantom{\begin{matrix} * \\ \vdots \\ * \end{matrix}}\right\} n_i - 1 \\ \} \, 1 \end{matrix} \qquad (i > j).$$

$$\underbrace{\qquad}_{n_i - 1} \; \underbrace{\;}_{1} \; \underbrace{\qquad}_{n_j - n_i}$$

This form can be derived by selecting $\nu_i = 1.0$ and $\theta_i = (n_1 + n_2 + \cdots + n_i)/n$ in μ_{pq}^{ij} of Eq. (13).

Case 2

$$A_{ij} = \overbrace{\begin{bmatrix} & \bigcirc & \\ * & \cdots & * \\ \vdots & & \vdots \\ * & \cdots & * \\ * & \cdots & * \end{bmatrix}}^{n_j} \begin{matrix} \}\ l_i - 1 \\ \\ \}\ n_i - l_i \\ \\ \}\ 1 \end{matrix} \qquad (i < j),$$

$$A_{ij} = \begin{bmatrix} * & & \\ \vdots & \ddots & \bigcirc \\ * & \cdots & * \end{bmatrix} \Big\}\ n_i\ (=n_j) \qquad (i = j),$$

$$A_{ij} = \begin{bmatrix} * & \cdots & * & & & \\ \vdots & & \vdots & & \bigcirc & \\ * & \cdots & * & & & \\ \underbrace{* \ \cdots \ *}_{l_i} & & & \underbrace{* \ \cdots \ *}_{n_j - l_i} & & \end{bmatrix} \begin{matrix} \}\ n_i - 1 \\ \\ \}\ 1 \end{matrix} \qquad (i > j)$$

where l_i is a positive integer. This form can be derived by selecting $\nu_i = 2n_1 \times 2n_2 \times \cdots \times 2n_i$ and $\theta_i = -l_i$.

B. *PROOF OF THEOREM*

First observe that the matrix A_i in Eq. (8) can be represented as

$$A_i = \hat{A}_i + b_i f_i^T \tag{16}$$

where

$$\hat{A}_i = \begin{bmatrix} 0 & 1 & \cdots & 0 \\ 0 & 0 & \cdots & 0 \\ \hline 0 & 0 & \cdots & 1 \\ 0 & 0 & \cdots & 0 \end{bmatrix}, \tag{17}$$

$$f_i^T = \begin{bmatrix} a_1^i & a_2^i & \cdots & a_{n_i}^i \end{bmatrix}. \tag{18}$$

With Eq. (18) and f_{ij}^T of Eq. (12), we define a block matrix $\hat{F}^T = [\hat{f}_{ij}^T]_{n\times n}$ as

$$\hat{f}_{ij}^T = \begin{cases} f_i^T + f_{ij}^T, & \text{if } i = j, \\ f_{ij}^T, & \text{if } i \neq j. \end{cases} \tag{19}$$

Then the system S of Eq. (3) can be rewritten as

$$S: \quad \dot{x} = \left(\hat{A}_D + \hat{A}_C + B_D\hat{F}^T\right)x + B_D u \tag{20}$$

where

$$\hat{A}_D = \text{block diag}\left[\hat{A}_1, \hat{A}_2, \ldots, \hat{A}_N\right],$$

$$\hat{A}_C = \text{block matrix}\left[\hat{A}_{ij}\right]_{n\times n}$$

We regard the system S in Eq. (20) as the interconnected system composed of subsystems

$$\hat{S}_D: \quad \dot{x} = \hat{A}_D x + B_D u \tag{21}$$

with the interconnections $\left(\hat{A}_C + B_D\hat{F}^T\right)x$. We note that $\hat{S}_D$ is an imaginary system and the real subsystems constituting the system S are described by

$$S_D: \quad \dot{x} = A_D x + B_D u. \tag{22}$$

Before discussing the optimal control problem for S, let us consider that for $\hat{S}_D$. With the system $\hat{S}_D$ we associate a performance index

$$\hat{J}_D = \int_0^\infty (x^T\hat{Q}x + u^T\hat{R}u)\, dt, \tag{23}$$

where $\hat{Q} = \text{block diag}\left[\hat{Q}_1, \hat{Q}_2, \ldots, \hat{Q}_N\right]$ is an $n \times n$ symmetric positive-definite matrix with blocks $\hat{Q}_i$ as $n_i \times n_i$ matrices, and $\hat{R} = \text{diag}\left[\hat{r}_1, \hat{r}_2, \ldots, \hat{r}_N\right]$ where $\hat{r}_i$ is a positive number. Since the pair $\left(\hat{A}_D, B_D\right)$ is obviously completely controllable, we can obtain the optimal control law, which is given by

$$u = -\hat{K}^T x, \tag{24}$$

where

$$\hat{K}^T = \hat{R}^{-1} B_D^T \hat{P}, \tag{25}$$

and $\hat{P}$ is the positive-definite solution of the Riccati equation

$$\hat{A}_D^T \hat{P} + \hat{P}\hat{A}_D - \hat{P}B_D\hat{R}^{-1}B_D^T\hat{P} + \hat{Q} = 0. \tag{26}$$

We note that due to the form of Eq. (26) we have $\hat{P}$ = block diag$\left[\hat{P}_1, \hat{P}_2, \ldots, \hat{P}_N\right]$, $\hat{K}$ = block diag$\left[\hat{k}_1, \hat{k}_2, \ldots, \hat{k}_N\right]$, and the control law (24) is decentralized, where submatrices $\hat{P}_i$ and $\hat{k}_i^T = \hat{r}_i^{-1} b_i^T \hat{P}_i$ are conformable with the dimension of the corresponding subsystem

$$\hat{S}_i: \quad \dot{x}_i = \hat{A}_i x_i + b_i u_i. \tag{27}$$

When the decentralized control law (24) with the gain $\hat{K}^T$ of Eq. (25) is applied to the system S of Eq. (20), it is not generally optimal for the performance index $\hat{J}_D$ of (23). We modify $\hat{J}_D$ and $\hat{K}^T$ to provide a suitable performance index and a decentralized optimal control law for the interconnected system S satisfying the condition of Theorem 1. For this purpose, we employ matrices

$$T_D = \text{block diag}[T_1, T_2, \ldots, T_N], \tag{28}$$

$$T_i = \text{diag}\left[\gamma_i^{-\theta_i - 1}, \gamma_i^{-\theta_i - 2}, \ldots, \gamma_i^{-\theta_i - n_i}\right],$$

$$T = \text{diag}\left[\gamma_1^{-\theta_1 - n_1}, \gamma_2^{-\theta_2 - n_2}, \ldots, \gamma_N^{-\theta_N - n_N}\right], \tag{29}$$

$$\Gamma_D = \text{block diag}[\gamma_1 I_{n_1}, \gamma_2 I_{n_2}, \ldots, \gamma_N I_{n_N}], \tag{30}$$

$$\Gamma = \text{diag}[\gamma_1, \gamma_2, \ldots, \gamma_N], \tag{31}$$

where $\gamma_i = \gamma^{1/\nu_i}$ with positive number γ, I_{n_i} is the $n_i \times n_i$ identity matrix, and ν_i, θ_i are constants specified in Theorem 1. The positive number γ is determined later so that we have a suitable performance index. With the matrices of Eqs. (28)-(31) we define the weights Q and R in the performance index J of Eq. (4) as

$$Q = Q_D - Q_C, \tag{32}$$

$$Q_D = \Gamma_D^{1/2}\left(T_D\hat{Q}T_D\right)\Gamma_D^{1/2} + (\beta - 1)\Gamma_D^{1/2}\left(T_D\hat{P}B_D\hat{R}^{-1}B_D^T\hat{P}T_D\right)\Gamma_D^{1/2}, \tag{33}$$

$$Q_C = \left(\hat{A}_C + B_D\hat{F}^T\right)^T T_D\hat{P}T_D + T_D\hat{P}T_D\left(\hat{A}_C + B_D\hat{F}^T\right), \tag{34}$$

$$R = \beta^{-1}\Gamma^{-1/2}T\hat{R}T\Gamma^{-1/2} \tag{35}$$

where β is a positive number, which is also determined later.

Now with this performance index let us consider the optimal control problem for the interconnected system S. Since R is obviously positive diagonal, if the matrix Q defined by Eqs. (32)-(34) is positive definite, this problem is well defined and then the optimal control law is obtained as

$$u = -K^T x, \quad K^T = R^{-1}B_D^T P \tag{36}$$

where P is the positive-definite solution of the Riccati equation

$$\left(\hat{A}_D + \hat{A}_C + B_D\hat{F}^T\right)^T P + P\left(\hat{A}_D + \hat{A}_C + B_D\hat{F}^T\right) - PB_D R^{-1}B_D^T P + Q = 0. \tag{37}$$

As shown in the Appendix, the solution is given by

$$P = T_D\hat{P}T_D. \tag{38}$$

Since P of Eq. (38), B_D, and R of Eq. (35) are block diagonal, the gain matrix K^T of Eq. (36) is also block diagonal. Thus, the optimal control law (36) is decentralized and the input u_i of the i-th subsystem can be calculated as

$$u_i = -k_i^T x, \quad k_i^T = \beta \hat{r}_i^{-1} b_i^T \hat{P}_i \hat{T}_i \tag{39}$$

where

$$\hat{T}_i = \mathrm{diag}[\gamma^{n_i/\nu_i}, \gamma^{(n_i-1)/\nu_i}, \ldots, \gamma^{1/\nu_i}]. \tag{40}$$

To conclude the existence of the decentralized optimal control law (36), it remains to show the positive definiteness of the matrix Q defined by Eqs. (32)-(34) for an appropriate choice of positive numbers β and γ. To do this, we observe that

$$\begin{aligned} Q = {} & T_D \Gamma_D^{1/2} \Big[\hat{Q} - \Gamma_D^{-1/2} \left(T_D \hat{A}_C T_D^{-1} \right)^T \hat{P} \Gamma_D^{-1/2} \\ & - \Gamma_D^{-1/2} \hat{P} \left(T_D \hat{A}_C T_D^{-1} \right) \Gamma_D^{-1/2} \Big] \Gamma_D^{1/2} T_D \\ & + (\beta - 1) \Big[T_D \hat{P} B_D \Gamma_D^{1/2} - (\beta - 1)^{-1} \hat{F} T B_D^T \Gamma_D^{-1/2} \hat{R} \Big] \hat{R}^{-1} \\ & \times \Big[\Gamma_D^{1/2} B_D^T \hat{P} T_D - (\beta - 1)^{-1} \hat{R} \Gamma_D^{-1/2} B_D T \hat{F}^T \Big] \\ & - (\beta - 1)^{-1} \hat{F} T B_D^T \Gamma_D^{-1/2} \hat{R} \Gamma_D^{-1/2} B_D T \hat{F}^T, \end{aligned} \tag{41}$$

which can easily be verified by using the equality $T_D B_D = B_D T$. This equality implies that we have a positive-definite Q if the first term on the right side is positive definite, because the second term is nonnegative definite for $\beta > 1$ and the third term can be made arbitrarily small by choosing a sufficiently large γ. We show the positive definiteness of the first term utilizing the inequality

$$\begin{aligned} & y^T \Big[\hat{Q} - \Gamma_D^{-1/2} \left(T_D \hat{A}_C T_D^{-1} \right)^T \hat{P} \Gamma_D^{-1/2} - \Gamma_D^{-1/2} \hat{P} \left(T_D \hat{A}_C T_D^{-1} \right) \Gamma_D^{-1/2} \Big] y \\ & \qquad \geqq y^T \hat{Q} y - 2 \|\hat{P}\| \, \|\tilde{A}_C\| y^T y \end{aligned} \tag{42}$$

where y is an n-dimensional nonzero vector, $||\cdot||$ is the matrix norm induced by the Euclidean vector norm, and

$$\tilde{A}_C = \Gamma_D^{-1/2} T_D \hat{A}_C T_D^{-1} \Gamma_D^{-1/2}. \tag{43}$$

Observing that the ij-th submatrix $\tilde{A}_{ij} = \left[\tilde{a}_{pq}^{ij}\right]$ of $\tilde{A}_C$ is calculated as

$$\tilde{A}_{ij} = (\gamma_i \gamma_j)^{-1/2} T_i \hat{A}_{ij} T_j^{-1}, \tag{44}$$

we obtain

$$\tilde{a}_{pq}^{ij} = \gamma^{\mu_{pq}^{ij}} \hat{a}_{pq}^{ij}. \tag{45}$$

Under the condition of Theorem 1, Eq. (45) implies that

$$\tilde{a}_{pq}^{ij} = 0, \quad \text{if} \quad \hat{a}_{pq}^{ij} = 0, \tag{46}$$

or

$$\lim_{\gamma\to\infty} \tilde{a}_{pq}^{ij} = 0, \quad \text{if} \quad \hat{a}_{pq}^{ij} \neq 0, \tag{47}$$

holds for any i, j, p, and q, so that we have

$$\lim_{\gamma\to\infty} ||\tilde{A}_C|| = 0. \tag{48}$$

This means that for sufficiently large γ, the left side of inequality (42) is positive definite and so is the first term of the right side of equality (41). Thus, we have a positive-definite Q by choosing appropriately the positive numbers β and γ, which completes the proof.

C. *SOME REMARKS*

(a) As follows from the proof of Theorem 1, the resulting closed-loop system

$$S_C: \quad \dot{x} = \left(A_D + A_C - B_D K^T\right)x \tag{49}$$

is connectively optimal. That is, the optimality of the decentralized control law is preserved for a modified performance index under perturbations in interconnections such that the strength of coupling does not increase, or more precisely, the changes ensure the positive definiteness of the matrix Q of Eq. (41). This implies that we can design satisfactorily the connectively optimal system by choosing appropriate numbers β and γ in advance for all possible interconnection patterns which might undergo perturbations.

(b) The optimal feedback gain k_i^T of Eq. (39) is related to the optimal feedback gain $\hat{k}_i^T$ for the imaginary subsystem $\hat{S}_i$ of Eq. (27) as $k_i^T = \beta\hat{k}_i^T\hat{T}_i$, which means that k_i is obtained from $\hat{k}_i$ by an appropriate tuning. This feature suggests that the decentralized optimal control law (39) is a kind of high-gain controller.

(c) The condition for decentral optimizability of Theorem 1 is also that for decentral stabilizability with the arbitrary stability degree α, which can be readily shown by observing that if the interconnection matrix $\hat{A}_C$ satisfies the condition, then so does $\hat{A}_C + \alpha I$ for any number α. The least restrictive condition for stabilizability in terms of the structure of interconnection reported so far is that of Yasuda and Hirai [7], and that of Sezer and Šiljak [8]. The author's result includes theirs, which follows from the fact that the author characterizes the interconnections using the matrix $\hat{A}_{ij}$, while they used A_{ij} that has more nonzero elements than $\hat{A}_{ij}$.

IV. MULTI-INPUT SUBSYSTEMS

In this section, we mention that Theorem 1 can also apply to the multi-input case by reducing a multi-input subsystem to a set of single-input subsystems. It is assumed that the multi-input subsystem S_i of Eq. (8) is completely controllable and that the matrices A_i, B_i of S_i are given in the controllable canonical form as

$$A_i = \begin{bmatrix} A_{i11} & A_{i12} & \cdots & A_{i1r_i} \\ A_{i21} & A_{i22} & \cdots & A_{i2r_i} \\ \hline A_{ir_i1} & A_{ir_i2} & \cdots & A_{ir_ir_i} \end{bmatrix}, \tag{50}$$

$$A_{ikk} = \begin{bmatrix} 0 & 1 & \cdots & 0 \\ 0 & 0 & \cdots & 0 \\ \hline 0 & 0 & \cdots & 1 \\ * & * & \cdots & * \end{bmatrix}$$

$$A_{ikl} = \begin{bmatrix} 0 & 0 & \cdots & 0 \\ 0 & 0 & \cdots & 0 \\ \hline 0 & 0 & \cdots & 0 \\ * & * & \cdots & * \end{bmatrix} \quad (k \neq l),$$

$$B_i = \begin{bmatrix} b_{i11} & b_{i12} & \cdots & b_{i1r_i} \\ b_{i21} & b_{i22} & \cdots & b_{i2r_i} \\ \hline b_{ir_i1} & b_{ir_i2} & \cdots & b_{ir_ir_i} \end{bmatrix}, \tag{51}$$

$$b_{ikk} = [0 \ \ 0 \ \cdots \ 0 \ \ 1]^T,$$

$$b_{ikl} = [0 \ \ 0 \ \cdots \ 0 \ \ *]^T \quad (k < l),$$

$$b_{ikl} = [0 \ \ 0 \ \cdots \ 0 \ \ 0]^T \quad (k > l)$$

where A_{ikl} is a $\sigma_{ik} \times \sigma_{il}$ constant matrix, b_{ikl} is a σ_{ik}-dimensional vector, and σ_{ik} is a positive constant such that $\Sigma_{k=1}^{r_i} \sigma_{ik} = n_i$. In Eqs. (50) and (51), the asterisks denote elements which may not be zeros. We also assume that the interconnection matrix A_{ij} is decomposed correspondingly as

$$A_{ij} = \left[\begin{array}{cccc} A_{ij11} & A_{ij12} & \cdots & A_{ij1r_j} \\ A_{ij21} & A_{ij22} & \cdots & A_{ij2r_j} \\ \hline A_{ijr_i1} & A_{ijr_i2} & \cdots & A_{ijr_ir_j} \end{array}\right], \tag{52}$$

where $A_{ijkl} = \left[a_{pq}^{ijkl}\right]$ is a $\sigma_{ik} \times \sigma_{jl}$ matrix.

Following the previous section, we represent the submatrices A_{ikl} and A_{ijkl} as

$$A_{ikl} = \begin{cases} \hat{A}_{ikk} + b_{ikk}f_{ikk}^T, & \text{if } k = l, \\ b_{ikk}f_{ikl}^T, & \text{if } k \neq l, \end{cases} \tag{53}$$

and

$$A_{ijkl} = \hat{A}_{ijkl} + b_{ikk}f_{ijkl}^T \tag{54}$$

where

$$\hat{A}_{ikk} = \left[\begin{array}{cccc} 0 & 1 & \cdots & 0 \\ 0 & 0 & \cdots & 0 \\ \hline 0 & 0 & \cdots & 1 \\ 0 & 0 & \cdots & 0 \end{array}\right], \tag{55}$$

f_{ikl}^T, f_{ijkl}^T are row vectors, and $\hat{A}_{ijkl} = \left[\hat{a}_{pq}^{ijkl}\right]$ is a $\sigma_{ik} \times \sigma_{jl}$ matrix defined as

$$\hat{a}_{pq}^{ijkl} = \begin{cases} a_{pq}^{ijkl}, & \text{if } p \neq \sigma_{ik}, \\ 0, & \text{if } p = \sigma_{ik}. \end{cases} \tag{56}$$

Defining $\tilde{A}_i$, $\tilde{B}_i$, and $\tilde{A}_{ij}$ as

$$\tilde{A}_i = \text{block diag}\left[\tilde{A}_{i11}, \tilde{A}_{i22}, \ldots, \tilde{A}_{ir_ir_i}\right], \tag{57}$$

$$\tilde{B}_i = \text{block diag}\left[b_{i11}, b_{i22}, \ldots, b_{ir_ir_i}\right], \tag{58}$$

$$\tilde{A}_{ij} = \text{block matrix}\left[\hat{A}_{ijkl}\right]_{r_i \times r_i}, \tag{59}$$

the matrices A_i, B_i, and A_{ij} of Eqs. (50)-(51) can be described in the form

$$A_i = \tilde{A}_i + \tilde{B}_i F_i^T, \tag{60}$$

$$B_i = \tilde{B}_i G_i, \tag{61}$$

$$A_{ij} = \tilde{A}_{ij} + \tilde{B}_i F_{ij}^T \tag{62}$$

where

$$F_i^T = \text{block matrix}\left[f_{ikl}^T\right]_{r_i \times r_i}, \tag{63}$$

$$F_{ij}^T = \text{block matrix}\left[f_{ijkl}^T\right]_{r_i \times r_i}, \tag{64}$$

and G_i is an $r_i \times r_i$ nonsingular, upper triangular matrix.

We also define the matrices

$$\tilde{A}_D = \text{block diag}\left[\tilde{A}_1, \tilde{A}_2, \ldots, \tilde{A}_N\right], \tag{65}$$

$$\tilde{A}_C = \text{block matrix}\left[\tilde{A}_{ij}\right]_{N \times N}, \tag{66}$$

$$\tilde{B}_D = \text{block diag}\left[\tilde{B}_1, \tilde{B}_2, \ldots, \tilde{B}_N\right], \tag{67}$$

$$\tilde{F}^T = \text{block matrix}\left[\tilde{F}_{ij}^T\right]_{N \times N}, \tag{68}$$

$$\tilde{G} = \text{block diag}[G_1, G_2, \ldots, G_N] \tag{69}$$

where $\tilde{F}_{ij}^T = \text{block matrix}\left[\tilde{f}_{ij}^T\right]_{r_i \times r_i}$, and

$$\tilde{f}_{ij}^T = \begin{cases} f_{ikl}^T + f_{iikl}^T, & \text{if } i = j, \\ f_{ijkl}^T, & \text{if } i \neq j. \end{cases} \tag{70}$$

Using these matrices, the overall system S of Eq. (3) is written as

$$S: \quad \dot{x} = \left(\tilde{A}_D + \tilde{A}_C + \tilde{B}_D \tilde{F}^T\right)x + \tilde{B}_D \tilde{G} u. \tag{71}$$

We now introduce the imaginary input $v = \tilde{G}u$ to reduce S to

$$\tilde{S}: \quad \dot{x} = \left(\tilde{A}_D + \tilde{A}_C + \tilde{B}_D\tilde{F}^T\right)x + \tilde{B}_D v, \tag{72}$$

which can be regarded as an interconnected system composed of $r \left(= \Sigma_{i=1}^{N} r_i\right)$ single-input subsystems

$$\tilde{S}_{ik}: \quad \dot{x}_{ik} = A_{ikk}x_{ik} + b_{ikk}v_{ik} \tag{73}$$

where x_{ik} is the σ_{ik}-dimensional state vector and v_{ik} is the scalar input of $\tilde{S}_{ik}$. Since the matrices A_{ikk} and b_{ikk} are of the controllable canonical form, the collection of $\tilde{S}_{ik}$,

$$\tilde{S}_D: \quad \dot{x} = \tilde{A}_D x + \tilde{B}_D v, \tag{74}$$

is of the form Eq. (21), and the overall system $\tilde{S}$ of Eq. (72) is of the form Eq. (20), so that the result obtained in the previous section for the case of single-input subsystems can be applied.

Finally, we note that the decentralized optimal control law for $\tilde{S}$ of Eq. (72) is in of the form

$$v = -\tilde{K}^T x, \tag{75}$$

$$\tilde{K} = \text{block diag}\left[\tilde{K}_1, \tilde{K}_2, \ldots, \tilde{K}_N\right],$$

$$\tilde{K}_i = \text{block diag}[k_{i1}, k_{i2}, \ldots, k_{iN}].$$

This implies that the real optimal control law for $\tilde{S}$ is given by

$$u = -\tilde{G}^{-1}\tilde{K}^T x \tag{76}$$

which is still decentralized, and is optimal with respect to the performance index

$$J = \int_0^\infty [x^T\tilde{Q}x + u^T(\tilde{G}^T\tilde{R}\tilde{G})u]\, dt \tag{77}$$

where $\tilde{Q}$ is a positive-definite matrix and $\tilde{R}$ is a positive-diagonal matrix.

V. ILLUSTRATIVE EXAMPLE

We provide here a simple example to illustrate the synthesis procedure for decentralized optimal control laws. Let us consider a system S composed of the completely controllable subsystems

$$S_1: \quad \begin{bmatrix} \dot{x}_{11} \\ \dot{x}_{12} \end{bmatrix} = \begin{bmatrix} 0 & 1 \\ 0 & 0 \end{bmatrix} \begin{bmatrix} x_{11} \\ x_{12} \end{bmatrix} + \begin{bmatrix} 0 \\ 1 \end{bmatrix} u_1$$

and

$$S_2: \quad \begin{bmatrix} \dot{x}_{21} \\ \dot{x}_{22} \end{bmatrix} = \begin{bmatrix} 0 & 1 \\ -1 & -1 \end{bmatrix} \begin{bmatrix} x_{21} \\ x_{22} \end{bmatrix} + \begin{bmatrix} 0 \\ 1 \end{bmatrix} u_2$$

with the interconnections

$$A_{12}x_2 = \begin{bmatrix} 1 & 0 \\ 1 & 0 \end{bmatrix} \begin{bmatrix} x_{21} \\ x_{22} \end{bmatrix}$$

and

$$A_{21}x_1 = \begin{bmatrix} 0 & 1 \\ 1 & 0 \end{bmatrix} \begin{bmatrix} x_{11} \\ x_{12} \end{bmatrix}.$$

The overall system S can be written in the compact form

$$S: \quad \dot{x} = \left(\hat{A}_D + \hat{A}_C + B_D\hat{F}^T\right)x + B_D u$$

where

$$\hat{A}_D = \left[\begin{array}{cc|cc} 0 & 1 & & \\ 0 & 0 & \multicolumn{2}{c}{\bigcirc} \\ \hline \multicolumn{2}{c|}{\bigcirc} & 0 & 1 \\ & & 0 & 0 \end{array}\right], \qquad B_D = \left[\begin{array}{c|c} 0 & \\ 1 & \bigcirc \\ \hline & 0 \\ \bigcirc & 1 \end{array}\right],$$

$$\hat{A}_C = \left[\begin{array}{cc|cc} & & 1 & 0 \\ \multicolumn{2}{c|}{\bigcirc} & 0 & 0 \\ \hline 0 & 1 & & \\ 0 & 0 & \multicolumn{2}{c}{\bigcirc} \end{array}\right], \qquad \hat{F}^T = \left[\begin{array}{cc|cc} 0 & 0 & 1 & 0 \\ \hline 1 & 0 & -1 & -1 \end{array}\right].$$

By selecting $\nu_1 = \nu_2 = 1.0$, $\theta_1 = 0.5$, and $\theta_2 = 1.0$, we can easily see from Case 1 of Example 1 that the interconnection matrix $\hat{A}_C$ satisfies the condition of Theorem 1, which means the overall system S is decentrally optimizable.

To get a decentralized optimal control law for S, we first give the matrices $\hat{Q}$ and $\hat{R}$ in $\hat{J}_D$ of Eq. (23) as

$$\hat{Q} = \left[\begin{array}{cc|cc} 1 & 0 & & \\ 0 & 2 & \multicolumn{2}{c}{\bigcirc} \\ \hline & & 1 & 0 \\ \multicolumn{2}{c|}{\bigcirc} & 0 & 2 \end{array}\right], \qquad \hat{R} = \left[\begin{array}{c|c} 1 & 0 \\ \hline 0 & 1 \end{array}\right].$$

For these $\hat{Q}$ and $\hat{R}$, the Riccati equation (26) has the positive-definite solution

$$\hat{P} = \left[\begin{array}{cc|cc} 2 & 1 & & \\ 1 & 2 & \multicolumn{2}{c}{\bigcirc} \\ \hline & & 2 & 1 \\ \multicolumn{2}{c|}{\bigcirc} & 1 & 2 \end{array}\right].$$

Using T_D, T, Γ_D, and Γ with $\nu_1 = \nu_2 = 1.0$, $\theta_1 = 0.5$, $\theta_2 = 1.0$, the matrices Q_D and Q_C are calculated as

$$Q_D = \left[\begin{array}{cc|cc} \beta\gamma^{-2} & 2(\beta - 1)\gamma^{-3} & & \\ 2(\beta - 1)\gamma^{-3} & 2(2\beta - 1)\gamma^{-4} & \multicolumn{2}{c}{\bigcirc} \\ \hline & & \beta\gamma^{-3} & 2(\beta - 1)\gamma^{-4} \\ \multicolumn{2}{c|}{\bigcirc} & 2(\beta - 1)\gamma^{-4} & 2(2\beta - 1)\gamma^{-5} \end{array}\right],$$

$$Q_C = \left[\begin{array}{cc|cc} & & 2\gamma^{-3} + \gamma^{-4} + \gamma^{-5} & 2\gamma^{-6} \\ \multicolumn{2}{c|}{\bigcirc} & 3\gamma^{-4} + 2\gamma^{-5} & \gamma^{-5} \\ \hline 2\gamma^{-3} + \gamma^{-4} + \gamma^{-5} & 3\gamma^{-4} + 2\gamma^{-5} & -2\gamma^{-5} & -\gamma^{-5} - 2\gamma^{-6} \\ 2\gamma^{-6} & \gamma^{-5} & -\gamma^{-3} - 2\gamma^{-6} & -4\gamma^{-6} \end{array}\right],$$

so that the quadratic weights Q and R in the performance index J of Eq. (4) associated with the overall system S are given by

$$Q = Q_D - Q_C$$

$$= \left[\begin{array}{cc|cc} \beta\gamma^{-2} & 2(\beta-1)\gamma^{-3} & -2\gamma^{-3}-\gamma^{-4}-\gamma^{-5} & -2\gamma^{-6} \\ 2(\beta-1)\gamma^{-3} & 2(2\beta-1)\gamma^{-4} & -3\gamma^{-4}-2\gamma^{-5} & -\gamma^{-5} \\ \hline -2\gamma^{-3}-\gamma^{-4}-\gamma^{-5} & -3\gamma^{-4}-2\gamma^{-5} & \beta\gamma^{-3}+2\gamma^{-5} & 2(\beta-1)\gamma^{-4}+\gamma^{-5}+2\gamma^{-6} \\ -2\gamma^{-6} & -\gamma^{-5} & 2(\beta-1)\gamma^{-4}+\gamma^{-5}+2\gamma^{-6} & 2(2\beta-1)\gamma^{-5}+4\gamma^{-6} \end{array}\right]$$

$$R = \left[\begin{array}{c|c} \beta^{-1}\gamma^{-6} & 0 \\ \hline 0 & \beta^{-1}\gamma^{-7} \end{array}\right].$$

Then, we have the decentralized optimal control

$$\begin{bmatrix} u_1 \\ u_2 \end{bmatrix} = -\left[\begin{array}{cc|cc} \beta\gamma^2 & 2\beta\gamma & 0 & 0 \\ \hline 0 & 0 & \beta\gamma^2 & 2\beta\gamma \end{array}\right] \left[\begin{array}{c} x_{11} \\ x_{12} \\ \hline x_{21} \\ x_{22} \end{array}\right],$$

provided that Q is positive definite. Choosing $\gamma = 1.0$ and $\beta \geqq 6.5$, for example, makes the matrix Q positive definite.

VI. CONCLUSION

A decentralized optimal control has been proposed for achieving a highly reliable control scheme for large-scale interconnected systems, and the class of large-scale systems has been provided for which such a decentralized optimal control can always be found. The overall closed-loop system has the robust stability properties which the optimal regulator system has. Furthermore, the optimality of the decentralized control is preserved under perturbations in interconnections such that the strength of coupling does not increase. The class of decentrally optimizable large-scale systems presented in Theorem 1 is also larger than any class of decentrally stabilizable large-scale systems described by the structure of interconnections so far.

APPENDIX

We first verify that the positive-definite matrix P of Eq. (38) is a solution of the Riccati equation (37). By substituting P of Eq. (38) into the left side of Eq. (37), we have

$$\begin{aligned}
&\left(\hat{A}_D + \hat{A}_C + B_D\hat{F}^T\right)^T\left(T_D\hat{P}T_D\right) + \left(T_D\hat{P}T_D\right)\left(\hat{A}_D + \hat{A}_C + B_D\hat{F}^T\right) \\
&\quad - \left(T_D\hat{P}T_D\right)B_D\left(\beta^{-1}\Gamma^{-1/2}T\hat{R}T\Gamma^{-1/2}\right)^{-1}B_D^T\left(T_D\hat{P}T_D\right) \\
&\quad + \Gamma_D^{1/2}\left(T_D\hat{Q}T_D\right)\Gamma_D^{1/2} + (\beta - 1)\Gamma_D^{1/2}\left(T_D\hat{P}B_D\hat{R}^{-1}B_D^T\hat{P}T_D\right)\Gamma_D^{1/2} \\
&\quad - \left(\hat{A}_C + B_D\hat{F}^T\right)^T P_D - P_D\left(\hat{A}_C + B_D\hat{F}^T\right) \\
&= \Gamma_D^{1/2}T_D\left(\hat{P}\hat{A}_D + \hat{A}_D^T\hat{P} - \hat{P}B_D\hat{R}^{-1}B_D^T\hat{P} + \hat{Q}\right)T_D\Gamma_D^{1/2} = 0.
\end{aligned}$$

The last equality follows from the matrix $\hat{P}$'s satisfying the Riccati equation (26). To show the uniqueness, we utilize the fact [15] that if the pair $\left(\hat{A}_D + \hat{A}_C + B_D\hat{F}^T, B_D\right)$ is stabilizable, then for any positive-definite Q, the positive-definite solution of the Riccati equation (37) is determined uniquely. The stabilizability of the pair $\left(\hat{A}_D + \hat{A}_C + B_D\hat{F}^T, B_D\right)$ is ascertained by observing the stability of the closed-loop system S_C of Eq. (49). Thus, we see that the matrix P of Eq. (38) is the unique positive-definite solution of the Riccati equation (37).

ACKNOWLEDGMENTS

The author wishes to express his gratitude to Professor Kazumasa Hirai and Professor Masao Ikeda of Kobe University for their helpful comments and valuable encouragement.

REFERENCES

1. D. D. ŠILJAK, "Large-Scale Dynamic Systems: Stability and Structure," North-Holland, New York, 1978.

2. N. R. SANDELL, JR., P. VARAIYA, M. ATHANS, and M. G. SAFONOV, "Survey of Decentralized Control Methods for Large Scale Systems," *IEEE Trans. Autom. Control AC-23*, No. 2, 108-128 (1978).

3. E. J. DAVISON, "The Decentralized Stabilization and Control of a Class of Unknown Nonlinear Time-Varying Systems," *Automatica 10*, 309-316 (1974).

4. M. IKEDA, O. UMEFUJI, and S. KODAMA, "Stabilization of Large-Scale Linear Systems," *Trans. IECE Japan (D) 59-D*, No. 5, 355-362 (1976) [in Japanese]; also in *Systems Computers Controls 7*, 34-41 (1976).

5. D. D. ŠILJAK and M. B. VUKČEVIĆ, "Decentrally Stabilizable Linear and Bilinear Large-Scale Systems," *Int. J. Control 26*, No. 2, 289-305 (1977).

6. M. IKEDA and D. D. ŠILJAK, "On Decentrally Stabilizable Large-Scale Systems," *Automatica 16*, 331-334 (1980).

7. K. YASUDA and K. HIRAI, "Stabilization of Linear Large-Scale Systems," *Trans. SICE 16*, No. 4, 504-510 (1980) [in Japanese].

8. M. E. SEZER and D. D. ŠILJAK, "On Decentralized Stabilization and Structure of Linear Large-Scale Systems," *Automatica 17*, No. 4, 641-644 (1981).

9. B. D. O. ANDERSON and J. B. MOORE, "Linear Optimal Control," Prentice-Hall, Englewood Cliffs, New Jersey, 1971.

10. M. G. SAFONOV and M. ATHANS, "Gain and Phase Margin for Multiloop LQG Regulators," *IEEE Trans. Autom. Control AC-22*, No. 2, 173-179 (1977).

11. R. E. KALMAN, "Contributions to the Theory of Optimal Control," *Boletin de la Sociedad Matematica Mexicana 5*, 102-119 (1960).

12. U. ÖZGÜNER, "Local Optimization in Large Scale Composite Dynamic Systems," *Proc. 9th Asilomar Conference on Circuits and Systems*, 3-5 Nov., 87-91 (1975).

13. D. D. ŠILJAK, "Reliable Control Using Multiple Control Systems," *Int. J. Control 31*, No. 2, 303-329 (1980).

14. K. YASUDA, T. HIKATA, and K. HIRAI, "On Decentrally Optimizable Interconnected Systems," *Proc. 19th IEEE Conference on Decision and Control*, 536-537 (1980).

15. W. M. WONHAM, "On a Matrix Riccati Equation of Stochastic Control," *SIAM J. Control 6*, No. 4, 681-697 (1968).

Techniques in Model Reduction for Large-Scale Systems

P. N. PARASKEVOPOULOS

Division of Computer Science
Department of Electrical Engineering
National Technical University of Athens
Athens, Greece

I. INTRODUCTION

The model-reduction or model-simplification problem may be defined as follows: Given a mathematical model of a system (e.g., state-space equations, transfer function matrix, etc.) which is considered to be quite complex, find a simpler mathematical model which adequately approximates the original model. Model reduction, therefore, simplifies the mathematical description of a system at the cost of having a less accurate model.

Model reduction appears to be a common procedure in engineering practice. The main reasons for this are:

(a) to simplify analysis of the original system,

(b) to simplify simulation of the original system,

(c) to reduce the computational effort in the design of controllers (optimal, adaptive, etc.), and

(d) to derive simpler control system structure.

The model-reduction problem can be formulated either in the time or in the frequency domain. In the time domain, the original system is assumed to be a linear time-invariant multivariable system described in state-space as

$$\dot{\underline{x}} = \underline{A}\underline{x} + \underline{B}\underline{u}, \tag{1a}$$

$$\underline{y} = \underline{C}\underline{x} \tag{1b}$$

where $\underline{x} \in R^n$, $\underline{y} \in R^p$, $\underline{u} \in R^m$, and $\underline{A}$, $\underline{B}$, and $\underline{C}$ are constant matrices of appropriate dimensions. The reduced-order model is assumed in the form

$$\dot{\underline{x}}_r = \underline{F}\underline{x}_r + \underline{G}\underline{u}, \tag{2a}$$

$$\underline{y}_r = \underline{H}\underline{x}_r \tag{2b}$$

where $\underline{x}_r \in R^r$, $\underline{y}_r \in R^p$, $r << n$, and $\underline{F}$, $\underline{G}$, and $\underline{H}$ are constant matrices of appropriate dimensions. In the time domain, the objective of model reduction is to obtain a set of model matrices $\underline{F}$, $\underline{G}$, and $\underline{H}$ so that $\underline{y}_r$ approximates $\underline{y}$, as close as possible, for all $\underline{u} \in \Omega$, where Ω is a set of admissible inputs.

In the frequency domain the original system is described by its $p \times m$ transfer function matrix $\underline{T}(s)$ having the form

$$\underline{T}(s) = \frac{\underline{B}_0 + \underline{B}_1 s + \underline{B}_2 s^2 + \cdots + \underline{B}_{n-1} s^{n-1}}{a_0 + a_1 s + a_2 s^2 + \cdots + a_{n-1} s^{n-1} + a_n s^n} \tag{3}$$

where $\underline{B}_i$, $i = 0, 1, \ldots, n - 1$, are $p \times m$ constant matrices. The reduced-order model transfer function matrix $\underline{T}_r(s)$ is also $p \times m$ and it is assumed of the form

$$\underline{T}_r(s) = \frac{\underline{D}_0 + \underline{D}_1 s + \underline{D}_2 s^2 + \cdots + \underline{D}_{r-1} s^{r-1}}{c_0 + c_1 s + c_2 s^2 + \cdots + c_{r-1} s^{r-1} + c_r s^r} \tag{4}$$

where $\underline{D}_i$, $i = 0, 1, \ldots, r - 1$, are $p \times m$ constant matrices. Here, the objective of model reduction is to obtain a set of coefficients $c_0, c_1, \ldots, c_r$ and $\underline{D}_0, \underline{D}_1, \ldots, \underline{D}_{r-1}$ such that $\underline{Y}_r(s)$ approximates $\underline{Y}(s)$, as close as possible, where

$$\underline{Y}(s) = \underline{T}(s)\underline{U}(s) \tag{5}$$

and

$$\underline{Y}_r(s) = \underline{T}_r(s)\underline{U}(s) \tag{6}$$

where $\underline{Y}(s)$, $\underline{Y}_r(s)$, and $\underline{U}(s)$ are the Laplace transforms of $\underline{y}(t)$, $\underline{y}_r(t)$, and $\underline{u}(t)$, respectively.

To solve the model-reduction problem several techniques have been reported. This chapter is devoted to reviewing and comparing these techniques. Other reviews have already been reported in the literature [1-6]. In [1] a comprehensive set of references is given.

To facilitate presentation, the model-reduction techniques are grouped under six main approaches:

(a) the theory of aggregation,

(b) the dominant-pole or eigenvalue approach,

(c) Padé-type approximant and partial realization,

(d) Routh approximation,

(e) perturbation method, and

(f) error minimization approach.

All six approaches will be reviewed in the sequel in separate sections. To give a very brief introduction here, we mention that the theory of aggregation [7-11] aims in deriving a simplified model with a coarser state-space description. The dominant-pole approach [12-21] yields a reduced-order model having as its poles the dominant poles of the original system. The Padé-type approximant [22,23] is based on the idea of deriving a simplified model whose first power series coefficients are exactly the same as those of the original system. The partial realization technique [24,25] is based on the idea of deriving a model by prematurely terminating the realization procedure. Related to the Padé approximant are the techniques of continued fraction expansion [26-29] and time moments [30]. The Routh approximation [31-33] yields a simplified model by truncating a particular form of an expansion of the original transfer function matrix, called the alpha-beta expansion. The perturbation method [34-38] derives a reduced-order model by neglecting the fast phenomena of the original system. Finally, the error minimization approach [39-54] yields a reduced-order model through minimizing the error difference between $\underline{y}$ and $\underline{y}_r$ of (1b) and (2b), respectively.

It is remarked that certain of the above techniques appear to be interrelated. This will be pointed out in appropriate places in the text.

It is also remarked that, besides the aformentioned six main approaches to model reduction, several other approaches have been reported such as the Chebyshev polynomial technique [55], the Walsh series approach [56], the l_1 and l_∞ norm minimization [57], the reduction over a frequency interval [58], the optimal Hankel-norm approximation [59], the model-following technique [60], and others [61,62]. Related to the model-reduction problem is also the problem of minimal-order observers [63,64].

It is finally pointed out that most of the reported results in the literature refer to linear time-invariant continuous systems. The present chapter refers to this type of system as well. There have been, however, certain results on model reduction for other types of systems such as time-varying [65-67]. discrete [68-70], two-dimensional [71-73], stochastic [74,75], and systems with time delays [76].

II. THE THEORY OF AGGREGATION

The theory of aggregation [7-11] is one of the most attractive techniques in model reduction. It originates from mathematical economics and it was introduced to the control of large-scale systems by Aoki [7].

The theory of aggregation is based on the intuitively appealing relationship between the state vector $\underline{x}$ of the original system (1) and $\underline{x}_r$ of the reduced-order model (2) having the form

$$\underline{x}_r = \underline{K}\underline{x} \tag{7}$$

where $\underline{K}$ is the $r \times n$ *aggregation* matrix. In order for system (2a) to be an aggregated model of system (1a) we require that (7) holds for all t. It is easily seen that aggregation is achieved if and only if the following matrix equations are satisfied:

$$\underline{F}\underline{K} = \underline{K}\underline{A}, \tag{8}$$

$$\underline{G} = \underline{K}\underline{B}. \tag{9}$$

Let rank $\underline{K} = r$. Then the Penrose solvability condition gives the unique $\underline{F}$ as

$$\underline{F} = \underline{KAK}^{+} \tag{10}$$

where

$$\underline{K}^{+} = \underline{K}^{T}(\underline{KK}^{T})^{-1} \tag{11}$$

is the Penrose pseudoinverse of $\underline{K}$.

Now, consider the error $\underline{e}(t) = \underline{x}_r(t) - \underline{Kx}(t)$. From (1a) and (2a) we have that the dynamics of the error $\underline{e}(t)$ are given by

$$\dot{\underline{e}}(t) = \underline{Fe}(t) + (\underline{FK} - \underline{KA})\underline{x}(t) + (\underline{G} - \underline{KB})\underline{u}(t). \tag{12}$$

Then, if (8) and (9) hold, relation (12) reduces to

$$\dot{\underline{e}}(t) = \underline{Fe}(t).$$

Therefore, if $\underline{e}(0) = \underline{0}$, i.e., if we impose the condition $\underline{x}_r(0) = \underline{Kx}(0)$, then $\underline{e}(t) = \underline{0}$ for all $t \geq 0$. This means that (7) holds for all t. This case is called *perfect aggregation*. In the case where $\underline{e}(0) \neq \underline{0}$ and $\underline{F}$ is an asymptotically stable matrix, then $\underline{e}(t) \to \underline{0}$ as $t \to \infty$. In this case relation (7) is asymptotically satisfied and the aggregation may be called *perfect asymptotic aggregation* [8].

With regard to the determination of the aggregation matrix $\underline{K}$, the following approach was first proposed by Aoki [7]. Let

$$\underline{Q}_1 = [\underline{B} \mid \underline{AB} \mid \cdots \mid \underline{A}^{n-1}\underline{B}],$$

$$\underline{Q}_2 = [\underline{G} \mid \underline{FG} \mid \cdots \mid \underline{F}^{n-1}\underline{G}].$$

On using (8) and (9) it can be readily shown that

$$\underline{KQ}_1 = \underline{Q}_2. \tag{13}$$

Under the assumption that rank $\underline{Q}_1 = n$, then (13) may be solved to yield the aggregation matrix

$$\underline{K} = \underline{Q}_2\underline{Q}_1^{+} = \underline{Q}_2\underline{Q}_1^{T}\left(\underline{Q}_1\underline{Q}_1^{T}\right)^{-1}. \tag{14}$$

Recently, more direct methods for determining the aggregation matrix $\underline{K}$ have been proposed [2,5,11]. We briefly present here the method given in [5]. Let

$$\underline{W} = [\underline{w}_1 \mid \underline{w}_2 \mid \cdots \mid \underline{w}_n],$$

$$\underline{V} = [\underline{v}_1 \mid \underline{v}_2 \mid \cdots \mid \underline{v}_n]$$

be the model matrices of $\underline{A}$ and $\underline{A}^T$, respectively. Here $\underline{w}_i$ and $\underline{v}_i$ are the eigenvectors of $\underline{A}$ and $\underline{A}^T$, respectively, corresponding to the eigenvalue λ_i. Furthermore, let $\underline{W}$ and $\underline{V}$ be scaled such that

$$\underline{V}^T = \underline{W}^{-1}. \tag{15}$$

Then, the aggregation matrix $\underline{K}$ is given by

$$\underline{K} = \underline{M}\hat{\underline{V}}^T, \quad \text{where} \quad \hat{\underline{V}} = [\underline{v}_1 \mid \underline{v}_2 \mid \cdots \mid \underline{v}_r] \tag{16}$$

where $\underline{M}$ is an arbitrary nonsingular $r \times r$ matrix. If, for simplicity, we let $\underline{M}$ be the unit matrix, then

$$\underline{K} = \hat{\underline{V}}^T = [\underline{v}_1 \mid \underline{v}_2 \mid \cdots \mid \underline{v}_r].$$

Using this particular $\underline{K}$, it can be shown that the reduced-order model matrix $\underline{F}$ reduces to

$$\underline{F} = \underline{KAK}^+ = \mathrm{diag}(\lambda_1, \lambda_2, \ldots, \lambda_r). \tag{17}$$

It is remarked that the notion of aggregation may be thought of as a form of generalization of the well-known approach of simplifying linear systems by retaining the dominant eigenvalues of the system (see next section). This becomes very clear from relation (17).

It is further remarked that the aggregation problem may also be thought of as a minimal realization problem [9]. Indeed, since (la) and (7) define a dynamic relationship between $\underline{u}(t)$

and $\underline{x}_r(t)$, their frequency domain relationship will be

$$\underline{X}_r(s) = \underline{T}_1(s)\underline{U}(s), \quad \text{where} \quad \underline{T}_1(s) = \underline{K}(s\underline{I} - \underline{A})^{-1}\underline{B}. \tag{18}$$

Similarly for the reduced-order model (2a), the frequency domain relationship between $\underline{u}(t)$ and $\underline{x}_r(t)$ will be

$$\underline{X}_r(s) = \underline{T}_2(s)\underline{U}(s), \quad \text{where} \quad \underline{T}_2(s) = (s\underline{I} - \underline{F})^{-1}\underline{G}. \tag{19}$$

Clearly, for perfect aggregation, there must be

$$\underline{T}_1(s) = \underline{T}_2(s). \tag{20}$$

Here, by assumption, $\underline{x}_r(t)$ is of lower dimension than $\underline{x}(t)$. This means that for (20) to hold, the system defined by (1a) and (7) is nonminimal, i.e., this system involves pole-zero cancellations. Consequently, the aggregation matrix $\underline{K}$ may be interpreted as that particular matrix (or class of matrices) which has the distinct characteristic in that it creates pole-zero cancellations in $\underline{T}_1(s)$ so that $\underline{T}_1(s)$ reduces to $\underline{T}_2(s)$. Note that the particular poles canceled are those not retained in $\underline{F}$.

Finally, consider the case where (1b) and (2b) are incorporated in the original system (1a) and the reduced-order model (2a), respectively. In this case, in addition to Eqs. (8) and (9), we have the relation

$$\underline{HK} \simeq \underline{C}. \tag{21}$$

As indicated, relation (21) may be satisfied, in general, only approximately. The model output matrix $\underline{H}$ is determined by the relationship

$$\underline{H} = \underline{CK}^+. \tag{22}$$

III. THE DOMINANT POLE APPROACH

The dominant-pole or eigenvalue approach consists of determining a lower-order model which retains the dominant (i.e., the slow) poles of the original system. This actually means that in the present approach the dynamic effects associated with the small time constants of the original system are neglected.

Consider the high-order system (1a) and assume that $\underline{A}$ has n distinct eigenvalues $\lambda_1, \lambda_2, \ldots, \lambda_n$. On using the transformation

$$\underline{x} = \underline{W}\underline{z} \quad \text{or} \quad \underline{z} = \underline{U}\underline{x} \tag{23}$$

where $\underline{W}$ is the model matrix of $\underline{A}$ and $\underline{U} = \underline{W}^{-1}$, system (1a) becomes

$$\dot{\underline{z}} = \underline{\Lambda}\underline{z} + \underline{B}^*\underline{u}, \quad \text{where} \quad \underline{\Lambda} = \underline{W}^{-1}\underline{A}\underline{W} \quad \text{and} \quad \underline{B}^* = \underline{W}^{-1}\underline{B}. \tag{24}$$

Suppose that the eigenvalues in $\underline{\Lambda}$ are in order of increasing moduli. Furthermore, assume that the first r of these eigenvalues are to be retained in the reduced-order model while the rest n - r are to be neglected. Also let (1), (23), and (24) be partitioned as

$$\begin{bmatrix} \dot{\underline{x}}_1 \\ \dot{\underline{x}}_2 \end{bmatrix} = \begin{bmatrix} \underline{A}_{11} & \underline{A}_{12} \\ \underline{A}_{21} & \underline{A}_{22} \end{bmatrix} \begin{bmatrix} \underline{x}_1 \\ \underline{x}_2 \end{bmatrix} + \begin{bmatrix} \underline{B}_1 \\ \underline{B}_2 \end{bmatrix} \underline{u}, \tag{25}$$

$$\begin{bmatrix} \underline{x}_1 \\ \underline{x}_2 \end{bmatrix} = \begin{bmatrix} \underline{W}_{11} & \underline{W}_{12} \\ \underline{W}_{21} & \underline{W}_{22} \end{bmatrix} \begin{bmatrix} \underline{z}_1 \\ \underline{z}_2 \end{bmatrix} \quad \text{or} \quad \begin{bmatrix} \underline{z}_1 \\ \underline{z}_2 \end{bmatrix} = \begin{bmatrix} \underline{U}_{11} & \underline{U}_{12} \\ \underline{U}_{21} & \underline{U}_{22} \end{bmatrix} \begin{bmatrix} \underline{x}_1 \\ \underline{x}_2 \end{bmatrix}, \tag{26}$$

$$\begin{bmatrix} \dot{\underline{z}}_1 \\ \dot{\underline{z}}_2 \end{bmatrix} = \begin{bmatrix} \underline{\Lambda}_1 & \underline{0} \\ \underline{0} & \underline{\Lambda}_2 \end{bmatrix} \begin{bmatrix} \underline{z}_1 \\ \underline{z}_2 \end{bmatrix} + \begin{bmatrix} \underline{B}_1^* \\ \underline{B}_2^* \end{bmatrix} \underline{u} \tag{27}$$

where subscript 1 refers to the dominant modes and subscript 2 refers to the negligible modes. Furthermore, (27) may be decoupled into the two sets of equations

$$\dot{\underline{z}}_1 = \underline{\Lambda}_1\underline{z}_1 + \underline{B}_1^*\underline{u}, \tag{28}$$

$$\dot{\underline{z}}_2 = \underline{\Lambda}_2 z_2 + \underline{B}_2^*\underline{u}. \tag{29}$$

To derive the reduced-order model (2a) it was first proposed by Davison [13] that the contribution of the fast modes be entirely neglected, i.e., assume that $\underline{z}_2 = \underline{0}$. Following this approach, from (26) we have that

$$\underline{x}_1 = \underline{W}_{11}\underline{z}_1 \quad \text{and} \quad \underline{x}_2 = \underline{W}_{21}\underline{z}_1. \tag{30}$$

Thus, making use of (30) we have

$$\underline{x}_2 = \underline{W}_{21}\underline{z}_1 = \underline{W}_{21}W_{11}^{-1}\underline{x}_1. \tag{31}$$

Application of (30) in (28) yields

$$\dot{\underline{x}}_1 = \underline{W}_{11}\underline{\Lambda}_1 W_{11}^{-1}\underline{x}_1 + \underline{W}_{11}\underline{B}_1^*\underline{u}. \tag{32}$$

Comparing (2a) with (32), it follows that the reduced-order model matrices $\underline{F}$ and $\underline{G}$ in (2a) will then be

$$\underline{F} = \underline{W}_{11}\underline{\Lambda}_1\underline{W}_{11}^{-1} \quad \text{and} \quad \underline{G} = \underline{W}_{11}B_1^*. \tag{33}$$

These results suffer from the disadvantage in that the reduced-order model steady-state response differs from that of the original system. To alleviate this discrepancy, Davison [14] further proposed a modified model which, in addition to (32), involves the relationship

$$\overline{\underline{x}}_1 = \underline{x}_1 + [\underline{F}^{-1}\underline{G} - \underline{A}^{-1}\underline{B}]\underline{u} \tag{34}$$

where $\overline{\underline{x}}_1$ is a new state vector for the reduced-order model. Then the model composed of (32) and (34) not only retains the first r dominant eigenvalues of the original system, but has the same steady-state response with the original system.

A similar approach to the problem was independently proposed by Marshall [16] where it was assumed that $\dot{\underline{z}}_2 = \underline{0}$ (rather than $\underline{z}_2 = \underline{0}$). In this case Eq. (29) becomes the algebraic equation

$$\underline{0} = \underline{\Lambda}_2 \underline{z}_2 + \underline{B}_2^* \underline{u}. \tag{35}$$

Upon manipulation of (28) and (35), together with (23)-(27), the reduced-order model matrices $\underline{F}$ and $\underline{G}$ are given by

$$\underline{F} = \underline{W}_{11} \underline{\Lambda}_1 \underline{W}_{11}^{-1} \quad \text{and} \quad \underline{G} = \underline{B}_1 - \underline{A}_{12} \underline{U}_{22}^{-1} \underline{\Lambda}_2^{-1} \underline{B}_2^*. \tag{36}$$

It is remarked that Marshall's model also exhibits the same steady-state response as that of the original system.

The results of Davison were further elaborated in [15] and [17]. An interesting unified derivation, together with a critical review, of the dominant-pole approaches have been reported in [12]. Finally, the problem of selecting the model order using the dominant-pole concept has also been considered (see, e.g., [18-21]).

IV. PADÉ-TYPE APPROXIMANT AND PARTIAL REALIZATION

The p × m transfer function matrices $\underline{T}(s)$ and $\underline{T}_r(s)$ of the original system (1) and of the reduced-order model (2), respectively, are given by

$$\underline{T}(s) = \underline{C}(s\underline{I} - \underline{A})^{-1}\underline{B}, \tag{37a}$$

$$\underline{T}_r(s) = \underline{H}(s\underline{I} - \underline{F})^{-1}\underline{G}. \tag{37b}$$

Assume that both $\underline{A}$ and $\underline{F}$ are nonsingular matrices. Then $\underline{T}(s)$ and $\underline{T}_r(s)$ may be expanded in Taylor series as

$$\underline{T}(s) = \underline{L}_0 + \underline{L}_1 s + \underline{L}_2 s^2 + \cdots, \tag{38a}$$

$$\underline{T}_r(s) = (\underline{L}_r)_0 + (\underline{L}_r)_1 s + (\underline{L}_r)_2 s^2 + \cdots \tag{38b}$$

where

$$\underline{L}_i = \underline{C}\underline{A}^{-(i+1)}\underline{B} \quad \text{and} \quad (\underline{L}_r)_i = \underline{H}\underline{F}^{-(i+1)}\underline{G}, \quad i = 0, 1, 2, \ldots . \tag{38c}$$

Similarly, $\underline{T}(s)$ and $\underline{T}_r(s)$ may be expanded in a Laurent series as

$$\underline{T}(s) = \underline{J}_0 s^{-1} + \underline{J}_1 s^{-2} + \underline{J}_2 s^{-3} + \cdots, \tag{39a}$$

$$\underline{T}_r(s) = (\underline{J}_r)_0 s^{-1} + (\underline{J}_r)_1 s^{-2} + (\underline{J}_r)_2 s^{-3} + \cdots \tag{39b}$$

where

$$\underline{J}_i = \underline{C}\underline{A}^i\underline{B} \quad \text{and} \quad (\underline{J}_r)_i = \underline{H}\underline{F}^i\underline{G}, \quad i = 0, 1, 2, \ldots . \tag{39c}$$

If $\underline{T}(s)$ and $\underline{T}_r(s)$ are given according to (3) and (4), respectively, then the series (38) and (39) may also be derived. For example, the corresponding Taylor series coefficients $\underline{L}_i$ of $\underline{T}(s)$ are now given by

$$\underline{L}_0 = \underline{B}_0/a_0, \tag{40a}$$

$$\underline{L}_i = (1/a_0)\left[\underline{B}_i - \sum_{j=0}^{i-1} a_{i-j}\underline{L}_j\right], \quad i = 1, 2, 3, \ldots, \tag{40b}$$

and $\underline{B}_i = \underline{0}$ for $i > n - 1$.

The Taylor and the Laurent series expansions of $\underline{T}(s)$ and $\underline{T}_r(s)$ given above have been used in connection with the model-reduction problem in two main different approaches, namely, the Padé-type approximant approach [6,22,23] and the partial realization approach [2,24,25]. To present the basic philosophy behind the Padé approach briefly, consider the case of single-input single-output systems. The transfer function matrices given by (3) and (4) are now scalar, having the form

$$T(s) = \frac{b_0 + b_1 s + b_2 s^2 + \cdots + b_{n-1} s^{n-1}}{a_0 + a_1 s + a_2 s^2 + \cdots + a_{n-1} s^{n-1} + a_n s^n}, \tag{41}$$

$$T_r(s) = \frac{d_0 + d_1 s + d_2 s^2 + \cdots + d_{r-1} s^{r-1}}{c_0 + c_1 s + c_2 s^2 + \cdots + c_{r-1} s^{r-1} + c_r s^r}, \tag{42}$$

and their corresponding Taylor series expansions will be

$$T(s) = L_0 + L_1 s + L_2 s^2 + \cdots, \tag{43}$$

$$T_r(s) = (L_r)_0 + (L_r)_1 s + (L_r)_2 s^2 + \cdots. \tag{44}$$

The Pade-type approximant $T_r(s)$ of $T(s)$ is obtained by equating the first 2r coefficients of the Taylor series of $T(s)$ and $T_r(s)$, i.e., by setting

$$L_i = (L_r)_i, \quad i = 0, 1, 2, \ldots, 2r - 1. \tag{45}$$

Relation (45) may be written more explicitly in terms of the known Taylor series coefficients $L_0, L_1, L_2, \ldots$ and the unknown reduced-order model parameters $d_0, d_1, \ldots, d_{r-1}$ and $c_0, c_1, \ldots, c_{r-1}$ as

$$\begin{aligned}
d_0 &= c_0 L_0, \\
d_1 &= c_0 L_1 + c_1 L_0, \\
d_2 &= c_0 L_2 + c_1 L_1 + c_2 L_0, \\
&\vdots \\
d_{r-1} &= c_0 L_{r-1} + c_1 L_{r-2} + \cdots + c_{r-1} L_0, \\
0 &= c_0 L_r + c_1 L_{r-1} + \cdots + c_r L_0, \\
&\vdots \\
0 &= c_0 L_{2r-1} + c_1 L_{2r-2} + \cdots + c_r L_r.
\end{aligned} \tag{46}$$

This set of equations is a linear system of 2r equations with 2r unknowns and can be readily solved to yield the unknown coefficients $d_0, d_1, \ldots, d_{r-1}$ and $c_0, c_1, \ldots, c_{r-1}$ of $T_r(s)$. Note that, without loss of generality, c_r can be chosen as $c_r = 1$.

With regard to the partial realization approach, it starts with the idea of using the Laurent series coefficient matrices $\underline{J}_i$ given in (39a) of the original system transfer function matrix (37a) to construct the Hankel matrix $\underline{H}_{ij}$, where

$$\underline{H}_{ij} = \begin{bmatrix} \underline{J}_0 & \underline{J}_1 & \underline{J}_2 & \cdots & \underline{J}_{i-1} \\ \underline{J}_1 & \underline{J}_2 & \underline{J}_3 & \cdots & \underline{J}_i \\ \vdots & \vdots & \vdots & & \vdots \\ \underline{J}_{j-1} & \underline{J}_j & \underline{J}_{j+1} & \cdots & \underline{J}_{i+j-2} \end{bmatrix}. \tag{47}$$

Let α and β be the controllability and the observability indices of the original system, respectively. Then the order n of the minimal realization is given by

$$n = \text{rank } \underline{H}_{ij}, \quad i \geq \alpha \quad \text{and} \quad j \geq \beta. \tag{48}$$

To go from the Hankel matrix to a state-space realization, several algorithms have been developed. If these algorithms are prematurely terminated, i.e., before they reach the integers α and β, then the state-space model so obtained is called a partial realization model [2,24,25].

Related to Padé-type approximation are the continued-fraction expansion and the time-moments approaches. In the continued-fraction approach [26-29] the transfer function matrix $\underline{T}(s)$ given in (3) is expanded into a continued fraction as [assume, for the moment, that $\underline{T}(s)$ is square]

$$\underline{T}(s) = [\underline{R}_1 + s[\underline{R}_2 + s[\underline{R}_3 + \cdots]^{-1}]^{-1}]^{-1}. \tag{49}$$

Note that this is the matrix continued-fraction form of the familiar scalar case

$$T(s) = \cfrac{1}{h_1 + \cfrac{s}{h_2 + \cfrac{s}{h_3 + \cfrac{s}{\vdots}}}} \tag{50}$$

The idea behind the continued-fraction approach is to truncate (49) retaining, say, the first r matrix coefficients $\underline{R}_i$. The resulting transfer function matrix is the reduced-order model matrix $\underline{T}_r(s)$ derived by this method. In particular, for i = 0, we get the crudest or zero-order model having the form

$$\underline{T}_r(s) = \underline{R}_1^{-1}.$$

From (3) we immediately have

$$\underline{T}_r(s) = \underline{R}_1^{-1} = \underline{B}_0/a_0.$$

For i = 1, we get the second simplest model having the form

$$\underline{T}_r(s) = \left[\underline{R}_1 + s\underline{R}_2^{-1}\right]^{-1}.$$

Similarly, we can determine higher-order models [27].

The time-moments approach [30] is based on the idea of matching the first moments of $\underline{T}(t)$ and $\underline{T}_r(t)$, where $\underline{T}(t)$ and $\underline{T}_r(t)$ are the impulse response matrices corresponding to $\underline{T}(s)$ and $\underline{T}_r(s)$. The moment $\underline{Q}_i$ of $\underline{T}(t)$ is defined by

$$\underline{Q}_i = \int_0^\infty t^i \underline{T}(t)\, dt, \quad i = 0, 1, 2, \ldots . \tag{51}$$

There are strong similarities among the various methods presented in this section. In particular, the continued-fraction-expansion approach and the time-moments approach are actually the same [77,78]. Furthermore, these two methods are essentially

Padé-type methods of the (38a) type [22]. Finally, the methods proposed in [26-28] and [24] are special cases of the minimal realization approach [2].

"Mixed-type" methods have also been proposed combining two or more different methods to achieve a better model. For example, in [79] the Padé approach is combined with the dominant-pole approach, in [80] the Padé approach with the Routh approach presented in the next section, and others [81-83].

The Padé-type approach, even though it is very simple to apply, suffers from a very serious disadvantage in that it does not guarantee stability even in cases where the original system is stable. This holds true for the continued-fraction-expansion and the time-moments approaches, as well. In [22], however, an algorithm is introduced which ensures that the reduced-order model is stable, if the original system is stable.

V. ROUTH APPROXIMATION

The Routh approximation approach has been proposed by Hutton and Friendland [31]. Due to its interesting properties (see end of this section) we feel that the Routh approximation technique deserves special attention. To simplify the presentation, we will treat only the scalar case where the transfer function of the original system is given by (41). Let (41) be asymptotically stable. Then it can always be expanded in a canonical form, called the *alpha-beta expansion* of T(s), as

$$T(s) = \beta_1 f_1(s) + \beta_2 f_1(s) f_2(s) + \cdots + \beta_n f_1(s) f_2(s) \cdots f_n(s) \tag{52}$$

where β_i, $i = 1, 2, \ldots, n$, are constants and the functions

$f_i(s)$, $i = 2, 3, \ldots, n$, are given by

$$f_i(s) = \cfrac{1}{\alpha_i s + \cfrac{1}{\alpha_{i+1} s + \cfrac{1}{\ddots \; \alpha_{n-1} s + (1/\alpha_n s)}}}.$$

The expression for $f_1(s)$ is modified slightly, as follows. In the above expression, the first term in the continued-fraction expansion is $1 + \alpha_1 s$ rather than $\alpha_1 s$. The coefficients α_i and β_i are computed using certain algorithms.

The basic idea behind the Routh approximation is to truncate the alpha-beta expansion (52) keeping only the first r terms. To this end, define the functions $p_i(s)$ as

$$p_i(s) = \cfrac{1}{\alpha_i s + \cfrac{1}{\alpha_{i+1} s + \cfrac{1}{\ddots \; \alpha_{r-1} s + (1/\alpha_r s)}}}$$

for $i = 2, 3, \ldots, r$. For $i = 1$, this definition is modified as in the case of $f_1(s)$, i.e., the first term in the continued-fraction expansion is $1 + \alpha_1 s$ rather than $\alpha_1 s$. Then, the Routh approximant $T_r(s)$ of $T(s)$ will be

$$\begin{aligned} T_r(s) &= \beta_1 p_1(s) + \beta_2 p_1(s) p_2(s) \\ &\quad + \cdots + \beta_r p_1(s) p_2(s) \cdots p_r(s). \end{aligned} \tag{53}$$

The Routh approximation technique has several interesting properties:

(a) It preserves stability.

(b) If $h_r(t)$ and $h_{r+1}(t)$ are the impulse responses which correspond to preserving the first r and r + 1 terms in the alpha-beta expansion, then their corresponding impulse response energies J_r and J_{r+1} defined by

$$J_i = \int_0^\infty h_i^2(t)\, dt, \quad i = r,\ r+1,$$

are related by $J_r \leq J_{r+1}$, for all $r = 1, 2, \ldots, n - 1$.

(c) It is a partial Padé approximation, namely, the first r coefficients of the Taylor series of T(s) and $T_r(s)$, about s = 0, are equal.

(d) The poles and the zeros of $T_r(s)$ approach those of T(s) as r approaches n.

(e) Finally, $T_r(s)$, as given in (53), preserves high-frequency behavior. If low-frequency preservation is preferable, then a suitable transformation is required.

For related references to the Routh approximation approach see [32,33,80].

VI. PERTURBATION METHOD

Consider system (1a) and let $\underline{\bar{x}} = \underline{M}\underline{x}$, $|\underline{M}| \neq 0$. Then, system (1a) becomes

$$\begin{bmatrix} \dot{\underline{\bar{x}}}_1 \\ \dot{\underline{\bar{x}}}_2 \end{bmatrix} = \begin{bmatrix} \underline{\bar{A}}_{11} & \underline{\bar{A}}_{12} \\ \underline{\bar{A}}_{21} & \underline{\bar{A}}_{22} \end{bmatrix} \begin{bmatrix} \underline{\bar{x}}_1 \\ \underline{\bar{x}}_2 \end{bmatrix} + \begin{bmatrix} \underline{\bar{B}}_1 \\ \underline{\bar{B}}_2 \end{bmatrix} \underline{u} \tag{54}$$

where

$$\underline{\bar{x}} = \begin{bmatrix} \underline{\bar{x}}_1 \\ \underline{\bar{x}}_2 \end{bmatrix}, \quad \underline{\bar{A}} = \underline{M}\underline{A}\underline{M}^{-1} = \begin{bmatrix} \underline{\bar{A}}_{11} & \underline{\bar{A}}_{12} \\ \underline{\bar{A}}_{21} & \underline{\bar{A}}_{22} \end{bmatrix}$$

and

$$\underline{\bar{B}} = \underline{M}\underline{B} = \begin{bmatrix} \underline{\bar{B}}_1 \\ \underline{\bar{B}}_2 \end{bmatrix}.$$

Assume that $\underline{M}$ is a permutation transformation matrix such that $\underline{\bar{x}}_2$ has the property that $\dot{\underline{\bar{x}}}_2 \simeq \underline{0}$, $\forall t > 0$, i.e., the dynamic behavior of the state vector portion $\underline{\bar{x}}_2$ is much faster than that of $\underline{\bar{x}}_1$. In this case, system (54) is usually designated as (for a rigorous justification see [34])

$$\dot{\underline{\bar{x}}}_1 = \underline{\bar{A}}_{11}\underline{\bar{x}}_1 + \underline{\bar{A}}_{12}\underline{\bar{x}}_2 + \underline{\bar{B}}_1\underline{u}, \tag{55a}$$

$$\epsilon\dot{\underline{\bar{x}}}_2 = \underline{\bar{A}}_{21}\underline{\bar{x}}_1 + \underline{\bar{A}}_{22}\underline{\bar{x}}_2 + \underline{\bar{B}}_2\underline{u} \tag{55b}$$

where (55a) is the slow system, (55b) is the fast system, ϵ is a small positive parameter, and $\underline{\bar{A}}_{22}$ is stable and invertible. If we set $\epsilon = 0$, i.e., if we assume $\dot{\underline{\bar{x}}}_2 = \underline{0}$, $\forall t > 0$, then (55b) becomes the algebraic equation

$$\underline{0} = \underline{\bar{A}}_{21}\underline{\bar{x}}_1 + \underline{\bar{A}}_{22}\underline{\bar{x}}_2 + \underline{\bar{B}}_2\underline{u}. \tag{56}$$

From (56) we have

$$\underline{\bar{x}}_2 = -\underline{\bar{A}}_{22}^{-1}\underline{\bar{A}}_{21}\underline{\bar{x}}_1 - \underline{\bar{A}}_{22}^{-1}\underline{\bar{B}}_2\underline{u}. \tag{57}$$

Substitution of (57) in (55a) yields

$$\dot{\underline{\bar{x}}}_1 = \left(\underline{\bar{A}}_{11} - \underline{\bar{A}}_{12}\underline{\bar{A}}_{22}^{-1}\underline{\bar{A}}_{21}\right)\underline{\bar{x}}_1 + \left(\underline{\bar{B}}_1 - \underline{\bar{A}}_{12}\underline{\bar{A}}_{22}^{-1}\underline{\bar{B}}_2\right)\underline{u}. \tag{58}$$

Clearly, (58) is a reduced-order model of the form (2a), where $\underline{x}_r = \underline{\bar{x}}_1$ and

$$\underline{F} = \underline{\bar{A}}_{11} - \underline{\bar{A}}_{12}\underline{\bar{A}}_{22}^{-1}\underline{\bar{A}}_{21}, \tag{59a}$$

$$\underline{G} = \underline{\bar{B}}_1 - \underline{\bar{A}}_{12}\underline{\bar{A}}_{22}^{-1}\bar{B}_2. \tag{59b}$$

It is remarked that if $\underline{M}$ were chosen to be the inverse of the model matrix $\underline{W}$, as in (23), then (54) takes on the form of (24). If, subsequently, the approach of Marshall [16] were applied, one should reach the same results as in (36).

The basic idea presented above is called the singular perturbation approach having as its main characteristic the fact that it simplifies the original system by neglecting its fast phenomena. It is thus essentially an approach similar to the dominant-pole approach reported in Section III. Furthermore, the perturbation approach is also related to the aggregation method as shown in [3]. Finally it is mentioned that the singular perturbation approach has been extensively applied to model reduction and control theory [3, 34-38].

VII. ERROR MINIMIZATION APPROACH

The present approach consists in minimizing certain error between the original system and the reduced-order model, thus leading to an optimal solution of the model-reduction problem. To this end, several techniques have been reported [39-52].

To give some idea of the error minimization approach, we will very briefly present the results reported by Wilson [39] wherein the cost function to be minimized is defined by

$$J = \int_0^\infty \underline{e}^T(t)\underline{Q}\underline{e}(t)\ dt \tag{60}$$

where $\underline{Q}$ is a positive-definite symmetric matrix and $\underline{e}(t)$ is the vector difference given by

$$\underline{e}(t) = \underline{y}(t) - \underline{y}_r(t). \tag{61}$$

On using (1b) and (2b), $\underline{e}(t)$ may be written as

$$\underline{e}(t) = \underline{C}\underline{x} - \underline{H}\underline{x}_r. \tag{62}$$

Substitution of (62) in (60) gives

$$J = \int_0^\infty \left(\underline{x}^T\underline{C}^T - \underline{x}_r^T\underline{H}^T\right)\underline{Q}(\underline{C}\underline{x} - \underline{H}\underline{x}_r)\ dt$$

$$= \int_0^\infty \left[\underline{x}^T\underline{C}^T QCx - \underline{x}^T\underline{C}^T QHx_r - \underline{x}_r^T\underline{H}^T QCx + \underline{x}_r^T\underline{H}^T QHx_r\right] dt$$

$$= \int_0^\infty \begin{bmatrix} \underline{x}^T & \underline{x}_r^T \end{bmatrix} \begin{bmatrix} \underline{C}^T\underline{Q}\underline{C} & -\underline{C}^T\underline{Q}\underline{H} \\ -\underline{H}^T\underline{Q}\underline{C} & \underline{H}^T\underline{Q}\underline{H} \end{bmatrix} \begin{bmatrix} \underline{x} \\ \underline{x}_r \end{bmatrix} dt$$

$$= \int_0^\infty \underline{z}^T\underline{N}\underline{z}\ dt \tag{63}$$

where

$$\underline{z} = \begin{bmatrix} \underline{x} \\ \underline{x}_r \end{bmatrix} \quad \text{and} \quad \underline{N} = \begin{bmatrix} \underline{C}^T\underline{Q}\underline{C} & -\underline{C}^T\underline{Q}\underline{H} \\ -\underline{H}^T\underline{Q}\underline{C} & \underline{H}^T\underline{Q}\underline{H} \end{bmatrix}.$$

Now, minimization of (63) leads to the two Lyapunov equations

$$\underline{\hat{A}}\underline{D} + \underline{D}\underline{\hat{A}}^T + \underline{R} = \underline{0}, \tag{64a}$$

$$\underline{\hat{A}}^T\underline{K} + \underline{K}\underline{\hat{A}} + \underline{N} = \underline{0} \tag{64b}$$

where

$$\underline{\hat{A}} = \begin{bmatrix} \underline{A} & \underline{0} \\ \underline{0} & \underline{F} \end{bmatrix} \quad \text{and} \quad \underline{R} = \begin{bmatrix} \underline{B}\underline{B}^T & \underline{B}\underline{G}^T \\ \underline{G}\underline{B}^T & \underline{G}\underline{G}^T \end{bmatrix}.$$

Clearly, (64) is nonlinear in the unknown model matrices $\underline{F}$, $\underline{G}$, and $\underline{H}$ as well as in the matrices $\underline{D}$ and $\underline{K}$. This nonlinearity is a severe drawback of the method. It has been shown, however, that in the particular case where the eigenvalues of $\underline{F}$ are prespecified, then the solution of (64) reduces to that of solving a linear system of equations [39]. Note that in (60)-(64) we have assumed that all the elements of the input vector $\underline{u}(t)$ are unit Dirac functions.

The preceding approach has further been investigated in [40] and [41]. Other related results involve the descrete-time systems [42], the geometrical approach [43], the W-matrix approach [44, 45], and others [46-52].

Recently, a new "error minimization" approach to the model-reduction problem has been proposed by Moore [53] based on principal component analysis. The error to be minimized here is of the form

$$J = \left\| \int_0^\infty \underline{E}(t)\underline{E}^T(t)\ dt \right\|_2^{1/2} \tag{65}$$

where $\underline{E}(t)$ is the error impulse response matrix defined by

$$\underline{E}(t) = \underline{T}(t) - \underline{T}_r(t) = \underline{C}e^{\underline{A}t}\underline{B} - \underline{H}e^{\underline{F}t}\underline{G} \tag{66}$$

where $\underline{T}(t)$ and $\underline{T}_r(t)$ are the impulse response matrices of the original system (1) and of the reduced-order model (2), respectively. Simply speaking, the objective here is to find $\underline{H}$, $\underline{F}$, and $\underline{G}$ such that $J \ll 1$. This means that the main idea in minimizing J is to eliminate any subsystems in (1) which contribute little to the impulse response matrix $\underline{T}(t)$. Even though the results in [53] are incomplete, they appear to be very promising. Some related results to those given in [53] have been subsequently reported in [54].

VIII. APPLICATIONS

As mentioned in the Introduction, reduced-order models may be used in several ways. From the literature, it appears that some very popular applications are those in optimal control and in eigenvalue assignment of large-scale systems. To give just a taste of the model simplification problem from the applications point of view, these two types of applications will be very briefly presented here.

With regard to the optimal control, we consider the linear regulator problem using the reduced-order model derived by the aggregation technique given in Section II. The optimal linear regulator problem for the original system (1a) is to find a control vector $\underline{u}(t)$ such that the criterion function

$$J = \int_0^\infty (\underline{x}^T\underline{Q}\underline{x} + \underline{u}^T\underline{R}\underline{u})\ dt \tag{67}$$

is minimized, where $\underline{Q} \geq \underline{0}$, $\underline{R} \geq \underline{0}$, and $\underline{R}^{-1}$ exists. For the reduced-order model (2a) the corresponding criterion function is

$$J_r = \int_0^\infty \left(\underline{x}_r^T \underline{Q}_r \underline{x}_r + \underline{u}^T \underline{R} \underline{u}\right) dt. \tag{68}$$

It is well known that the optimal control vector which minimizes J_r is given by

$$\underline{u}(t) = -\underline{L}\underline{x}_r \tag{69}$$

where $\underline{L}$ is an $n \times r$ matrix given by

$$\underline{L} = \underline{R}^{-1}\underline{G}^T\underline{P}$$

where $\underline{P}$ is the solution of the algebraic Riccati equation

$$\underline{F}^T\underline{P} + \underline{P}\underline{F} - \underline{P}\underline{G}\underline{R}^{-1}\underline{G}^T\underline{P} = -\underline{Q}_r. \tag{70}$$

Now, consider controlling the original system (1a) by the state feedback law applied above to control the reduced-order model (2a), i.e., consider controlling system (1a) by the state feedback law

$$\underline{u} = -\underline{L}\underline{x}_r = -\underline{L}\underline{K}\underline{x}. \tag{71}$$

It has been shown by Aoki [7] that if $\underline{Q}_r$ is chosen as

$$\underline{Q}_r = (\underline{K}\underline{K}^T)^{-1}\underline{K}\underline{Q}\underline{K}^T(\underline{K}\underline{K}^T)^{-1}, \tag{72}$$

then the feedback law (71) is a suboptimal control for the original system (1a). This is a very interesting result having the distinct advantage in that it greatly simplifies the computational effort in determining the suboptimal control. For a more complete treatment of the problem of suboptimal control, as well as for related bibliography, see [3,7,8].

With regard to the eigenvalue assignment problem we consider the case of state feedback controllers. In this case, the feedback law applied to the reduced-order model (2a) is of the form (69) in which case the closed-loop system will be

$$\dot{\underline{x}}_r = (\underline{F} - \underline{GL})\underline{x}_r. \tag{73}$$

For the original system (1a) the feedback law is of the form (71) and thus the closed-loop systems will be

$$\dot{\underline{x}} = (\underline{A} - \underline{BLK})x. \tag{74}$$

It can be shown [7,84,85] that the r eigenvalues of $\underline{F} - \underline{GL}$ are also eigenvalues of $\underline{A} - \underline{BLK}$. The remaining n - r eigenvalues of $\underline{A} - \underline{BLK}$ are unaffected by the feedback and thus remain unchanged. Therefore, using the known results on eigenvalue assignment by state feedback [86, 87] one may readily determine an appropriate controller matrix $\underline{L}$ such that the eigenvalues of $\underline{F} - \underline{GL}$, or equivalently, r eigenvalues of $\underline{A} - \underline{BLK}$, have new desirable positions in the s plane. For more on the subject of eigenvalue assignment, as well as on the subject of stability, see, for example, [3].

IX. CONCLUSIONS

The problem of model reduction has great practical importance since it makes it possible to simplify various engineering problems such as analysis, simulation, and control. This is why the model-reduction problem has received considerable attention, particularly in the last 20 years.

Generally speaking, the underlying philosophy of most of the model-reduction techniques presented in this chapter is based on the idea of neglecting the fast phenomena involved in the original mathematical model. This approach results in a reduced-order model involving the dominant (i.e., the slow) phenomena of the physical system. Model reduction, therefore, may be thought of as a trade-off between model order and the degree to which the various characteristics of the physical system are described by the model.

From the material presented in this chapter, it is evident that up to now there has not been developed a universal model-reduction approach. One main difficulty for this is that the relative importance of the various characteristics of the physical system depend very much upon the particular application. The need, however, for establishing a universal model-reduction technique is obvious, and any contribution toward this end will be of great theoretical as well as practical value.

REFERENCES

1. R. GENESIO and M. MILANESE, *IEEE Trans. Autom. Control 21*, 118 (1976).
2. J. HICKIN and N. K. SINHA, *IEEE Trans. Autom. Control 25*, 1121 (1980).
3. N. R. SANDELL, JR., P. VARAIYA, M. ATHANS, and M. G. SAFANOV, *IEEE Trans. Autom. Control 23*, 108 (1978).
4. M. J. BOSLEY and F. P. LEES, *Automatica 8*, 765 (1972).
5. Z. ELRAZAZ and N. K. SINHA, *Canadian Elec. Eng. J. 6*, 34 (1981).
6. S. J. VAROUFAKIS and P. N. PARASKEVOPOULOS, *Proceedings 1st International Conference on Applied Modeling and Simulation, Lyon, France 1*, 38 (1981).
7. M. AOKI, *IEEE Trans. Autom. Control 13*, 246 (1981).
8. M. AOKI, *IEEE Trans. Autom. Control 23*, 173 (1978).
9. J. HICKIN and N. K. SINHA, *Int. J. Control 27*, 473 (1978).
10. G. MICHAILESCO, J. M. SIRET, and P. BERTRAND, *Electronics Letters 11*, 398 (1975).
11. J. HICKIN and N. K. SINHA, *Electronics Letters 11*, 186 (1975).
12. D. BONVIN and D. A. MELLICHAMP, *Int. J. Control 35*, 829 (1982).

13. E. J. DAVISON, *IEEE Trans. Autom. Control 11*, 93 (1966).

14. E. J. DAVISON, *Control 12*, 418 (1968).

15. E. J. DAVISON, *IEEE Trans. Autom. Control 12*, 120, 214, 799, 800 (1967).

16. S. A. MARSHALL, *Control 10*, 642 (1966).

17. M. R. CHIDAMBARA, *IEEE Trans. Autom. Control 12*, 119 (1967); *ibid, 12*, 213 (1967); *ibid, 12*, 799 (1967).

18. G. B. MAHAPATRA, *IEEE Trans. Autom. Control 22*, 677 (1977); *ibid, 24*, 135 (1979).

19. Z. ELRAZAZ and N. K. SINHA, *IEEE Trans. Autom. Control 24*, 792 (1979).

20. W. H. ENRIGHT and M. S. KAMEL, *IEEE Trans. Autom. Control 25*, 976 (1980).

21. A. S. RAO, S. S. LAMBA, AND S. V. RAO, *IEEE Trans. Autom. Control 26*, 604 (1981).

22. Y. SHAMASH, *IEEE Trans. Autom. Control 19*, 615 (1974).

23. K. C. DALY and A. P. COLEBOURN, *Int. J. Control 30*, 37 (1979).

24. Y. SHAMASH, *Electronics Letters 11*, 385 (1975).

25. J. HICKIN and N. K. SINHA, *Electronics Letters 12*, 90 (1976).

26. C. F. CHEN and L. S. SHIEH, *Int. J. Control 8*, 561 (1968).

27. C. F. CHEN, *Int. J. Control 20*, 225 (1974).

28. S. C. CHUANG, *Electronics Letters 6*, 861 (1970).

29. M. R. CALFE and M. HEALEY, *Proc. IEE 121*, 393 (1974).

30. V. ZAKIAN, *Int. J. Control 18*, 455 (1973).

31. M. F. HUTTON and B. FRIEDLAND, *IEEE Trans. Autom. Control 20*, 329 (1975).

32. Y. SHAMASH, *IEEE Trans. Autom. Control 23*, 940 (1978).

33. M. HUTTON and M. J. RABINS, *J. of Dynamic Systems, Measurement, and Control 97*, 383 (1975).

34. P. V. KOKOTOVIC, R. E. O'MALLEY, JR., and P. SANNUTI, *Automatica 12*, 123 (1976).

35. P. V. KOKOTOVIC, W. R. PERKINS, and J. B. CRUZ, *Proc. IEE 116*, 889 (1969).

36. P. SANNUTI and P. V. KOKOTOVIC, *IEEE Trans. Autom. Control 14*, 15 (1969).

37. P. V. KOKOTOVIC and R. A. YACKEL, *IEEE Trans. Autom. Control 17*, 29 (1972).

38. P. V. KOKOTOVIC, J. J. ALEMONG, J. R. WINKELMAN, and J. H. CHOW, *Automatica 16*, 23 (1980).

39. D. A. WILSON, *Proc. IEE 117*, 1161 (1970).

40. D. A. WILSON, *Int. J. Control 20*, 57 (1974).

41. D. A. WILSON and R. N. MISHRA, *Int. J. Control 29*, 267 (1979).

42. J. D. APLEVICH, *Int. J. Control 17*, 565 (1973).

43. J. H. ANDERSON, *Proc. IEE 114*, 1014 (1967).

44. D. MITRA, *Proc. IEE 116*, 1101 (1969).

45. D. MITRA, *Proc. IEE 116*, 1439 (1969).

46. F. D. GALIANA, *Int. J. Control 17*, 1313 (1973).

47. J. M. SIRET, M. MICHAILESCO, and P. BERTRAND, *Int. J. Control 26*, 963 (1977).

48. J. B. RIGGS and T. F. EDGAR, *Int. J. Control 20*, 213 (1974).

49. G. HIRZINGER and K. KREISSELMEIER, *Int. J. Control 22*, 399 (1975).

50. N. K. SINHA and W. PILLE, *Int. J. Control 14*, 111 (1971).

51. L. MEIER and D. G. LUENBERGER, *IEEE Trans. Autom. Control 12*, 585 (1967).

52. N. K. SINHA and G. T. BEREZNAI, *Int. J. Control 14*, 951 (1971).

53. B. C. MOORE, *IEEE Trans. Autom. Control 26*, 17 (1981).

54. L. PERNEBO and L. M. SILVERMAN, *IEEE Trans. Autom. Control 27*, 382 (1982).

55. Y. BISTRITZ and G. LANGHOLZ, *IEEE Trans. Autom. Control 24*, 741 (1979).

56. R. SUBBAYYAN and M. C. VAITHILINGAM, *Proc. IEEE 67*, 1676 (1979).

57. R. A. EL-ATTAR and M. VIDYASAGAR, *IEEE Trans. Autom. Control 23*, 731 (1978).

58. G. LANGHOLZ and Y. BISTRITZ, *Int. J. Control 31*, 51 (1980).

59. S. Y. KUNG and D. W. Lin, *IEEE Trans. Autom. Control 26*, 832 (1981).

60. M. M. M. HASSAN and P. A. COOK, *Int. J. Control 34*, 465 (1981).

61. J. W. BANDLER and T. V. SRINIVASAN, *Int. J. Control 5*, 1097 (1974).

62. Y. BISTRITZ and G. LANGHOLZ, *Int. J. Control 30*, 277 (1979).

63. C. T. LEONDES and L. M. NOVAK, *Automatica 8*, 379 (1972).

64. A. ARBEL and E. TSE, *Int. J. Control 30*, 513 (1979).

65. A. S. RAO, S. S. LAMBA, and S. VITAL RAO, *IEEE Trans. Autom. Control 25*, 110 (1980).

66. N. NOSRATI and H. E. MEADOWS, *IEEE Trans. Autom. Control 18*, 50 (1973).

67. M. Y. WU, *IEEE Trans. Autom. Control 19*, 619 (1974); *ibid, 20*, 159 (1975).

68. Y. SHAMASH and D. FEINMESSER, *Int. J. Systems Science 9*, 53 (1978).

69. L. S. SHIEH, K. M. DADKHAH, and R. E. YATES, *IEEE Trans. Industrial Electronics and Control Instrumentation 23*, 371 (1976).

70. Y. P. SHIH and W. T. WU, *Int. J. Control 17*, 1089 (1973).

71. P. N. PARASKEVOPOULOS, *IEEE Trans. Circuits and Systems 27*, 413 (1980).

72. N. K. BOSE and S. BASU, *IEEE Trans. Autom. Control 25*, 509 (1980).

73. S. J. VAROUFAKIS and P. N. PARASKEVOPOULOS, *Proceedings Conference on Applied Modeling and Simulation, Paris, France* (1982).

74. Y. BARAM and Y. BE'ERI, *IEEE Trans. Autom. Control 26*, 379 (1981).

75. Y. BARAM, *IEEE Trans. Autom. Control 26*, 1225 (1981).

76. S. A. MARSHALL, *Int. J. Control 31*, 677 (1980).

77. M. J. BOSLEY, H. W. KROPHOLLER, AND F. P. LEES, *Int. J. Control 18*, 461 (1973).

78. M. LAL and R. MITRA, *IEEE Trans. Autom. Control 19*, 617 (1974).

79. Y. SHAMASH, *Int. J. Control 21*, 257 (1975).

80. Y. SHAMASH, *Int. J. Control 21*, 475 (1975).

81. S. J. VAROUFAKIS and P. N. PARASKEVOPOULOS, *Electronics Letters 15*, 789 (1979).

82. L. S. SHIEH and Y. G. WEI, *IEEE Trans. Autom. Control 20*, 429 (1975).

83. C. HWANG, Y. P. SHIH, and R. Y. HWANG, *J. Franklin Institute 311*, 391 (1981).

84. S. V. RAO and S. S. LAMBA, *Proc. IEE 122*, 197 (1975).

85. J. HICKIN and N. K. SINHA, *Electronics Letters 11*, 318 (1975); *J. Cybernetics 8*, 159 (1978).

86. W. M. WONHAN, *IEEE Trans. Autom. Control 6*, 660 (1967).

87. S. G. TZAFESTAS and P. N. PARASKEVOPOULOS, *Int. J. Control 21*, 911 (1975).

Optimal Estimation Theory for Distributed Parameter Systems

SHIGERU OMATU
Department of Information Science and Systems Engineering University of Tokushima Tokushima, Japan

I. INTRODUCTION

When considering system analysis or controller design, the engineer has at his disposal a wealth of knowledge derived from deterministic system and control theories. One would then naturally ask why we have to go beyond these results and propose stochastic system models, with the ensuing concepts of estimation and control based on these stochastic models. There are three basic reasons why deterministic and control theories do not provide a totally sufficient means of performing the physical system analysis and design. First, no mathematical system model is perfect. Any such model depicts only those characteristics of direct interest to the engineer's purpose. A second shortcoming of deterministic models is that dynamic systems are deriven not only by our own control inputs, but also by disturbances which we can neither control nor model deterministically. A final shortcoming is that sensors do not provide perfect and complete data about a system. As can be seen from the preceding discussion, to assume perfect control over the system is a naive and often inadequate approach and/or to assume perfect knowledge of all quantities necessary to describe a system completely is almost impossible in the real systems.

The practical application of feedback control to a given physical system requires knowledge of the state functions which must be fed back into the controller input. More often, only some of these state functions are accessible to direct measurement, and hence arises the problem of estimating and computing the nonmeasured states by using the measured outputs of the system at hand. Also, in almost all practical situations the measurements are influenced by errors, due to the measurement instruments and methods or other reasons, and the systems are affected by internal and external disturbances of a random nature. These facts have naturally led to the evolution of stochastic state estimation or state identification theory of dynamic and control systems. Of course, in many situations the mathematical model of the system under consideration contains unknown structural paramteters which must also be estimated by using the same measured quantities. This requirement has led to the parameter estimation problem which has been examined either on its own or as a subproblem of state estimation.

There are two major avenues which have been followed in control theory, depending on whether the system under study is assumed to be concentrated at a single spatial point (lumped parameter system, LPS) or is assumed to occupy a certain spatial domain (distributed parameter system, DPS). Actually, all real physical systems are DPS. LPS is modeled by an ordinary differential equation (ODE), whereas DPS is modeled by a partial differential equation (PDE).

Our purpose in this chapter is to give a unified derivation of the DP state estimation theory based on the Wiener-Hopf theory. The chapter will naturally include works dealing with an optimal sensor location.

II. SYSTEM MODELING

The mathematical model of linear DPS has the following form. The dynamic system is described by a stochastic PDE,

$$\partial u(t, x)/\partial t = A_x u(t, x) + B(t, x) w(t, x), \qquad x \in D, \tag{1}$$

$$\Gamma_\xi u(t, \xi) = 0, \qquad \xi \in \partial D, \tag{2}$$

$$u(t_0, x) = u_0(x), \qquad x \in D, \tag{3}$$

where D is an open spatial r-dimensional domain with smooth boundary ∂D, $u(t, x)$, $x \in D$, is the state function of the system, $u_0(x)$ is the initial state function, assumed to be a Gaussian random variable with mean $\hat{u}_0(x)$ and covariance function $p_0(x, y)$, $x, y \in D$. A_x is a well-posed linear spatial differential operator, and Γ_ξ is a boundary operator defined on ∂D. The noise $w(t, x)$ has been assumed to be a white Gaussian process in time and independent of the initial state $u_0(x)$.

The measurement system is described by a linear algebraic relation to the state. The m-dimensional measurement vector z(t) is given by

$$z(t) = H(t)u_m(t) + v(t), \tag{4}$$

$$u_m(t) = \mathrm{Col}[u(t, x^1), \ldots, u(t, x^m)] \tag{5}$$

where $x^i \in \overline{D} = D \cup \partial D$, $i = 1, 2, \ldots, m$, denote measurement points, H(t) is a $p \times m$ matrix, and v(t) is a white Gaussian measurement noise. It is assumed that w(t, x), v(t), and $u_0(x)$ are mutually independent and

$$E[w(t, x)] = 0, \quad E[v(t)] = 0, \tag{6}$$

$$E[w(t, x)w(s, y)] = \tilde{Q}(t, x, y)\,\delta(t - s),$$
$$E[v(t)v'(s)] = \tilde{R}(t)\,\delta(t - s) \tag{7}$$

where ' and E are transpose and mathematical expectation operators, respectively, and δ is the Dirac delta function. Let $\tilde{Q}(t)$ be an operator such that

$$\tilde{Q}(t)u(t) = \int_D \tilde{Q}(t, x, y)u(t, y)\,dy \tag{8}$$

and let us define an inner product by

$$\langle u(t), w(t) \rangle = \int_D u(t, x)w(t, x)\,dx. \tag{9}$$

$\tilde{Q}(t, x, y) = \tilde{Q}(t, y, x)$ and it is assumed to be semipositive definite in the sense that $\langle u(t), \tilde{Q}(t)u(t) \rangle \geqq 0$ for all u(t). Similarly, $\tilde{R}(t)$ is assumed to be positive definite. Since the Dirac delta function is not an ordinary function, we see that, although useful, the white Gaussian process is a mathematical fiction. In most references, all white Gaussian processes are assumed to be defined as formal derivatives of Wiener processes interpreted in the Ito sense [1,2]. Hence, we call these approaches in which the DP stochastic processes are defined in appropriate rigorous ways [2-4]. In order to avoid the use of high-level mathematical sophistications, we adopt the formal approach to derive the optimal estimation algorithms since both approaches result in the same algorithms.

In what follows, let us make two assumptions:

(i) The system of equations (1)-(3) is well posed in the sense of Hadamard; that is, the solution exists uniquely and depends continuously on the initial and boundary data.

(ii) There exists a fundamental solution $G(t, x, y)$ of Eqs. (1) and (2), defined for $t \geqq 0$ and $x, y \in \overline{D}$ such that

$$\partial G(t, x, y)/\partial t = A_x G(t, x, y), \tag{10}$$

$$\Gamma_\xi G(t, \xi, y) = 0, \qquad \xi \in \partial D, \quad y \in \overline{D}, \tag{11}$$

$$\lim_{t \to 0} G(t, x, y) = \delta(x - y), \tag{12}$$

and that the solution of Eqs. (1)-(3) is expressed as

$$u(t, x) = \int_D G(t - t_0, x, y) u_0(y)\, dy + \int_{t_0}^{t} \int_D G(t - s, x, y) B(s, y) w(s, y)\, dy\, ds. \tag{13}$$

If $w(t, x)$ is a smooth function and A_x is given by

$$A_x = \Delta - q(x) \tag{14}$$

where Δ is Laplacian and $q(x)$ is a Hölder continuous function, it is well known that the foregoing assumptions are satisfied [5].

III. DESCRIPTION OF THE ESTIMATION PROBLEMS

The general problem considered here is to find an estimate $\hat{u}(s, x/t)$ of the state $u(s, x)$ at time s based on the measurement data $Z_0^t = \{z(\sigma), t_0 \leq \sigma \leq t\}$. Specifically, for $s > t$ we have the prediction problem, for $s = t$ the filtering problem, and for $s < t$ the smoothing problem. As in the Kalman-Bucy approach, an estimate $\hat{u}(s, x/t)$ of $u(s, x)$ is sought through a linear operation on the past and present measurement data Z_0^t as

$$\hat{u}(s, x/t) = \int_{t_0}^{t} \tilde{F}(s, x, \sigma) z(\sigma)\, d\sigma \tag{15}$$

where $\tilde{F}(s, x, \sigma)$ is a p-dimensional kernel function.

To differentiate among the prediction, filtering, and smoothing problems, we replace Eq. (15) with different notation for each problem:

Prediction $(s > t)$

$$\hat{u}(s, x/t) = \int_{t_0}^{t} F_e(s, x, \sigma) z(\sigma)\, d\sigma. \tag{16}$$

Filtering $(s = t)$

$$\hat{u}(t, x/t) = \int_{t_0}^{t} F(t, x, \sigma) z(\sigma)\, d\sigma. \tag{17}$$

Smoothing $(s < t)$

$$\hat{u}(s, x/t) = \int_{t_0}^{t} F_i(s, t, x, \sigma) z(\sigma)\, d\sigma. \tag{18}$$

The estimation error is denoted by $\tilde{u}(s, x/t)$,

$$\tilde{u}(s, x/t) = u(s, x) - \hat{u}(s, x/t). \tag{19}$$

The estimate $u(s, x/t)$ that minimizes

$$J(\hat{u}) = E[|\tilde{u}(s, x/t)|^2] \tag{20}$$

is said to be optimal.

IV. WIENER-HOPF THEOREM

Let us derive the optimal estimators by a unified method based on the Wiener-Hopf theory.

Theorem 1 (Wiener-Hopf Theorem)

A necessary and sufficient condition for the estimate $\hat{u}(s, x/t)$ to be optimal is that the following Wiener-Hopf equation holds for $t_0 \leqq \alpha \leqq t$ and $x \in \bar{D}$:

$$\int_{t_0}^{t} \tilde{F}(s, x, \sigma) E[z(\sigma) z'(\alpha)] \, d\sigma = E[u(s, x) z'(\alpha)]. \tag{21}$$

Furthermore, Eq. (21) is equivalent to

$$E[\tilde{u}(s, x/t) z'(\alpha)] = 0 \tag{22}$$

for $t_0 \leqq \alpha \leqq t$ and $x \in \bar{D}$.

Proof. Let $F_\Delta(s, x, \alpha)$ be a p-dimensional vector function and let ϵ be a scalar-valued parameter. The trace of the covariance of the estimate

$$\hat{u}_\epsilon(s, x/t) = \int_{t_0}^{t} (\tilde{F}(s, x, \alpha) + \epsilon F_\Delta(s, x, \alpha)) z(\alpha) \, d\alpha$$

is given by

$$\begin{aligned} J(\hat{u}_\epsilon) &= E\left[|u(s, x) - \hat{u}_\epsilon(s, x/t)|^2\right] \\ &= E\left[\left|u(s, x) - \hat{u}(s, x/t) - \epsilon \int_{t_0}^{t} F_\Delta(s, x, \alpha) z(\alpha) \, d\alpha\right|^2\right] \\ &= J(\hat{u}) - 2\epsilon E\left[\tilde{u}(s, x/t) \int_{t_0}^{t} F_\Delta(s, x, \alpha) z(\alpha) \, d\alpha\right] \\ &\quad + \epsilon^2 E\left[\left|\int_{t_0}^{t} F_\Delta(s, x, \alpha) z(\alpha) \, d\alpha\right|^2\right]. \end{aligned}$$

A necessary and sufficient condition for $u(s, x/t)$ to be optimal is that

$$E\left[\tilde{u}(s, x/t) \int_{t_0}^{t} F_\Delta(s, x, \alpha) z(\alpha)\, d\alpha\right] = 0$$

for any p-dimensional vector function $F_\Delta(s, x, \alpha)$. Then we get

$$\int_{t_0}^{t} E[\tilde{u}(s, x/t) z'(\alpha)] F_\Delta'(s, x, \alpha)\, d\alpha = 0$$

and setting $F_\Delta(s, x, \alpha) = E[\tilde{u}(s, x/t) z'(\alpha)]$ in the preceding equation, it follows that Eq. (22) is a necessary condition for $\hat{u}(s, x/t)$ to be optimal. Sufficiency of Eq. (22) also follows from the above equation. Thus, the proof of the theorem is complete. QED

Corollary 1 (Orthogonal Projection Lemma)

The following orthogonality condition holds:

$$E[\tilde{u}(s, x/t) \hat{u}(\tau, y/t)] = 0, \quad x, y \in \overline{D}, \tag{23}$$

where τ is any time instant, for example, $\tau < t$, $\tau = t$, or $\tau > t$.

Proof. Multiplying each side of Eq. (22) by $\tilde{F}'(\tau, y, \alpha)$ and integrating from $\alpha = t_0$ to $\alpha = t$, we obtain

$$E\left[\tilde{u}(s, x/t) \int_{t_0}^{t} z'(\alpha) \tilde{F}'(\tau, y, \alpha)\, d\alpha\right] = 0.$$

Substituting Eq. (15) into the above equation yields Eq. (23). Thus, the proof of the corollary is complete. QED

Then the following lemma can be proved.

Lemma 1 (Uniqueness of the Optimal Kernel)

Let $\tilde{F}(s, x, \sigma)$ and $\tilde{F}(s, x, \sigma) + N(s, x, \sigma)$ be optimal kernel functions satisfying the Wiener-Hopf equation (21). Then it follows that

$$N(s, x, \sigma) = 0, \quad t_0 \leqq \sigma < t \quad \text{and} \quad x \in \bar{D}. \tag{24}$$

In other words, the optimal kernel function $\tilde{F}(s, x, \sigma)$ is unique.

Proof. From Eq. (21) we get

$$\int_{t_0}^{t} \tilde{F}(s, x, \sigma)E[z(\sigma)z'(\alpha)]\, d\sigma = E[u(s, x)z'(\alpha)]$$

$$= \int_{t_0}^{t} (\tilde{F}(s, x, \sigma) + N(s, x, \sigma))E[z(\sigma)z'(\alpha)]\, d\sigma.$$

Thus, we get

$$\int_{t_0}^{t} N(s, x, \sigma)E[z(\sigma)z'(\alpha)]\, d\sigma = 0. \tag{25}$$

Multiplying each side of this equation by $N'(s, x, \alpha)$ and integrating from $\alpha = t_0$ to $\alpha = t$ we have

$$\int_{t_0}^{t} \int_{t_0}^{t} N(s, x, \sigma)E[z(\sigma)z'(\alpha)]N'(s, x, \alpha)\, d\sigma\, d\alpha = 0.$$

On the other hand, from Eqs. (4) and (7) we get

$$E[z(\sigma)z'(\alpha)] = H(\sigma)E\left[u_m(\sigma)u_m'(\alpha)\right]H'(\alpha) + \tilde{R}(\sigma)\ \delta(\sigma - \alpha).$$

Then it follows that

$$\int_{t_0}^{t} \int_{t_0}^{t} N(s, x, \sigma)H(\sigma)E\left[u_m(\sigma)u_m'(\alpha)\right]H'(\alpha)N'(s, x, \alpha)\, d\sigma\, d\alpha$$

$$+ \int_{t_0}^{t} N(s, x, \sigma)H(\sigma)\tilde{R}(\sigma)H'(\sigma)N'(s, x, \sigma)\, d\sigma = 0.$$

Since the right-hand side of the preceding equation is positive semidefinite because of the positive-definiteness of $\tilde{R}(\sigma)$, a necessary and sufficient condition for the above equation to hold is $N(s, x, \sigma) = 0$ for $t_0 \leqq \sigma < t$ and $x \in \bar{D}$. Thus, the proof of the lemma is complete. QED

Note that the uniqueness of the kernel function means that Eq. (25) implies Eq. (24).

In order to facilitate the derivation of the optimal estimators, we rewrite Eq. (21) in terms of the following corollary.

Corollary 2

The Wiener-Hopf equation (21) is rewritten for the prediction, filtering, and smoothing problems as follows:

Prediction $(s > t)$

$$\int_{t_0}^{t} F_e(s, x, \sigma)E[z(\sigma)z'(\alpha)]\, d\sigma = E[u(s, x)z'(\alpha)] \tag{26}$$

for $t_0 \leqq \alpha < t$ and $x \in \bar{D}$.

Filtering $(s = t)$

$$\int_{t_0}^{t} F(t, x, \sigma)E[z(\sigma)z'(\alpha)]\, d\sigma = E[u(t, x)z'(\alpha)] \tag{27}$$

for $t_0 \leqq \alpha < t$ and $x \in \bar{D}$.

Smoothing $(s < t)$

$$\int_{t_0}^{t} F_i(s, t, x, \sigma)E[z(\sigma)z'(\alpha)]\, d\sigma = E[u(s, x)z'(\alpha)] \tag{28}$$

for $t_0 \leqq \alpha < t$ and $x \in \bar{D}$.

In what follows, let us denote the estimation error covariance function by

$$p(s, x, y/t) = E[\tilde{u}(s, x/t)\tilde{u}(s, y/t)]. \tag{29}$$

V. DERIVATION OF THE OPTIMAL PREDICTOR

In this section, we derive the optimal prediction estimator by using the Wiener-Hopf theory in the previous section.

Theorem 2

The optimal prediction estimator is given by

$$\partial\hat{u}(s, x/t)/\partial s = A_x\hat{u}(s, x/t), \tag{30}$$

$$\Gamma_\xi\hat{u}(s, \xi/t) = 0, \quad \xi \in \partial D, \quad s \geq t, \tag{31}$$

where the initial value of $\hat{u}(s, x/t)$ is $\hat{u}(t, x/t)$.

Proof. From Eqs. (1) and (26) we get

$$\int_{t_0}^{t} \frac{\partial F_e(s, x, \sigma)}{\partial s} E[z(\sigma)z'(\alpha)]\, d\sigma = E\left[\frac{\partial u(s, x)}{\partial s} z'(\alpha)\right]$$

$$= E\left[(A_x u(s, x) + B(s, x)w(s, x))z'(\alpha)\right]$$

$$= A_x E[u(s, x)z'(\alpha)]$$

since $w(s, x)$ is independent of $z(\alpha)$, $t_0 \leq \alpha < t$.

From the Wiener-Hopf equation (26) for the optimal prediction problem, we get

$$\int_{t_0}^{t}\left(\frac{\partial F_e(s, x, \sigma)}{\partial s} - A_x F_e(s, x, \sigma)\right)E[z(\sigma)z'(\alpha)]\, d\sigma = 0.$$

On defining $N(s, x, \sigma)$ by

$$N(s, x, \sigma) = \frac{\partial F_e(s, x, \sigma)}{\partial s} - A_x F_e(s, x, \sigma),$$

it is clear that $F_e(s, x, \sigma) + N(s, x, \sigma)$ also satisfies the Wiener-Hopf equation (26). From the uniqueness of $F_e(s, x, \sigma)$ by Lemma 1 it follows that $N(s, x, \sigma) = 0$; that is,

$$\partial F_e(s, x, \sigma)/\partial s = A_x F_e(s, x, \sigma). \tag{32}$$

Thus, from Eq. (16) we get

$$\partial\hat{u}(s, x/t)/\partial s = A_x\hat{u}(s, x/t).$$

Letting $x = \xi \in \partial D$ in Eq. (26), it follows from Eq. (2) that

$$\int_{t_0}^{t} \Gamma_\xi F_e(s, \xi, \sigma)E[z(\sigma)z'(\alpha)]\, d\sigma = E\left[\Gamma_\xi u(s, \xi)z'(\alpha)\right] = 0.$$

Thus, from Lemma 1 we get

$$\Gamma_\xi F_e(s, \xi, \sigma) = 0, \quad \xi \in \partial D. \tag{33}$$

Therefore, we get from Eq. (16)

$$\Gamma_\xi \int_{t_0}^{t} F_e(s, \xi, \sigma) z(\sigma)\, d\sigma = \Gamma_\xi \hat{u}(s, \xi/t) = 0.$$

Since it is clear that the initial value of $\hat{u}(s, x/t)$ is $\hat{u}(t, x/t)$, the proof of the theorem is complete. QED

Let us denote the prediction error covariance function by $p(s, x, y/t)$,

$$p(s, x, y/t) = E[\tilde{u}(s, x/t)\tilde{u}(s, y/t)]. \tag{34}$$

Theorem 3

The optimal prediction error covariance function $p(s, x, y/t)$ is given by

$$\partial p(s, x, y/t)/\partial s = A_x p(s, x, y/t) + A_y p(s, x, y/t) + Q(s, x, y),$$

$$\Gamma_\xi p(s, \xi, y/t) = 0, \quad \xi \in \partial D, \quad y \in \bar{D},$$

where $Q(s, x, y) = B(s, x)\tilde{Q}(s, x, y)B(s, y)$ and the initial value of $p(s, x, y/t)$ is $p(t, x, y/t)$.

Proof. From Eqs. (1), (19), and (30) it follows that

$$\partial \tilde{u}(x, x/t)/\partial s = A_x \tilde{u}(s, x/t) + B(s, x)w(s, x) \tag{35}$$

and from Eqs. (2), (19), and (31)

$$\Gamma_\xi \tilde{u}(s, \xi/t) = 0, \quad \xi \in \partial D. \tag{36}$$

The solution of Eq. (35) is given by using the fundamental solution $G(t, x, y)$ as

$$\tilde{u}(s, x/t) = \int_D G(s - t, x, a)\tilde{u}(t, a/t)\, da + \int_t^s \int_D G(s - \tau, x, b)B(\tau, b)\, db\, d\tau. \tag{37}$$

Differentiating Eq. (35) with respect to s and using Eqs. (34) and (35) we obtain

$$\partial p(s, x, y/t)/\partial s = A_x p(s, x, y/t) + A_y p(s, x, y/t) + B(s, x)E[w(s, x)\tilde{u}(s, y/t)] + E[\tilde{u}(s, x/t)w(s, y)]B(s, y).$$

From Eqs. (7) and (37) we get for s > t

$$E[w(s, x)\tilde{u}(s, y/t)] = \int_t^s \int_D G(s - \tau, y, b)B(\tau, b) \times \tilde{Q}(\tau, x, b)\ \delta(s - \tau)\ db\ d\tau$$

$$= \frac{1}{2}\int_D \delta(y - b)B(s, b)\tilde{Q}(s, x, b)\ db$$

$$= \frac{1}{2}\ B(s, y)\tilde{Q}(s, x, y)$$

and similarly

$$E[\tilde{u}(s, x/t)w(s, y)] = \frac{1}{2}\ B(s, x)\tilde{Q}(s, x, y).$$

Thus, we get

$$\partial p(s, x, y/t)/\partial s = A_x p(s, x, y/t) + A_y p(s, x, y/t) + Q(s, x, y).$$

From Eq. (36) we get

$$E\left[\Gamma_\xi \tilde{u}(s, \xi/t)\tilde{u}(s, y/t)\right] = \Gamma_\xi E[\tilde{u}(s, \xi/t)\tilde{u}(s, y/t)]$$

$$= \Gamma_\xi p(s, \xi, y/t) = 0.$$

Thus, the proof of the theorem is complete. QED

VI. DERIVATION OF THE OPTIMAL FILTER

Let us derive the optimal filter by using the Wiener-Hopf theorem for the filtering problem. From Eq. (27) it follows that

$$\int_{t_0}^{t} \frac{\partial F(t, x, \sigma)}{\partial t} E[z(\sigma)z'(\alpha)]\, d\sigma + F(t, x, t)E[z(t)z'(\alpha)]$$

$$= E\left[\frac{\partial u(t, x)}{\partial t} z'(\alpha)\right].$$

Substituting Eq. (1) into the above equation and using Eq. (27) we get

$$\int_{t_0}^{t} \frac{\partial F(t, x, \sigma)}{\partial t} E[z(\sigma)z'(\alpha)]\, d\sigma + F(t, x, t)E[z(t)z'(\alpha)]$$

$$= \int_{t_0}^{t} A_x F(t, x, \sigma)E[z(\sigma)z'(\alpha)]\, d\sigma.$$

It follows from Eqs. (4) and (27) that

$$E[z(t)z'(\alpha)] = H(t)E\left[u_m(t)z'(\alpha)\right]$$

$$= H(t)\int_{t_0}^{t} F_m(t, \sigma)E[z(\sigma)z'(\alpha)]\, d\sigma \tag{38}$$

where

$$F_m(t, \sigma) = \begin{bmatrix} F(t, x^1, \sigma) \\ \vdots \\ F(t, x^m, \sigma) \end{bmatrix}. \tag{39}$$

Thus, we get

$$\int_{t_0}^{t} N(s, x, \sigma)E[z(\sigma)z'(\alpha)]\, d\sigma = 0$$

where

$$N(s, x, \sigma) = \frac{\partial F(t, x, \sigma)}{\partial t} + F(t, x, t)H(t)F_m(t, \sigma) - A_x F(t, x, \sigma).$$

From Lemma 1 it follows that $N(s, x, \sigma) = 0$; that is,

$$\partial F(t, x, \sigma)/\partial t = A_x F(t, x, \sigma) - F(t, x, t)H(t)F_m(t, \sigma). \tag{40}$$

Then we have

Lemma 2

The optimal kernel function $F(t, x, \sigma)$ is given by Eq. (40).

Theorem 4

The optimal filtering estimate $\hat{u}(t, x/t)$ is given by

$$\partial\hat{u}(t, x/t)/\partial t = A_x\hat{u}(t, x/t) + F(t, x, t)\nu(t), \tag{41}$$

$$\nu(t) = z(t) - H(t)\hat{u}_m(t/t), \tag{42}$$

$$\hat{u}(t_0, x/t_0) = \hat{u}_0(x), \tag{43}$$

$$\Gamma_\xi\hat{u}(t, \xi/t) = 0, \qquad \xi \in \partial D, \tag{44}$$

where

$$\hat{u}_m(t/t) = \mathrm{Col}[\hat{u}(t, x^1/t), \ldots, \hat{u}(t, x^m/t)]. \tag{45}$$

Proof. Differentiating Eq. (17) with respect to t and making use of Eq. (40) we get

$$\frac{\partial\hat{u}(t, x/t)}{\partial t} = F(t, x, t)z(t) + \int_{t_0}^{t} \frac{\partial F(t, x, \sigma)}{\partial t} z(\sigma)\, d\sigma$$

$$= A_x\hat{u}(t, x/t) + F(t, x, t)(z(t) - H(t)\hat{u}_m(t/t)).$$

Letting $x = \xi \in \partial D$ in Eq. (27) and using Eq. (2) we obtain

$$\int_{t_0}^{t} \Gamma_\xi F(t, \xi, \sigma)E[z(\sigma)z'(\alpha)]\, d\sigma = E\left[\Gamma_\xi u(t, \xi)z'(\alpha)\right] = 0.$$

From Lemma 1 we get

$$\Gamma_\xi F(t, \xi, \sigma) = 0, \qquad \xi \in \partial D.$$

Therefore, we obtain the boundary condition

$$\Gamma_\xi\hat{u}(t, \xi/t) = 0, \qquad \xi \in \partial D.$$

Since we have no information at the initial time t_0, it is suitable to assume an initial value of $\hat{u}(t, x/t)$ as $\hat{u}(t_0, x/t_0) = \hat{u}_0(x)$. Thus, the proof of the theorem is complete. QED

In order to find the optimal kernel function $F(t, x, t)$ for the filtering problem, we introduce the notation

$$p_m(t, x/t) = [p(t, x, x^1/t), \ldots, p(t, x, x^m/t)], \quad (46)$$

$$p(t, x, y/t) = E[\tilde{u}(t, x/t)\tilde{u}(t, y/t)]. \quad (47)$$

From the definition of $p_m(t, x/t)$ it follows that

$$p_m(t, x/t) = E\left[\tilde{u}(t, x/t)\tilde{u}_m'(t/t)\right]. \quad (48)$$

It follows from Eqs. (4) and (7) that

$$\begin{aligned} E[z(\sigma)z'(\alpha)] &= E\left[z(\sigma)u_m'(\alpha)\right]H'(\alpha) + \tilde{R}(\alpha)\delta(\sigma - \alpha), \\ E[u(t, x)z'(\alpha)] &= E\left[u(t, x)u_m'(\alpha)\right]H'(\alpha). \end{aligned} \quad (49)$$

Substituting the above equations into Eq. (27) we get

$$\int_{t_0}^{t} F(t, x, \sigma)E\left[z(\sigma)u_m'(\alpha)\right]H'(\alpha)\, d\sigma + F(t, x, \alpha)\tilde{R}(\alpha)$$
$$= E\left[u(t, x)u_m'(\alpha)\right]H'(\alpha), \quad t_0 \leqq \alpha < t.$$

By virtue of Eq. (17), the preceding equation can be rewritten as

$$\begin{aligned} F(t, x, \alpha)\tilde{R}(\alpha) &= E\left[(u(t, x) - \hat{u}(t, x/t))u_m'(\alpha)\right]H'(\alpha) \\ &= E\left[\tilde{u}(t, x/t)u_m'(\alpha)\right]H'(\alpha) \end{aligned} \quad (50)$$

where the following relation of Corollary 1,

$$E\left[\tilde{u}(t, x/t)\hat{u}_m'(\alpha)\right] = 0, \quad (51)$$

was employed.

Letting $\tau \to t$ in Eq. (50) we get

$$F(t, x, t) = p_m(t, x/t)H'(t)\tilde{R}^{-1}(t). \quad (52)$$

Thus, we have

Theorem 5

The optimal filtering kernel function $F(t, x, t)$ is given by Eq. (52).

Let us derive the equation of the optimal filtering error covariance function $p(t, x, y/t)$. It follows from Eqs. (1)-(3) and (41)-(45) that

$$\partial\tilde{u}(t, x/t)/\partial t = A_x\tilde{u}(t, x/t) - F(t, x, t)\nu(t) + B(t, x)w(t, x), \tag{53}$$

$$\Gamma_\xi\tilde{u}(t, \xi/t) = 0, \quad \xi \in \partial D, \tag{54}$$

$$\tilde{u}(t_0, x/t_0) = \hat{u}_0(x) - u_0(x). \tag{55}$$

Then we have

Theorem 6

The optimal filtering error covariance function $p(t, x, y/t)$ satisfies the following PDE of Riccati type:

$$\partial p(t, x, y/t)/\partial t = A_x p(t, x, y/t) + A_y p(t, x, y/t) + Q(t, x, y) - p_m(t, x/t)R(t)p_m'(t, y/t), \tag{56}$$

$$\Gamma_\xi p(t, \xi, y/t) = 0, \quad \xi \in \partial D, \tag{57}$$

$$p(t_0, x, y/t_0) = p_0(x, y) \tag{58}$$

where

$$R(t) = H'(t)\tilde{R}^{-1}(t)H(t).$$

Proof. Differentiating Eq. (47) with respect to t we obtain

$$\frac{\partial p(t, x, y/t)}{\partial t} = E\left[\frac{\partial\tilde{u}(t, x/t)}{\partial t}\tilde{u}(t, y/t)\right] + E\left[\tilde{u}(t, x/t)\frac{\partial\tilde{u}(t, y/t)}{\partial t}\right].$$

From Eq. (53) we get

$$E\left[\frac{\partial \tilde{u}(t, x/t)}{\partial t} \tilde{u}(t, y/t)\right] = A_x p(t, x, y/t) - F(t, x, t)E[\nu(t)\tilde{u}(t, y/t)] + B(t, x)E[w(t, x)\tilde{u}(t, y/t)]. \tag{59}$$

But we have from Eqs. (4) and (42)

$$\nu(t) = H(t)\tilde{u}_m(t/t) + v(t). \tag{60}$$

Then we have from Eq. (52)

$$\begin{aligned} E[\nu(t)\tilde{u}(t, y/t)] &= H(t)E\left[\tilde{u}_m(t/t)\tilde{u}(t, y/t)\right] + E[v(t)\tilde{u}(t, y/t)] \\ &= H(t)p_m'(t, y/t) - \int_{t_0}^{t} E[v(t)z'(\sigma)]F'(t, y, \sigma)\, d\sigma \\ &= H(t)p_m'(t, y/t) - \int_{t_0}^{t} \tilde{R}(t)\ \delta(t - \sigma)F'(t, y, \sigma)\, d\sigma \\ &= \frac{1}{2} H(t)p_m'(t, y/t). \end{aligned} \tag{61}$$

It follows from Eqs. (10) and (53) that

$$\tilde{u}(t, y/t) = \int_D G(t - t_0, y, a)(u_0(a) - \hat{u}_0(a))\, da + \int_{t_0}^{t} \int_D G(t - \tau, y, a)(-F(\tau, a, \tau)\nu(\tau) + B(\tau, a)w(\tau, a))\, da\, d\tau. \tag{62}$$

Then we get from Eqs. (7) and (12)

$$E[w(t, x)\tilde{u}(t, y/t)] = \int_{t_0}^{t} \int_D G(t - \tau, y, a)B(\tau, a) \times E[w(t, x)w(\tau, a)] \, da \, d\tau$$
$$= \int_{t_0}^{t} \int_D G(t - \tau, y, a)B(\tau, a) \times \tilde{Q}(\tau, x, a) \, \delta(t - \tau) \, da \, d\tau$$
$$= \frac{1}{2} \tilde{Q}(t, x, y)B(t, y). \tag{63}$$

Thus, from Eqs. (59), (61), and (63) we get

$$E\left[\frac{\partial \tilde{u}(t, x/t)}{\partial t} \tilde{u}(t, y/t)\right]$$
$$= A_x p(t, x, y/t) - \frac{1}{2} F(t, x, t)H(t)p_m'(t, y/t) + \frac{1}{2} Q(t, x, y).$$

Analogously, we get

$$E\left[\tilde{u}(t, x/t)\frac{\partial \tilde{u}(t, y/t)}{\partial t}\right]$$
$$= A_y p(t, x, y/t) - \frac{1}{2} F(t, y, t)H(t)p_m'(t, x/t) + \frac{1}{2} Q(t, y, x).$$

But from Eqs. (7) and (52) it follows that

$$Q(t, x, y) = Q(t, y, x), \tag{64}$$

$$F(t, x, t)H(t)p_m'(t, y/t) = F(t, y, t)H(t)p_m'(t, x/t)$$
$$= p_m(t, x/t)R(t)p_m'(t, y/t). \tag{65}$$

Thus, we get

$$\partial p(t, x, y/t)/\partial t = A_x p(t, x, y/t) + A_y p(t, x, y/t) + Q(t, x, y) - p_m(t, x/t)R(t)p_m'(t, y/t).$$

From Eq. (54) we get

$$E\left[\Gamma_\xi \tilde{u}(t, \xi/t)\tilde{u}(t, y/t)\right] = \Gamma_\xi p(t, \xi, y/t) = 0$$

and from Eq. (55)

$$p(t_0, x, y/t_0) = p_0(x, y).$$

Thus, the proof of the theorem is complete. QED

VII. DERIVATION OF THE OPTIMAL SMOOTHING ESTIMATOR

In this section, we derive the basic equations for the optimal smoothing estimator by using the Wiener-Hopf theory. Differentiating Eq. (28) with respect to t we get

$$F_i(s, t, x, t)E[z(t)z'(\alpha)] + \int_{t_0}^{t} \frac{\partial F_i(s, t, x, \sigma)}{\partial t} E[z(\sigma)z'(\alpha)]\, d\sigma = 0.$$

It follows from Eq. (4) that for $t_0 \leqq \alpha < t$

$$E[z(t)z'(\alpha)] = H(t)E\left[u_m(t)z'(\alpha)\right].$$

From Eq. (5) and the Wiener-Hopf equation (27) for the filtering problem we get

$$E\left[u_m(t)z'(\alpha)\right] = \int_{t_0}^{t} F_m(t, \sigma)E[z(\sigma)z'(\alpha)]\, d\sigma.$$

Hence, we have

$$\int_{t_0}^{t} N(s, t, x, \sigma)E[z(\sigma)z'(\alpha)]\, d\sigma = 0$$

where

$$N(s, t, x, \sigma) = \frac{\partial F_i(s, t, x, \sigma)}{\partial t} + F_i(s, t, x, \sigma)H(t)F_m(t, \sigma).$$

Since it is easily seen that $F_i(s, t, x, \sigma) + N(s, t, x, \sigma)$ also satisfies the Wiener-Hopf equation (28), from Lemma 1 we have $N(s, t, x, \sigma) = 0$. Thus, we have

Lemma 3

The optimal smoothing kernel function $F_i(s, t, x, \sigma)$ is given by

$$\partial F_i(s, t, x, \sigma)/\partial t = F_i(s, t, x, \sigma)H(t)F_m(t, \sigma). \tag{66}$$

Theorem 7

The optimal smoothing estimate $\hat{u}(s, x/t)$ is given by

$$\partial \hat{u}(s, x/t)/\partial t = F_i(s, t, x, t)\nu(t), \tag{67}$$

$$\Gamma_\xi \hat{u}(s, \xi/t) = 0, \quad \xi \in \partial D, \tag{68}$$

where the initial value of $\hat{u}(s, x/t)$ is $\hat{u}(s, x/s$ and

$$F_i(s, t, x, t) = c_m(s, x/t)H'(t)\tilde{R}^{-1}(t), \tag{69}$$

$$c_m(s, x/t) = (c(s, x, x^1/t), \ldots, c(s, x, x^m/t)), \tag{70}$$

$$c(s, x, y/t) = E[\tilde{u}(s, x/t)u(t, y)]. \tag{71}$$

Proof. Differentiating Eq. (18) with respect to t and using Eqs. (17) and (66) we have

$$\frac{\partial \hat{u}(s, x/t)}{\partial t} = F_i(s, t, x, t)z(t) + \int_{t_0}^{t} \frac{\partial F_i(s, t, x, \sigma)}{\partial t} z(\sigma)\, d\sigma$$

$$= F_i(s, t, x, t)(z(t) - H(t)\hat{u}_m(t/t))$$

$$= F_i(s, t, x, t)\nu(t).$$

Letting $x = \xi \in \partial D$ in Eq. (28) we get

$$\int_{t_0}^{t} \Gamma_\xi F_i(s, t, \xi, \sigma)E[z(\sigma)z'(\alpha)]\, d\sigma$$

$$= E[\Gamma_\xi u(s, \xi)z'(\alpha)] = 0.$$

From Lemma 1 and the above equation we obtain

$$\Gamma_\xi F_i(s, t, \xi, \sigma) = 0, \quad \xi \in \partial D.$$

Thus, from Eq. (18) and the preceding equation we get

$$\Gamma_\xi \hat{u}(s, \xi/t) = 0, \quad \xi \in \partial D.$$

From Eq. (49) we obtain

$$E[z(\sigma)z'(\alpha)] = E\left[z(\sigma)u_m'(\alpha)\right]H'(\alpha) + \tilde{R}(\sigma)\,\delta(\sigma - \alpha). \tag{72}$$

It follows from Eq. (4) and the Wiener-Hopf equation (28) that for $s < \alpha < t$

$$E[u(s, x)z'(\alpha)] = E\left[u(s, x)u_m'(\alpha)\right]H'(\alpha)$$

$$= \int_{t_0}^{t} F_i(s, t, x, \sigma)E[z(\sigma)z'(\alpha)]\,d\sigma.$$

Substituting Eq. (72) into the above equation we have

$$E\left[u(s, x)u_m'(\alpha)\right]H'(\alpha)$$

$$= E\left[\int_{t_0}^{t} F_i(s, t, x, \sigma)z(\sigma)\,d\sigma\; u_m'(\alpha)\right]H'(\alpha)$$

$$+ F_i(s, t, x, \alpha)\tilde{R}(\alpha)$$

$$= E\left[\hat{u}(s, x/t)u_m'(\alpha)\right]H'(\alpha) + F_i(s, t, x, \alpha)\tilde{R}(\alpha).$$

Thus, we get

$$E\left[\tilde{u}(s, x/t)u_m'(\alpha)\right]H'(\alpha) = F_i(s, t, x, \alpha)\tilde{R}(\alpha).$$

Letting $\alpha \to t$ we get

$$c_m(s, x/t)H'(t) = F_i(s, t, x, t)\tilde{R}(t)$$

where

$$c_m(s, x/t) = E\left[\tilde{u}(s, x/t)u_m'(\alpha)\right].$$

Since $\tilde{R}(t)$ is positive definite, the proof of the theorem is complete. QED

Let us derive the equation satisfied by $c(s, x, y/t)$. On using the orthogonality between $\tilde{u}(s, x/t)$ and $\hat{u}(s, y/t)$ of Corollary 1, $c(s, x, y/t)$ can be rewritten as

$$c(s, x, y/t) = E[\tilde{u}(s, x/t)\tilde{u}(t, y/t)]$$
$$= E[\tilde{u}(s, x/s)\tilde{u}(t, y/t)] + r_c$$

where

$$r_c = E[(\tilde{u}(s, x/t) - \tilde{u}(s, x/s))\hat{u}(t, y/t)]$$
$$= E[(\hat{u}(s, x/s) - \hat{u}(s, x/t))\tilde{u}(t, y/t)].$$

Use of the orthogonality condition of Corollary 1 yields $r_c = 0$ and $c(s, x, y/t)$ is given by

$$c(s, x, y/t) = E[\tilde{u}(s, x/s)\tilde{u}(t, y/t)]. \tag{73}$$

On the other hand, from Eqs. (53) and (60) it follows that

$$\partial\tilde{u}(t, y/t)/\partial t = A_y\tilde{u}(t, y/t) + B(t, y)w(t, y)$$
$$- F(t, y, t)H(t)\tilde{u}_m(t/t) - F(t, y, t)v(t), \tag{74}$$

$$\Gamma_\xi\tilde{u}(t, \xi/t) = 0, \quad \xi \in \partial D, \tag{75}$$

$$\tilde{u}(t_0, x/t_0) = \tilde{u}_0(x) \tag{76}$$

where

$$\tilde{u}_0(x) = u_0(x) - \hat{u}_0(x).$$

Let $G(t, t_0, y, a)$ be the fundamental solution of Eqs. (74) and (75); that is,

$$\partial\tilde{G}(t, t_0, y, a)/\partial t = A_y\tilde{G}(t, t_0, y, a)$$
$$- F(t, y, t)H(t)\tilde{G}'_m(t, t_0, a), \tag{77}$$

$$\Gamma_\xi G(t, t_0, \xi, a) = 0, \quad \xi \in \partial D, \tag{78}$$

$$\lim_{t\to t_0} G(t, t_0, \xi, a) = \delta(\xi - a) \tag{79}$$

where

$$\tilde{G}_m(t, t_0, a) = \left(\tilde{G}\left(t, t_0, x^1, a\right), \ldots, \tilde{G}\left(t, t_0, x^m, a\right)\right). \tag{80}$$

Then the solution $\tilde{u}(t, y/t)$ of Eqs. (74)-(76) is given by

$$\tilde{u}(t, y/t) = \int_D \tilde{G}(t, t_0, y, a)\tilde{u}_0(a)\, da + \int_{t_0}^{t} \int_D \tilde{G}(t, \sigma, y, a) \times [B(\sigma, a)w(\sigma, a) - F(\sigma, a, \sigma)v(\sigma)]\, da\, d\sigma. \tag{81}$$

Theorem 8

$c(s, x, y/t)$ satisfies the equations

$$\partial c(s, x, y/t)/\partial t = A_y c(s, x, y/t) - c_m(s, x/t)R(t)p_m'(t, y/t) \tag{82}$$

or

$$\partial c(s, x, y/t)/\partial s = A_x c(s, x, y/t) + \int_D \tilde{G}(t, s, y, a)Q(s, a, x)\, da, \tag{83}$$

$$\Gamma_\xi c(s, \xi, y/t) = 0, \quad \xi \in \partial D, \tag{84}$$

$$c(s, x, y/s) = p(s, x, y/s). \tag{85}$$

Proof. On using the orthogonality between $\hat{u}(s, x/s)$ and $u(t, y/t)$, $c(s, x, y/t)$ of Eq. (73) is given by

$$c(s, x, y/t) = E[u(s, x)\tilde{u}(t, y/t)]. \tag{86}$$

Differentiating the above equation with respect to s and using Eq. (1) and the independent assumption between $v(t)$ and $u(s, x)$ we obtain

$$\partial c(s, x, y/t)/\partial s = A_x c(s, x, y/t) + B(s, x)r_w, \tag{87}$$

$$r_w = E[w(s, x)\tilde{u}(t, y/t)].$$

Substituting Eq. (81) into r_w and using the assumption that $w(s, x)$ is independent of $u_0(a)$ and $v(a)$, r_w is given by

$$r_w = \int_{t_0}^{t} \int_D \tilde{G}(t, \sigma, y, a) B(s, a) E[w(s, x) w(\sigma, a)] \, da \, d\sigma$$

$$= \int_D \tilde{G}(t, s, y, a) B(s, a) \tilde{Q}(s, x, a) \, da. \tag{88}$$

Hence, Eq. (83) is obtained from Eqs. (87) and (88).

Differentiating Eq. (73) with respect to t we get

$$\frac{\partial c(s, x, y/t)}{\partial t} = E\left[\tilde{u}(s, x/s) \frac{\partial \tilde{u}(t, x/t)}{\partial t}\right].$$

Substituting Eq. (74) into the above equation, we get for $s < t$

$$\begin{aligned}\partial c(s, x, y/t)/\partial t &= A_y c(s, x, y/t) \\ &\quad - F(t, y, t) H(t) E\left[\tilde{u}(s, x/s) \tilde{u}_m(t/t)\right] \\ &= A_y c(s, x, y/t) \\ &\quad - F(t, y, t) H(t) c_m'(s, x/t).\end{aligned}$$

But from Eq. (52) we get

$$\begin{aligned}F(t, y, t) H(t) c_m'(s, x/t) &= c_m(s, x/t) H'(t) F'(t, y, t) \\ &= c_m(s, x/t) R(t) p_m'(t, y/t).\end{aligned}$$

Thus, we have derived Eq. (82). From Eqs. (2) and (68) we get

$$\Gamma_\xi \tilde{u}(s, \xi/t) = 0, \quad \xi \in \partial D. \tag{89}$$

Multiplying each side of Eq. (89) by $u(t, y)$ and taking the expectation we get Eq. (84). Since the initial value of $\tilde{u}(s, x/t)$ is $\tilde{u}(s, x/s)$, it is clear that the initial value of $c(s, x, y/t)$ is given by Eq. (85). Thus, the proof of the theorem is complete. QED

Then the following corollary is obtained.

Corollary 3

c(s, x, y/t) is given by

$$c(s, x, y/t) = \int_D \tilde{G}(t, s, y, a) p(s, a, x/s)\, da. \tag{90}$$

Proof. Since Eq. (82) with Eqs. (84) and (85) is a linear PDE, it is proved in [5] that there exists a unique solution of Eq. (82) under some conditions. By direct differentiation of Eq. (90) with respect to t, it is clear that Eq. (90) satisfies Eq. (82). Furthermore, from Eqs. (77)-(79) it follows that c(s, x, y/t) given by Eq. (90) satisfies Eqs. (84) and (85). Thus, the proof of the corollary is complete. QED

Theorem 9

The optimal smoothing estimate $\hat{u}(s, x/t)$ is given by

$$\hat{u}(s, x/t) = \hat{u}(s, x/s) + \int_s^t c_m(s, x/\sigma) \nu_m(\sigma)\, d\sigma, \tag{91}$$

$$\nu_m(\sigma) = H'(\sigma) \tilde{R}^{-1}(\sigma) \nu(\sigma). \tag{92}$$

Proof. Substituting Eq. (69) into Eq. (67) and integrating Eq. (67) with respect to t we get Eq. (91). Thus, the proof of the theorem is complete. QED

Theorem 10

The optimal smoothing estimation error covariance function p(s, x, y/t) is given by

$$\partial p(s, x, y/t)/\partial t = -c_m(s, x/t) R(t) c_m'(s, y/t), \tag{93}$$

$$\Gamma_\xi p(s, \xi, y/t) = 0, \quad \xi \in \partial D, \tag{94}$$

with the initial value p(s, x, y/s). Equivalently, we get the relation

$$p(s, x, y/t) = p(s, x, y/s) - \int_s^t c_m(s, x/\sigma) R(\sigma) c_m'(s, y/\sigma)\, d\sigma. \tag{95}$$

Proof. Using the orthogonality between $\tilde{u}(s, y/t)$ and and $\hat{u}(s, y/t)$ we obtain

$$p(s, x, y/t) = E[\tilde{u}(s, x/t)u(s, y)]. \tag{96}$$

Differentiating Eq. (96) with respect to t and using the relation

$$\partial\tilde{u}(s, x/t)/\partial t = -\partial\hat{u}(s, x/t)/\partial t,$$

we get from Eq. (67)

$$\partial p(s, x, y/t)/\partial t = -F_i(s, t, x, t)E[\nu(t)u(s, y)] \tag{97}$$

and from Eq. (60), Corollary 1, and Eq. (73) it follows that

$$\begin{aligned} E[\nu(t)u(s, y)] &= H(t)E\left[\tilde{u}_m(t/t)u(s, y)\right] \\ &= H(t)E\left[\tilde{u}_m(t/t)\tilde{u}(s, y/s)\right] \\ &= H(t)c_m'(s, y/t). \end{aligned}$$

Then it follows from Eqs. (69), (97), and the above equation that Eq. (93) holds. Multiplying each side of Eq. (89) by $\tilde{u}(s, y/t)$ and taking the expectation we have Eq. (94). Since it is clear that the initial value of $p(s, x, y/t)$ is $p(s, x, y/s)$, we get Eq. (95) by direct integration of Eq. (93) with respect to t. Thus, the proof of the theorem is complete. QED

Based on the preceding results of the smoothing estimators, we can derive three kinds of the optimal smoothing estimators; that is, fixed-point, fixed-interval, and fixed-lag smoothing estimators.

Let t_1 be a fixed time such that $t_1 < t$. Then we have

Theorem 11 (Fixed-Point Smoothing)

The optimal fixed-point smoothing estimate $\hat{u}(t_1, x/t)$ and the smoothing error covariance function $p(t_1, x, y/t)$ are given by

$$\partial \hat{u}(t_1, x/t)/\partial t = c_m(t_1, x/t)\nu_m(t), \tag{98}$$

$$\partial p(t_1, x, y/t)/\partial t = -c_m(t_1, x/t)R(t)c_m'(t_1, y/t), \tag{99}$$

$$c_m(t_1, x/t) = \left(c\left(t_1, x, x^1/t\right), \ldots, c\left(t_1, x, x^m/t\right)\right),$$

$$\partial c(t_1, x, y/t)/\partial t = A_x c(t_1, x, y/t) - c_m(t_1, x/t)R(t)p_m(t, y/t), \tag{100}$$

$$c(t_1, x, y/t_1) = p(t_1, x, y/t_1), \tag{101}$$

$$\Gamma_\xi f = 0, \quad f = \hat{u}(t_1, \xi/t), \quad p(t_1, \xi, y/t), \quad \text{or} \quad c(t_1, \xi, y/t) \tag{102}$$

where the initial values of $\hat{u}(t_1, x/t)$ and $p(t_1, x, y/t)$ are $\hat{u}(t_1, x/t_1)$ and $p(t_1, x, y/t_1)$, respectively.

Proof. Letting $s = t_1$ in Theorems 7-9 we get Eqs. (98)-(102. Thus, the proof of the theorem is complete. QED

Letting T be a fixed time and setting $s = t$ and $t = T$ in Eqs. (91) and (95), we have

$$\hat{u}(t, x/T) = \hat{u}(t, x/t) + \int_t^T c_m(t, x/\sigma)\nu_m(\sigma)\, d\sigma, \tag{103}$$

$$p(t, x, y/T) = p(t, x, y/t) - \int_t^T c_m(t, x/\sigma)R(\sigma)c_m'(t, y/\sigma)\, d\sigma. \tag{104}$$

Then we have

Theorem 12 (Fixed-Interval Smoothing)

The fixed-interval optimal smoothing estimate $\hat{u}(t, x/T)$ and the smoothing error covariance function $p(t, x, y/T)$ are given by by

$$\partial \hat{u}(t, x/T)/\partial t = A_x \hat{u}(t, x/T) + \int_D \int_D (\hat{u}(t, a/T) - \hat{u}(t, a/t)) \times \overline{p}(t, a, b/t)Q(t, b, x)\, da\, db, \tag{105}$$

$$\begin{aligned}\partial p(t, x, y/T)/\partial t = {} & A_x p(t, x, y/T) + A_y p(t, x, y/T) \\ & - Q(t, x, y) \\ & + \int_D \int_D p(t, a, y/T)\bar{p}(t, b, a/t) \\ & \qquad \times Q(t, x, b)\, da\, db \\ & + \int_D \int_D p(t, x, a/T)\bar{p}(t, a, b/t) \\ & \qquad \times Q(t, b, y)\, da\, db \end{aligned} \tag{106}$$

$$\Gamma_\xi f = 0, \quad f = \hat{u}(t, \xi/T), \quad \text{or} \quad p(t, \xi, y/T), \quad \xi \in \partial D, \tag{107}$$

where the terminal conditions for Eqs. (105) and (106) are $\hat{u}(T, x/T)$ and $p(t, x, y/T)$, respectively, and $\bar{p}(t, a, b/t)$ denotes the inverse kernel function of $p(t, a, b/t)$ such that

$$\int_D p(t, b, a/t)\bar{p}(t, a, x/t)\, da = \delta(b - x). \tag{108}$$

Proof. Differentiating Eq. (103) with respect to t we obtain

$$\begin{aligned}\frac{\partial \hat{u}(t, x/T)}{\partial t} = {} & \frac{\partial \hat{u}(t, x/t)}{\partial t} - c_m(t, x/t)\nu_m(t) \\ & + \int_t^T \frac{\partial c_m(t, x/\sigma)}{\partial t} \nu_m(\sigma)\, d\sigma. \end{aligned} \tag{109}$$

From Eq. (41) we get

$$\partial \hat{u}(t, x/t)/\partial t = A_x \hat{u}(t, x/t) + F(t, x, t)\nu(t) \tag{110}$$

and from Eqs. (70) and (83)

$$\begin{aligned}\partial c_m(t, x/\sigma)/\partial t = {} & A_x c_m(t, x/\sigma) \\ & + \int_D \tilde{G}_m(\sigma, t, b)Q(t, b, x)\, db. \end{aligned} \tag{111}$$

From Eqs. (90) and (103) we get

$$\hat{u}(t, a/T) - \hat{u}(t, a/t)$$
$$= \int_t^T \int_D \tilde{G}_m(\sigma, t, h)p(t, h, a/t)\nu_m(\sigma)\, dh\, d\sigma.$$

Multiplying each side of the above equation by $\overline{p}(t, a, b/t)$ and integrating each side with respect to a, we get from Eq. (108)

$$\int_t^T \tilde{G}_m(\sigma, t, b)\nu_m(\sigma)\, d\sigma = \int_D (\hat{u}(t, a/T) - \hat{u}(t, a/t)) \times \overline{p}(t, a, b/t)\, da. \qquad (112)$$

Substituting Eqs. (110)-(112) into Eq. (109) and using Eq. (103) we get Eq. (105). Differentiating p(t, x, y/T) of Eq. (104) with respect to t we have

$$\frac{\partial p(t, x, y/T)}{\partial t} = \frac{\partial p(t, x, y/t)}{\partial t} + c_m(t, x/t)R(t)c_m'(t, y/t)$$
$$- \int_t^T \frac{\partial c_m(t, x/\sigma)}{\partial t} R(\sigma)c_m'(t, y/\sigma)\, d\sigma$$
$$- \int_t^T c_m(t, x/\sigma)R(\sigma) \frac{\partial c_m'(t, y/\sigma)}{\partial t}\, d\sigma. \qquad (113)$$

From Eq. (56) it follows that

$$\partial p(t, x, y/t)/\partial t = A_x p(t, x, y/t) + A_y p(t, x, y/t)$$
$$+ Q(t, x, y) - p_m(t, x/t)$$
$$\times p_m'(t, y/t). \qquad (114)$$

Substituting Eq. (114) into Eq. (113) and using Eq. (104) we have

$$\partial p(t, x, y/T)/\partial t$$
$$= A_x p(t, x, y/T) + A_y p(t, x, y/T) + Q(t, x, y)$$
$$- \int_t^T \int_D \tilde{G}_m(\sigma, t, b)Q(t, b, x)R(\sigma)c_m'(t, y/\sigma)\, db\, d\sigma$$
$$- \int_t^T \int_D c_m(t, x/\sigma)R(\sigma)Q(t, b, y)G_m'(\sigma, t, b)\, db\, d\sigma. \qquad (115)$$

Multiplying Eq. (90) by $\bar{p}(s, x, b/s)$ and integrating each side with respect to x we get from Eq. (108)

$$\tilde{G}(t, s, y, b) = \int_D c(s, x, y/t)\bar{p}(s, x, b/s)\, dx. \tag{116}$$

From Eqs. (70) and (80) it follows that

$$\tilde{G}_m(\sigma, t, b) = \int_D c_m(s, a/\sigma)p(t, a, b/t)\, da. \tag{117}$$

From Eqs. (104), (108), and (116) we get

$$Q(t, x, y) - \int_t^T \int_D \tilde{G}_m(\sigma, t, b)Q(t, b, x)R(\sigma)c_m'(t, y/\sigma)\, db\, d\sigma$$

$$= \int_D \int_D Q(t, b, x)p(t, a, b/t)\bar{p}(t, a, y/T)\, da\, db. \tag{118}$$

Since $Q(t, b, x) = Q(t, x, b)$ and $\bar{p}(t, a, b/t) = \bar{p}(t, b, a/t)$, we get Eq. (106) from Eqs. (115) and (118). It is easily seen that the initial and boundary conditions of the theorem are satisfied. Thus, the proof of the theorem is complete. QED

Let ∇ be a fixed-time interval. Setting $s = t$ and $t = t + \nabla$ in Eqs. (91) and (95) we obtain

$$\hat{u}(t, x/t + \nabla) = \hat{u}(t, x/t) + \int_t^{t+\nabla} c_m(t, x/\sigma)\nu_m(\sigma)\, d\sigma \tag{119}$$

and

$$p(t, x, y/t + \nabla = p(t, x, y/t) - \int_t^{t+\nabla} c_m(t, x/\sigma)R(\sigma)c_m'(t, y/\sigma)\, d\sigma. \tag{120}$$

Then we have

Theorem 13 (Fixed-Lag Smoothing)

The optimal fixed-lag smoothing estimate $\hat{u}(t, x/t + \nabla)$ and smoothing error covariance function $p(t, x, y/t + \nabla)$ are given by

$$\partial\hat{u}(t, x/t + \nabla)/\partial t$$
$$= A_x\hat{u}(t, x/t + \nabla) + c_m(t, x/t + \nabla)\nu_m(t + \nabla)$$
$$+ \int_D \int_D Q(t, x, a)\overline{p}(t, a, b/t)(\hat{u}(t, b/t + \nabla)$$
$$- \hat{u}(t, b/t))\, da\, db, \tag{121}$$

$$\partial c(t, x, y/t + \nabla)/\partial t$$
$$= A_x c(t, x, y/t + \nabla) - c_m(t, x/t + \nabla)R(t + \nabla)$$
$$\times p_m'(t + \nabla, y/t + \nabla) + A_y c(t, x, y/t + \nabla)$$
$$+ \int_D \int_D c(t, a, y/t + \nabla)\overline{p}(t, a, b/t)Q(t, b, x)\, da\, db, \tag{122}$$

$$\partial p(t, x, y/t + \nabla)/\partial t$$
$$= A_x p(t, x, y/t + \nabla) - Q(t, x, y) + A_y p(t, x, y/t + \nabla)$$
$$+ \int_D \int_D Q(t, x, a)\overline{p}(t, a, b/t)p(t, b, y/t + \nabla)\, da\, db$$
$$+ \int_D \int_D Q(t, y, a)\overline{p}(t, a, b/t)p(t, b, x/t + \nabla)\, da\, db$$
$$- c_m(t, x/t + \nabla)R(t + \nabla)c_m'(t, y/t + \nabla), \tag{123}$$

$$\Gamma_\xi f = 0, \quad f = \hat{u}(t, \xi/t + \nabla), \quad c(t, \xi, y/t + \nabla),$$
$$\text{or} \quad p(t, \xi, y/t + \nabla), \quad \xi \in \partial D, \tag{124}$$

where the initial conditions of Eqs. (121)-(123) are $\hat{u}(t_0, x/t_0 + \nabla)$, $c(t_0, x, y/t_0 + \nabla)$, and $p(t_0, x, y/t_0 + \nabla)$, respectively.

Proof. Differentiating Eq. (119) with respect to t we obtain

$$\frac{\partial\hat{u}(t, x/t + \nabla)}{\partial t} = \frac{\partial\hat{u}(t, x/t)}{\partial t} - c_m(t, x/t)\nu_m(t)$$
$$+ c_m(t, x/t + \nabla)\nu_m(t + \nabla)$$
$$+ \int_t^{t+\nabla} \frac{\partial c_m(t, x/\sigma)}{\partial t}\, \nu_m(\sigma)\, d\sigma.$$

From Eqs. (83) and (112) we get

$$\int_t^{t+\nabla} \frac{\partial c_m(t, x/\sigma)}{\partial t} \nu_m(\sigma)\, d\sigma$$

$$= \int_t^{t+\nabla} A_x c_m(t, x/\sigma)\nu_m(\sigma)\, d\sigma$$

$$+ \int_D \int_D (\hat{u}(t, a/t + \nabla) - \hat{u}(t, a/t))\overline{p}(t, a, b/t)$$

$$\times Q(t, b, x)\, da\, db.$$

Use of Eqs. (85), (110), (119), and the above equation yields

$$\partial \hat{u}(t, x/t + \nabla)/\partial t$$

$$= A_x \hat{u}(t, x/t + \nabla) + c_m(t, x/t + \nabla)\nu_m(t + \nabla)$$

$$+ \int_D \int_D (\hat{u}(t, a/t + \nabla) - \hat{u}(t, a/t))\overline{p}(t, a, b/t)$$

$$\times Q(t, b, x)\, da\, db.$$

Since $Q(t, b, x) = Q(t, x, b)$ and $\overline{p}(t, a, b/t) = \overline{p}(t, b, a/t)$, Eq. (121) is obtained. From Eqs. (82) and (83) we get

$$\partial c(t, x, y/t + \nabla)/\partial t$$

$$= A_y c(t, x, y/t + \nabla) - c_m(t, x/t + \nabla)R(t + \nabla)$$

$$\times p_m(t + \nabla, y/t + \nabla) + A_x c(t, x, y/t + \nabla)$$

$$+ \int_D \tilde{G}(t + \nabla, t, y, a)Q(t, a, x)\, da.$$

Substituting Eq. (116) into the preceding equation we obtain Eq. (122).

Differentiating Eq. (120) with respect to t and using Eqs. (83), (114), and (120) we get

$$\partial p(t, x, y/t + \nabla)/\partial t$$

$$= A_x p(t, x, y/t + \nabla) + A_y p(t, x, y/t + \nabla) + Q(t, x, y)$$

$$- \int_D^{t+\nabla} \int_D \tilde{G}_m(\sigma, t, b)Q(t, b, x)R(\sigma)c_m'(t, y/\sigma)\, db\, d\sigma$$

$$- c_m(t, x/t + \nabla) R(t + \nabla) c_m'(t, y/t + \nabla)$$

$$- \int_t^{t+\nabla} \int_D c_m(t, x/\sigma) R(\sigma) \tilde{G}_m'(\sigma, t, a) Q(t, a, y) \, da \, d\sigma.$$

From Eqs. (117) and (120) it follows that

$$\int_t^{t+\nabla} \int_D \int_D cm(t, a/\sigma) \overline{p}(t, a, b/t) Q(t, b, x) R(\sigma) \times c_m'(t, y/\sigma) \, da \, db \, d\sigma$$

$$= \int_D \int_D \overline{p}(t, a, b/t) Q(t, b, x) \times [p(t, a, y/t) - p(t, a, y/t + \nabla)] \, da \, db$$

$$= Q(t, y, x) - \int_D \int_D Q(t, b, x) \overline{p}(t, b, a/t) \times p(t, a, y/t + \nabla) \, da \, db.$$

Thus, Eq. (23) is obtained. It is easily seen that the initial and boundary conditions of the theorem are satisfied. Thus, the proof of the theorem is complete. QED

Let us define $K(t + \nabla, x, h)$ as the solution of the equation

$$\partial K(t + \nabla, x, h)/\partial t = A_x K(t + \nabla, x, h) + \int_D \int_D Q(t, x, a) p(t, a, b/t) K(t + \nabla, b, h) \, da \, db - \int_D \int_D K(t + \nabla, x, a) Q(t + \nabla, a, b) \times \overline{p}(t + \nabla, b, h/t + \nabla) \, da \, db - A_h K(t + \nabla, x, h),$$

$$\Gamma_\xi K(t + \nabla, \xi, h) = 0, \quad \xi \in \partial D,$$

$$K(t_0 + \nabla, x, h) = \int_D c(t_0, x, a/t_0 + \nabla) \times \overline{p}(t_0 + \nabla, a, h/t_0 + \nabla) \, da.$$

Then it is easy to see that

$$c(t, x, y/t + \nabla) = \int_D K(t + \nabla, x, a)p(t + \nabla, a, y/t + \nabla)\, da. \tag{125}$$

Thus, the following corollary holds.

Corollary 4

The optimal fixed-lag smoothing estimator is given by

$$\begin{aligned} \partial\hat{u}(t,\ & x/t + \nabla)/\partial t \\ &= A_x\hat{u}(t, x/t + \nabla) \\ &\quad + \int_D K(t + \nabla, x, a)p_m(t + \nabla, a/t + \nabla)\, da\, \nu_m(t + \nabla) \\ &\quad + \int_D \int_D Q(t, x, a)\overline{p}(t, a, b/t)(\hat{u}(t, b/t + \nabla) \\ &\qquad - \hat{u}(t, b/t))\, da\, db. \end{aligned} \tag{126}$$

Therefore, three kinds of the optimal estimators were derived based on the Wiener-Hopf theory. A new feature of the present derivation for the optimal smoothing estimators is that three kinds of the smoothing estimators can be derived only from the Wiener-Hopf theoretical viewpoints although this fact was not pointed out even for a finite-dimensional system in the original works by Kalman [6,7].

VIII. OPTIMAL SENSOR LOCATION

In this section, we consider the optimal sensor location problem for a linear distributed parameter system. Based on the comparison theorem for PDE of Riccati type, we derive necessary and sufficient conditions for the optimal sensor location.

In order to define the optimal sensor location problem a performance index must be specified which is to be minimized by choice of x^i, i = 1, 2, ..., m. Since the location criterion is that of obtaining the best possible estimate of the state u(t, x), it is adopted here to minimize the trace of the estimation error covariance function p(t, x, x/t) for the optimal filter. Hence, for any fixed time t_f the performance index $J(t_f)$ is defined as

$$J(t_f) = \int_D p(t_f, x, x/t_f)\, dx = \mathrm{tr}[p].$$

In order to avoid the possibility that several measurement points might be clustered in a point of the spatial domain, it is assumed that $x^i \neq x^j$ for $i \neq j$.

From Theorem 6 we get

$$\partial p(t, x, y/t)/\partial t = A_x p(t, x, y/t) + A_y p(t, x, y/t) + Q(t, x, y) - M(t, x, y, p), \tag{127}$$

$$\Gamma_\xi p(t, \xi, y/t) = 0, \quad \xi \in \partial D, \tag{128}$$

$$p(t_0, x, y/t_0) = p_0(x, y) \tag{129}$$

where

$$M(t, x, y, p) = p_m(t, x/t) R(t) p_m'(t, y/t). \tag{130}$$

Since the existence and uniqueness theorem of the solution of Eqs. (127)-(129) has been proved [3,4,8], we denote the function space of the solution by $\mathscr{H}$. Let us consider the following PDE of Riccati type:

$$\partial q(t, x, y/t)/\partial t = A_x q(t, x, y/t) + A_y q(t, x, y/t) + Q(t, x, y) - L(t, x, y, q), \tag{131}$$

$$\Gamma_\xi q(t, \xi, y/t) = 0, \quad \xi \in \partial D, \tag{132}$$

$$q(t_0, x, y/t_0) = p_0(x, y) \tag{133}$$

where y^i, $i = 1, 2, \ldots, m$, denote observation points different from x^i and

$$L(t, x, y, q) = q_m(t, x/t)R(t)q_m'(t, y/t), \tag{134}$$

$$q_m(t, x/t) = (q(t, x, y^1/t), \ldots, q(t, x, y^m/t)).$$

Note that $q(t, x, y/t)$ denotes the optimal filtering error covariance function with pointwise observations at $(y^1, y^2, \ldots, y^m)$. Then the following theorem can be proved.

Theorem 14 (Comparison Theorem)

If the nonlinear terms $M(t, x, y, p)$ and $L(t, x, y, q)$ in Eqs. (127) and (131) satisfy, for all $p \in \mathscr{H}$,

$$M(t, x, y, p) \geqq L(t, x, y, p), \tag{135}$$

then we get

$$p(t, x, y/t) \leqq q(t, x, y/t), \quad t \in [t_0, t_f]. \tag{136}$$

Proof. Let $d(t, x, y)$ be the difference between $p(t, x, y/t)$ and $q(t, x, y/t)$; that is

$$d(t, x, y) = q(t, x, y/t) - p(t, x, y/t). \tag{137}$$

Let us define $e(t, x, y)$ by

$$e(t, x, y) = d(t, x, y)\exp(kt), \quad k = 2KJ \tag{138}$$

where

$$K = \sup_{p \in \mathscr{H}} |p(t, x, y/t)| \quad \text{and} \quad J = \sup_{t \in [t_0, t_f]} ||R(t)||. \tag{139}$$

Then we get from Eq. (130)

$$\begin{aligned} &|M(t, x, y, p) - M(t, x, y, q)| \\ &\quad \leqq k/2\Big(\sup_i |p(t, x, x^i/t) - q(t, x, x^i/t)| \\ &\qquad + \sup_i |p(t, x^i, y/t) - q(t, x^i, y/t)|\Big). \end{aligned} \tag{140}$$

It follows from Eqs. (127), (131), (137), and (138) that

$$\partial e(t, x, y)/\partial t = A_x e(t, x, y) + A_y e(t, x, y) + ke(t, x, y) + \exp(kt)(M(t, x, y, p) - L(t, x, y, q)). \tag{141}$$

It follows from Eqs. (135) and (140) that

$$\begin{aligned} &\exp(ks)(M(s, a, b, p) - L(s, a, b, q)) \\ &\quad \geqq \exp(ks)(M(s, a, b, p) - M(s, a, b, q)) \\ &\quad \geqq -k/2 \exp(ks)\Big[\sup_i |p(s, a, x^i/s) - q(s, a, x^i/s)| \\ &\qquad + \sup_i |p(s, x^i, b/s) - q(s, x^i, b/s)|\Big] \\ &\quad \geqq -k/2\Big[\sup_i |e(s, a, y^i)| + \sup_i |e(s, x^i, b)|\Big]. \end{aligned} \tag{142}$$

Let us define $n_\Delta(t)$ and $n(t)$ by

$$-n_\Delta(t) = \inf_{\substack{s \leqq t \\ a,b,i}} [e(s, a, b) - |e(s, a, x^i)|] \tag{143}$$

$$-n(t) = \inf_{\substack{s \leqq t \\ a,b}} [e(s, a, b) - |e(s, a, b)|]. \tag{144}$$

Since $e(t, x, y)$ is symmetric with respect to x and y, it follows from Eqs. (142)-(144) that

$$\begin{aligned} &ke(t, x, y) + \exp(kt)(M(t, x, y, p) - L(t, x, y, q)) \\ &\quad \geqq k/2\Big(\inf_{\substack{s \leqq t \\ a,b,i}} [e(s, a, b) - |e(s, a, x^i)|] \\ &\qquad + \inf_{\substack{s \leqq t \\ a,b,i}} [e(s, a, b) - |e(s, x^i, b)|]\Big) \\ &\quad = -kn_\Delta(t) \end{aligned}$$

and

$$e(t, x, y) \geqq -k\int_{t_0}^{t}\int_D\int_D G(t - s, x, a)n_\Delta(s) \times G(t - s, b, y)\, da\, db\, ds. \tag{145}$$

But it was proved in [5] that

$$\int_D G(t, x, y)\, dy = \int_D G(t, x, y)\, dx \leqq 1. \tag{146}$$

Since $-n(t) \leqq -n_\Delta(t)$ from Eqs. (143)-(144), we get

$$e(t, x, y) - |e(t, x, y)| \geqq -2k \int_{t_0}^{t} n_\Delta(s)\, ds$$

$$\geqq -2k \int_{t_0}^{t} n(s)\, ds$$

and

$$-n(t) \geqq -2k \int_{t_0}^{t} n(s)\, ds.$$

It is clear from Eq. (144) that $n(t)$ is a nonnegative increasing function of t. Thus, we get

$$0 \leqq n(t) \leqq 2k \int_{t_0}^{t} n(s)\, ds \leqq 2kn(t).$$

Hence, it follows that

$$n(t) = 0, \quad t \in [t_0, 1/2k].$$

Repeating the same procedure by taking $1/2k$ as the initial time, and so on, it follows that

$$n(t) = 0, \quad t \in [t_0, t_f].$$

Thus, we get from Eqs. (137), (138), and (144)

$$e(t, x, y) \geqq 0;$$

that is,

$$q(t, x, y/t) \geqq p(t, x, y/t).$$

Thus, the proof of the theorem is complete. QED

Let us apply the preceding theorem to derive the necessary and sufficient conditions for the optimal sensor location. Let $(x^1, x^2, \ldots, x^m)$ be the optimal measurement points that minimize the trace of $p(t, x, x/t)$ and let $(y^1, y^2, \ldots, y^m)$ be any other measurement points. Then the sufficient condition follows from Theorem 14.

Theorem 15

If the measurement points $(x^1, x^2, \ldots, x^m)$ satisfy the inequality

$$M(t, x, y, p) \geqq L(t, x, y, p) \tag{147}$$

for all $p \in \mathscr{H}$ and any measurement points $(y^1, y^2, \ldots, y^m)$, then $(x^1, x^2, \ldots, x^m)$ are optimal.

Let us define the partial differential operator E_x,

$$E_x u = A_x u - M(t, x, y, u), \tag{148}$$

and let the evolution operator of E_x be $\hat{G}(t, s, x, y)$; that is,

$$\partial \hat{G}(t, s, x, y)/\partial t = E_x \hat{G}(t, s, x, y), \tag{149}$$

$$\Gamma_\xi \hat{G}(t, s, \xi, y) = 0, \quad \xi \in \partial D \tag{150}$$

$$\lim_{t \to s} \hat{G}(t, s, x, y) = \delta(x - y). \tag{151}$$

Then we have

Theorem 16

For the measurement points $(x^1, x^2, \ldots, x^m)$ to be optimal, it is necessary that

$$\int_{t_0}^{t} \int_D \int_D G(t, s, x, a)[M(s, a, b, p) - L(s, a, b, p)] \times G(t, s, b, x)\, da\, db\, ds \geqq 0 \tag{152}$$

where p denotes the minimum filtering error covariance function $p(t, x, y/t)$ of Eq. (127) for the optimal sensor location x^1, $x^2, \ldots, x^m)$.

Proof. From Eq. (137) it follows that

$$\partial d(t, x, y)/\partial t = E_x d(t, x, y) + E_y d(t, x, y) + M(t, x, y, p)$$
$$- L(t, x, y, d) - L(t, x, y, p), \quad (153)$$

$$\Gamma_\xi d(t, \xi, y) = 0, \quad \xi \in \partial D, \quad (154)$$

$$d(t_0, x, y) = 0. \quad (155)$$

Use of the assumption that $\tilde{R}(t)$ is positive definite yields

$$\int_{t_0}^{t} \int_D \int_D G(t, s, x, a)(M(s, a, b, p) - L(s, a, b, p))$$
$$\times G(t, s, b, x)\, da\, db\, ds$$
$$\geqq d(t, x, x). \quad (156)$$

Since it is necessary for the measurement points $(x^1, x^2, \ldots, x^m)$ to be optimal that

$$d(t, x, x) = q(t, x, x/t) - p(t, x, x/t) \geqq 0, \quad (157)$$

it is clear from Eqs. (156)-(157) that Eq. (152) holds. Thus, the proof of the theorem is complete.

Note that the present results for the optimal senosr location problem coincide with those of Bensoussan [9] which were derived by using variational inequality.

It is difficult to solve the optimal sensor location problem by using the optimality condition derived here. Thus, we consider an approximation technique based on the preceding theorems. Let us assume that there exist the eigenvalues λ_i and the corresponding eigenfunctions $\phi_i(x)$ of A_x such that

$$A_x \phi_i(x) = \lambda_i \phi_i(x), \quad i = 1, 2, \ldots, \quad (158)$$

$$\Gamma_\xi \phi_i(\xi) = 0, \quad \xi \in \partial D, \quad (159)$$

$$\lambda_1 \geqq \lambda_2 \geqq \cdots \geqq \lambda_i \geqq \cdots \to -\infty.$$

Let us expand $p(t, x, y/t)$ and $Q(t, x, y)$ by using these eigenfunctions $\{\phi_i(x)\}$ as follows:

$$p(t, x, y/t) = \sum_{i,j=1}^{\infty} p_{ij}(t/t)\phi_i(x)\phi_j(y), \tag{160}$$

$$Q(t, x, y) = \sum_{i,j=1}^{\infty} q_{ij}(t)\phi_i(x)\phi_j(y). \tag{161}$$

If we truncate $p(t, x, y/t)$ and $Q(t, x, y)$ by N-dimensional system, we get from Eq. (127)

$$dP(t)/dt = \Lambda P(t) + P(t)\Lambda - P(t)\Phi'(x)R(t)\Phi(x)P(t) + Q(t) \tag{162}$$

where

$$P(t) = \begin{bmatrix} p_{11}(t/t) & \cdots & p_{1N}(t/t) \\ \vdots & & \vdots \\ p_{N1}(t/t) & \cdots & p_{NN}(t/t) \end{bmatrix}, \quad Q(t) = \begin{bmatrix} q_{11}(t) & \cdots & q_{1N}(t) \\ \vdots & & \vdots \\ q_{N1}(t) & \cdots & q_{NN}(t) \end{bmatrix}$$

$$\Phi(x) = \begin{bmatrix} \phi_1(x^1) & \cdots & \phi_N(x^1) \\ \vdots & & \\ \phi_1(x^m) & \cdots & \phi_N(x^m) \end{bmatrix}, \quad \Lambda = \mathrm{diag}(\lambda_1, \lambda_2, \ldots, \lambda_N)$$

and the performance index $J(t_f)$ is approximated as

$$J(t_f) \cong \sum_{i=1}^{N} p_{ii}(t_f) = \mathrm{tr}[P(t)].$$

Then we have the following theorems from Theorems 15 and 16.

Theorem 17

If the following inequality holds for all $t \in [t_0, t_f]$ amd any measurement points $(y^1, y^2, \ldots, y^m)$,

$$\Phi'(x)R(t)\Phi(x) \geqq \Phi'(y)R(t)\Phi(y), \tag{163}$$

then the measurement points $(x^1, x^2, \ldots, x^m)$ are optimal.

Theorem 18

It is necessary for the measurement points $(x^1, x^2, \ldots, x^m)$ to be optimal that

$$\int_{t_0}^{t_f} \Psi_\Lambda(t_f, t)P(t)[\Phi'(x)R(t)\Phi(x) - \Phi'(y)R(t)\Phi(y)] \times P(t)\Psi_\Lambda'(t_f, t)\,dt \geqq 0 \qquad (164)$$

where $\Psi_\Lambda(t_f, t)$ is the transition matrix of $\Lambda - P(t)\Phi'(y)R(t)\Phi(y)$.

Note that the necessary condition of Theorem 18 corresponds to that of Athans's work [10] which was derived by using the matrix maximum principle. It can be seen that the new matrix $\Phi(x)$ is contained in the conditions of Theorems 17 and 18 compared with that of Athans's work [10]. This difference results from the fact that Athans [10] considers only optimal switching time determination problem for the sensor location.

Let us consider the optimal actuator location problem of linear quadratic control systems. Let the cost functional $J(g(\cdot))$ be given by

$$J(g(\cdot)) = E\left[\left\langle u(t_f), Fu(t_f)\right\rangle + \int_{t_0}^{t_f} \left\langle u(t), F(t)u(t)\right\rangle + \left\langle g(t), G(t)g(t)\right\rangle\right] dt \qquad (165)$$

where F and F(t) are nonnegative operators and G(t) is a positive-definite operator. Furthermore, g(t) is a control input and the optimal control problem is to minimize $J(g(\cdot))$. For this problem the optimal actuator location is determined by the relation [11]

$$B(t)\Phi(c)G^{-1}(t)\Phi'(c)B'(t) \geqq B(t)\Phi(d)G^{-1}(t)\Phi'(d)B'(t) \qquad (166)$$

where B(t) is a coefficient of control input g(t) and c is the optimal actuator locations. Therefore, from Eqs. (163) and (166) it is shown that there exists a duality between sensor and actuator locations.

IX. CONCLUSIONS

In this chapter we have derived the optimal estimators, that is, optimal prediction, filtering, and smoothing estimators by a unified approach based on the Wiener-Hopf theory. It has been well-known that the optimal prediction and filtering problem can be solved by using the Wiener-Hopf theory. But for the optimal smoothing problem the Wiener-Hopf theory has not been applied to derive the estimator. Thus, a notable point of the present work is that the smoothing estimators have been derived by the same approach as the predictor and filter, thus providing a unified approach for DPS state estimation problems. This approach can be easily extended to the case of discrete-time DPS [12-14]. Furthermore, we have considered the optimal sensor location problem and derived the necessary and sufficient conditions for optimal sensor locations. Finally, it has been shown that there is a duality between sensor and actuator location problems just as the duality between the optimal filtering and control problems. The sensor location problem discussed here may be applied to the determination of the monitoring stations for the environmental monitoring system where the available information is obtained only from the finite discrete measurement points on the spatial domain. An important open problem concerning the sensor location is the stochastic observabili problem for the pointwise observation system. It seems that this problem can be solved by extending the results of [15] for the deterministic DPS.

REFERENCES

1. A. H. JAZWINSKI, "Stochastic Processes and Filtering Theory," Academic Press, New York, 1970.
2. Y. SAWARAGI, T. SOEDA, and S. OMATU, "Modeling, Estimation, and Their Applications for Distributed Parameter Systems." Lecture Notes in Control and Information Sciences, Vol. 11, Springer-Verlag, Berlin, 1978.
3. A. BENSOUSSAN, "Filtrage Optimal des Systèmes Linéaires," Dunod, Paris, 1971.
4. R. F. CURTAIN and A. J. PRITCHARD, "Functional Analysis in Modern Applied Mathematics," Academic Press, New York, 1977.
5. S. ITO, "Fundamental Solutions of Parabolic Differential Equations and Boundary Value Problems," *Japan J. Math. 27*, 55-102 (1957).
6. R. E. KALMAN, "A New Approach to Linear Filtering and Prediction Problems," *Trans. ASME Ser. D: J. Basic Eng. 82*, 35-45 (1960).
7. R. E. KALMAN, "New Results in Linear Filtering and Prediction Theory," *Trans. ASME, Ser. D: J. Basic Eng. 83*, 95-108 (1961).
8. S. OMATU and J. H. SEINFELD, "Existence and Comparison Theorems for Partial Differential Equations of Riccati type," *J. Optimization Theory Appl. 36*, 263-276 (1982).
9. A. BENSOUSSAN, "Optimization of Sensors Location in a Linear Filtering Problem," *Proc. Int. Symp. Stab. of Stoch. Dyn. Systems*, 62-84 (1972).
10. M. ATHANS, "On the Determination of Optimal Costly Measurement Strategies for Linear Stochastic Systems," *Prep. of IFAC V Conf.* (1972).
11. S. OMATU and J. H. SEINFELD, "Optimization of Sensor and Actuator Locations in a Distributed Parameter System," *J. Franklin Institute 315*, 407-421 (1982).
12. S. OMATU and J. H. Seinfeld, "A Unified Approach to Discrete-Time Distributed Parameter Estimation by the Least-Squares Method," *Int. J. Systems Sci. 12*, 665-686 (1981).

13. S. OMATU and J. H. SEINFELD, "Filtering and Smoothing for Linear Discrete-Time Distributed Parameter Systems Based on Wiener-Hopf Theory With Application to Estimation of Air Pollution," *IEEE Trans. Systems, Man, and Cybernetics SMC-11*, 785-801 (1981).

14. S. OMATU and J. H. SEINFELD, "Estimation of Atmospheric Species Concentrations from Remote Sensing Data," *IEEE Trans. GeoScience and Remote Sensing GE-20*, 142-153 (1982).

15. Y. SAKAWA, "Observability and Related Problems for Partial Differential Equations of Parabolic Type," *SIAM J. Control 13*, 14-27 (1975).

The Linear–Quadratic Control Problem

JASON L. SPEYER

Department of Aerospace Engineering
and Engineering Mechanics
University of Texas
Austin, Texas

I. INTRODUCTION

Probably the most used result in optimal control theory is that of the solution to the linear-quadratic problem; the dynamic equations and terminal constraints are linear and the performance criterion is a quadratic function of the state and control variables. The solution to this problem produces a control variable as a linear function of the state variables. This solution forms the basis of modern control synthesis techniques because it produces controllers for multi-input/multi-output systems for both time varying and time-invariant systems [1-5]. Furthermore, this problem also forms the basis of the accessory problem in calculus of variations [1,6-11].

The results presented here are for the most part already given elsewhere [1-13]. The presentation here is intended to be tutorial by uniting previous results through a derivation which makes explicit use of the symplectic property of Hamiltonian systems. In this way our derivation of the solution to the linear-quadratic problem is different from previous derivations. The reference list is not exhaustive.

The first-order necessary conditions in the calculus of variations for the terminally constrained linear-quadratic problem are derived. These first order necessary conditions are applied first to the terminally unconstrained linear-quadratic problem. From these necessary conditions a 2n vector linear differential equation is obtained in the state and multiplier variables whose solution is presented in terms of a transition matrix. The symplectic property of the Hamiltonian transition matrix is demonstrated. By partitioning the transition matrix into four $n \times n$ blocks, a two-point boundary value problem is solved which results in a linear controller whose gains are obtained as a nonlinear function of these blocks. It is then shown that the nonlinear function of these partitioned blocks can be propagated by a matrix Riccati differential equation. The existence of the solution to this Riccati differential equation is a necessary and sufficient condition for the quadratic performance criterion to be positive definite. Also dependent upon the existence of the solution of the Riccati differential equation is a canonical similarity transformation which elegantly relates the original Hamiltonian system to the feedback dynamic system.

The linear-quadratic problem with terminal constraints is formulated by using the first-order necessary conditions. Again, the block partition form of the transition matrix enters the controller gain in a nonlinear form. Now, it is shown that the partitioned matrix nonlinear functions can be represented by combining the solution of the Riccati differential equation, obtained from the unconstrained problem, with the solution of a linear matrix differential equation and a quadrature integration. The invertibility of the quadrature integration is shown to be related to a controllability condition for reaching the specified terminal manifold. Additional properties of the Riccati differential equation are given which lead to obtaining results for the infinite-time, autonomous, linear-quadratic problem, called the linear regulator problem. In this problem, the symplectic property requires the $2n \times 2n$ Hamiltonian matrix to have eigenvalues that are symmetric about the origin. By the canonical similarity transformations introduced earlier, it is seen that the dynamic feedback contains all the left-half plane poles of the Hamiltonian matrix.

II. PRELIMINARIES AND PROBLEM FORMULATION

The problem of minimizing the quadratic performance criterion

$$J[u(\cdot); x(t_0), t_0]$$

$$= \frac{1}{2} x(t_f)^T S_f x(t_f) + \frac{1}{2}\int_{t_0}^{t_f} [x(t)^T Q(t) x(t)$$

$$+ 2u(t)^T C(t) x(t) + u(t)^T R(t) u(t)]\, dt \quad (1)$$

where $t \in \mathbb{R}$, $x(t) \in \mathbb{R}^n$ and $u(t) \in \mathbb{R}^m$, subject to the linear dynamic constraint

$$\dot{x}(t) = A(t)x(t) + B(t)u(t) \quad (2)$$

with initial condition

$$x(t_0) = x_0 \quad (3)$$

and terminal constraints

$$Dx(t_f) = 0 \quad (4)$$

where D is a $p \times n$ matrix, is to be studied in detail. The matrices $Q(t)$, $C(t)$, $R(t)$, $A(t)$, and $B(t)$ are assumed to be piecewise continuous functions of time and, without loss of generality, $R(t) = R(t)^T$, $Q(t) = Q(t)^T$, and $S_f = S_f^T$.

Assumption 1. $R(t) > 0$ for all t in the interval $t_0 \leq t \leq t_f$. The implication of relaxing this assumption to positive semidefinite R is discussed in Section XIV.

Assumption 2. The control function $u(\cdot)$ belongs to the class $\mathscr{U}$ of piecewise continuous m-vector functions of t in the interval $[t_0, t_f]$.

Initially, no additional restrictions are required for $Q(t)$ and S_f other than symmetry. However, in later sections special but important results are obtained by requiring that $Q(t)$ and

S_f be at least positive semidefinite. The initial time t_0, on occasion throughout this chapter, is considered to be a variable and not a fixed value. To denote this occurrence, the dummy variable t will be substituted for t_0.

III. FIRST-ORDER NECESSARY CONDITIONS FOR OPTIMALITY*

To include the dynamic and terminal constraints explicitly in the cost criterion, $J[u(\cdot); x(t_0), t_0]$ given by (1) is augmented by adjoining (2) by means of a continuously differentiable n-vector function of time $\lambda(\cdot)$ and (4) by means of a p-vector ν as

$$\begin{aligned}\hat{J}&[u(\cdot); \lambda(\cdot), \nu, x_0, t_0]\\ &\triangleq J[u(\cdot); x_0, t_0]\\ &\quad + \int_{t_0}^{t_f} \lambda(t)^T[A(t)x(t) + B(t)u(t) - \dot{x}(t)]\,dt\\ &\qquad + \nu^T Dx(t_f).\end{aligned} \tag{5}$$

Note that

$$\hat{J}[u(\cdot); \lambda(\cdot), \nu, x_0, t_0] = J[u(\cdot); x_0, t_0] \tag{6}$$

when (1) and (4) hold.

For convenience define the variational Hamiltonian as

$$\begin{aligned}\mathscr{H}&(x(t), \lambda(t), u(t), t)\\ &= \frac{1}{2}[x(t)^T Q(t)x(t) + 2u(t)^T C(t)x(t) + u(t)^T R(t)u(t)]\\ &\quad + \lambda(t)^T[A(t)x(t) + B(t)u(t)].\end{aligned} \tag{7}$$

**The approach taken in this section was partially extracted from some unpublished notes of D. H. Jacobson.*

Integration by parts and using (7) gives for (5)

$$\hat{J}[u(\cdot);\ \lambda(\cdot),\ \nu,\ x_0,\ t_0]$$

$$= \int_{t_0}^{t_f} [\mathscr{H}(x(t),\ \lambda(t),\ u(t),\ t) + \dot{\lambda}(t)^T x(t)]\ dt$$

$$+ \lambda(t_0)^T x_0 - \lambda(t_f)^T x(t_f) + \frac{1}{2}\ x(t_f)^T S_f x(t_f)$$

$$+ \nu^T D x(t_f). \qquad (8)$$

Suppose there is a control $u^0(\cdot) \in \mathscr{U}$ that minimizes (1) and causes the resulting optimal state trajectory $x^0(\cdot)$ to satisfy

$$Dx^0(t_f) = 0. \qquad (9)$$

The objective is to determine necessary conditions for which the cost is a minimum. This is done by evaluating changes in $\hat{J}$ brought about by changing $u^0(\cdot)$ to $u(\cdot) \in \mathscr{U}$. Denote the change in the control as $\delta u(t) \triangleq u(t) - u^0(t)$ and the resulting change in the state as $\delta x(t) \triangleq x(t) - x^0(t)$. Therefore,

$$\Delta J(u(\cdot),\ u^0(\cdot);\ \lambda(\cdot),\ \nu,\ x_0,\ t_0)$$

$$\triangleq \Delta J$$

$$= \hat{J}(u(\cdot);\ \lambda(\cdot),\ \nu,\ x_0,\ t_0) - \hat{J}(u^0(\cdot);\ \lambda(\cdot),\ \nu,\ x_0,\ t_0)$$

$$= \int_{t_0}^{t_f} \Big[\frac{1}{2}\ \delta x(t)^T Q(t)\ \delta x(t) + x^0(t)^T Q(t)\ \delta x(t)$$

$$+ u^0(t)^T C(t)\ \delta x(t) + \delta u(t)^T C(t)\ \delta x(t)$$

$$+ x^0(t)^T C(t)^T\ \delta u(t) + \frac{1}{2}\ \delta u(t)^T R(t)\ \delta u(t)$$

$$+ u^0(t)^T R(t)\ \delta u(t) + \dot{\lambda}(t)^T\ \delta x(t) + \lambda(t)^T A(t)\ \delta x(t)$$

$$+ \lambda(t)^T B(t)\ \delta u(t)\Big]\ dt$$

$$- \lambda(t_f)^T\ \delta x(t_f) + \frac{1}{2}\ \delta x(t_f)^T S_f\ \delta x(t_f)$$

$$+ x^0(t_f)^T S_f\ \delta x(t_f) + \nu^T D\ \delta x(t_f). \qquad (10)$$

Now set

$$-\dot{\lambda}(t)^T = x^0(t)^T Q(t) + u^0(t)^T C(t) + \lambda(t)^T A(t),$$
$$\lambda(t_f)^T = x^0(t_f)^T S_f + \nu^T D. \tag{11}$$

For fixed ν this is a legitimate choice for $\lambda(\cdot)$, since (11) is a linear differential equation in $\lambda(t)$ with continuous coefficients, having a unique solution [14]. Then (10) becomes

$$\Delta J = \int_{t_0}^{t_f} \left[\frac{1}{2}\,\delta x(t)^T Q(t)\,\delta x(t) + \delta u(t)^T C(t)\,\delta x(t) + \frac{1}{2}\,\delta u(t)^T R(t)\,\delta u(t) + (u^0(t)^T R(t) + x^0(t)^T C(t)^T + \lambda(t)^T B(t))\,\delta u(t)\right] dt + \frac{1}{2}\,\delta x(t_f)^T S_f\,\delta x(t_f). \tag{12}$$

We require conditions that guarantee that $\Delta J \geq 0$. First, the variations are limited to those for which $\delta x(t)$ remains small, i.e., $\|\delta x(t)\| \leq \bar{\epsilon}$ for all $t \in [t_0, t_f]$. However, strong variations in δu are allowed. For example, $\delta u(\cdot)$ can be chosen as

$$\delta u(t) = \epsilon(t)\eta(t) \tag{13}$$

where $\eta(t) \in \mathscr{U}$ and

$$\epsilon(t) = \begin{cases} 1, & t_i \leq t \leq t_i + \epsilon\delta_i, \quad i = 1, \ldots, N, \\ \epsilon, & t \in I_\epsilon \triangleq \{[0, T] - \bigcup_i [t_i, t_i + \epsilon\delta_i]\} \end{cases} \tag{14}$$

where $\epsilon > 0$ is sufficiently small, the δ_i's are positive constants, and t_i, $t_i + \epsilon\delta_i \in [t_0, t_f]$ are arbitrary so that

$$\int_{t_0}^{t_f} \left[\frac{1}{2}\,\delta x(t)^T Q(t)\,\delta x(t) + \delta u(t)^T C(t)\,\delta x(t)\right] dt + \frac{1}{2}\,\delta x(t_f)^T S_f\,\delta x(t_f) = O(\epsilon) \tag{15}$$

where

$$O(\epsilon)/\epsilon \to 0 \quad \text{as} \quad \epsilon \to 0. \tag{16}$$

For ϵ sufficiently small (12) is rewritten using (7) as*

$$\Delta J = \int_{t_0}^{t_f} \left[\frac{1}{2}\, \delta u(t)^T R(t)\, \delta u(t) + \mathscr{H}_u(x^0(t), \lambda(t), u^0(t), t)\, \delta u\right] dt + O(\epsilon). \tag{17}$$

Since $R(t) > 0$ for $t \in [t_0, t_f]$, the cost function can be reduced if the second term is made negative. This is easily done by choosing $\eta(t) \in \mathscr{U}$ as

$$\eta(t) = -R(t)^{-1} \mathscr{H}_u(x^0(t), \lambda(t), u^0(t), t)^T. \tag{18}$$

Note that in arbitrary small intervals where $\epsilon(t) = 1$, this choice minimizes the integral in (17).

This choice of η is particularly significant since it can be shown under an additional assumption that there exists a ν such that $\eta(\cdot)$ given by (18) causes (9) to hold.

Assumption 3. The $p \times p$ matrix $\overline{W}(t_0, t_f)$ is positive definite where**

$$\overline{W}(t_0, t_f) \triangleq \sum_{i=1}^{N} D\Phi_A(t_f, t_i)B(t_i)R(t_i)^{-1}B(t_i)^T\Phi_A(t_f, t_i)^T D^T \delta_i + \int_{I_0} D\Phi_A(t_f, t)B(t)R(t)^{-1}B(t)^T\Phi_A(t_f, t)^T\, dt\, D^T. \tag{19}$$

where I_0 is I_ϵ evaluated at $\epsilon = 0$. This assumption is essentially the controllability condition [13] when $p = n$ and D has rank n.

*The subscript on $\mathscr{H}$ denotes partial differentiation.

**Let $\Phi_A(\cdot, \cdot)$ denote the transition matrix of the system $\dot{y}(t) = A(t)y(t)$, where $\dot{\Phi}_A(t, t_0) = A(t)\Phi_A(t, t_0)$, $\Phi_A(t_0, t_0) = I$.

From the linearity of (2), $z(t;\ \eta(\cdot))$ satisfies the equation

$$z(t_f;\ \eta(\cdot)) = \sum_{i=1}^{N} \Phi_A(t_f,\ t_i)B(t_i)\eta(t_i)\ \delta_i + \int_{I_o} \Phi_A(t_f,\ t)B(t)\eta(t)\ dt \tag{20}$$

where the state perturbation is

$$\delta x(t_f) = \epsilon z(t_f;\ \eta(\cdot)) + O(\epsilon). \tag{21}$$

Therefore, $z(t_f;\ (\eta(\cdot))$ is the gradient of $x(t_f)$ with respect to ϵ when using (13). By using (18) it is shown that to first order there exists a ν such that $Dz(t_f;\ \eta(\cdot)) = 0$. This requires solving the linear forced equation (11) as

$$\lambda(t) = \underline{\lambda}(t) + \Phi_A(t_f,\ t)^T D^T \nu \tag{22}$$

where

$$\underline{\lambda}(t) = \Phi_A(t_f,\ t)^T S_f x^0(t_f) + \Phi_A(t_f,\ t)^T D^T \nu + \int_t^{t_f} \Phi_A(\tau,\ t)^T (Q(\tau)x^0(\tau)^T + C(\tau)^T u^0(\tau)^T)\ d\tau. \tag{23}$$

By premultiplying (20) by D and using (18) for $\eta(\cdot)$, then

$$\begin{aligned} Dz(t_f;\ \eta(\cdot)) = &-\sum_{i=1}^{N} D\Phi_A(t_f,\ t_i)B(t_i)\ \delta_i R(t_i)^{-1} \\ &\times \left[R(t_i)u(t_i) + C(t_i)x^0(t_i) + B(t_i)^T \underline{\lambda}(t_i)\right] \\ &- \int_{I_0} D\Phi_A(t_f,\ t)^T B(t)R(t)^{-1} \\ &\times \left[R(t)u^0(t) + C(t)x^0(t) + B(t)^T \underline{\lambda}(t)\right] dt \\ &- \overline{W}(t_0,\ t_f)\nu = 0. \end{aligned} \tag{24}$$

By Assumption 3 the coefficient of ν can be inverted and ν can be determined indpendent of ϵ. Furthermore, by Assumption 3 and the implicit function theorem, for $\epsilon > 0$ and sufficiently small there exists a ν such that

$$D\ \delta x(t_f) = \epsilon D z(t_f;\ \eta(\cdot)) + DO(\epsilon) = 0 \tag{25}$$

when using $\eta(\cdot)$ given in (18). Consequently, with this choice of $\eta(\cdot)$, (6) holds and the change in J is

$$\Delta J = -\frac{1}{2}\left[\sum_{i=1}^{N} \|\mathscr{H}_u\|^2_{R(t)^{-1}}\ \delta_i + \int_{I_0} \|\mathscr{H}_u\|^2_{R(t)^{-1}}\ dt\right]\epsilon + O(\epsilon). \tag{26}$$

Note that $O(\epsilon)$ includes all higher-order variations such that (16) holds. Since the time intervals in (14) are arbitrary, the control is not restricted to only small variations. Therefore, a necessary condition for the cost J to be nonnegative for arbitrary strong variations $\delta u(t)$ is that

$$H_u(x^0(t),\ \lambda(t),\ u^0(t),\ t) = 0. \tag{27}$$

The above results are summarized in the following theorem.

Theorem 1

Suppose that Assumptions 1-3 are satisfied. Then the necessary conditions for J to be nonnegative to first order for strong perturbations in the control (13) is that

$$\dot{x}^0(t) = A(t)x^0(t) + B(t)u^0(t), \quad x^0(t_0) = x_0, \tag{28}$$

$$\dot{\lambda}(t) = -A(t)^T\lambda(t) - Q(t)x^0(t) - C(t)^T u^0(t),$$
$$\lambda(t_f) = S_f x^0(t_f) + D^T\nu, \tag{29}$$

$$0 = R(t)u^0(t) + C(t)x^0(t) + B(t)^T\lambda(t). \tag{30}$$

The remaining difficulty resides with the convexity of the cost associated with the neglected second-order terms. The objective of the remaining sections is to give necessary and sufficient conditions for optimality and to understand more deeply the character of the optimal solution when it exists.

IV. SOLUTION OF THE LINEAR-QUADRATIC PROBLEM USING THE FIRST-ORDER NECESSARY CONDITIONS--A TRANSITION MATRIX APPROACH

By applying the first-order necessary conditions of Theorem 1 to the problem of Eqs. (1)-(3), the resulting necessary conditions for the unconstrained terminal problem are given by (28)-(30) where D = 0 in (29). By Assumption 1, the extremal $u^0(t)$ can be determined from (30) as a function of $x^0(t)$ and $\lambda(t)$, as

$$u^0(t) = -R(t)^{-1}[C(t)x^0(t) + B(t)^T\lambda(t)]. \tag{31}$$

Substitution of $u^0(t)$ given by (31) into (28) and (29) results in the linear homogeneous 2n-vector differential equation

$$\begin{bmatrix} \dot{x}^0(t) \\ \dot{\lambda}(t) \end{bmatrix} = \begin{bmatrix} A(t) - B(t)R(t)^{-1}C(t) & -B(t)R(t)^{-1}B(t)^T \\ -Q(t) + C(t)^T R(t)^{-1}C(t) & -(A(t) - B(t)R(t)^{-1}C(t))^T \end{bmatrix} \times \begin{bmatrix} x^0(t) \\ \lambda(t) \end{bmatrix}. \tag{32}$$

Equation (32) is solved as a two-point boundary value problem where n conditions are given at the initial time (28) and n conditions are specified at the final time as $\lambda(t_f) = S_f x^0(t_f)$.

For convenience, define the Hamiltonian matrix as

$$H(t) \triangleq \begin{bmatrix} A(t) - B(t)R(t)^{-1}C(t) & -B(t)R(t)^{-1}B(t)^T \\ -Q(t) + C(t)^T R(t)^{-1}C(t) & -(A(t) - B(t)R(t)^{-1}C(t))^T \end{bmatrix} \tag{33}$$

and the transition matrix associated with the solution of Eq. (32) in a block-partitioned form [see footnote associated with (19)].

$$\Phi_H(t, \tau) \triangleq \begin{bmatrix} \Phi_{11}(t, \tau) & \Phi_{12}(t, \tau) \\ \Phi_{21}(t, \tau) & \Phi_{22}(t, \tau) \end{bmatrix} \tag{34}$$

where t is the output time and τ is the input time. Using this block-partitioned transition matrix, the solution to (32) is represented as

$$\begin{bmatrix} x^0(t_f) \\ \lambda(t_f) \end{bmatrix} = \begin{bmatrix} x^0(t_f) \\ S_f x^0(t_f) \end{bmatrix}$$

$$= \begin{bmatrix} \Phi_{11}(t_f, t_0) & \Phi_{12}(t_f, t_0) \\ \Phi_{21}(t_f, t_0) & \Phi_{22}(t_f, t_0) \end{bmatrix} \begin{bmatrix} x^0(t_0) \\ \lambda(t_0) \end{bmatrix}. \tag{35}$$

The objective is to obtain a unique relation between $\lambda(t_0)$ and $x^0(t_0)$ using (35). From (35), the first matrix equation gives

$$x^0(t_f) = \Phi_{11}(t_f, t_0)x^0(t_0) + \Phi_{12}(t_f, t_0)\lambda(t_0). \tag{36}$$

The second matrix equation of (35), using (36) to eliminate $x^0(t_f)$, becomes

$$S_f\left[\Phi_{11}(t_f, t_0)x^0(t_0) + \Phi_{12}(t_f, t_0)\lambda(t_0)\right]$$
$$= \Phi_{21}(t_f, t_0)x^0(t_0) + \Phi_{22}(t_f, t_0)\lambda(t_0). \tag{37}$$

By solving for $\lambda(t_0)$, assuming all necessary matrix inverses exist,

$$\lambda(t_0) = [S_f\Phi_{12}(t_f, t_0) - \Phi_{22}(t_f, t_0)]^{-1}$$
$$\times [\Phi_{21}(t_f, t_0) - S_f\Phi_{11}(t_f, t_0)]x^0(t_0). \tag{38}$$

The invertibility of this matrix is crucial to the problem solution and is discussed in detail in the following sections. The result (38) is of central importance to the linear-quadratic theory because this allows the optimal control (31) to be expressed as an explicit linear function of the state. For convenience, define the variable

$$S(t_f, t; S_f) \triangleq [S_f\Phi_{12}(t_f, t) - \Phi_{22}(t_f, t)]^{-1} \times [\Phi_{21}(t_f, t) - S_f\Phi_{11}(t_f, t)]. \tag{39}$$

If the transition matrix is evaluated over the interval $[t_0, t]$, where $t_0 \leq t \leq t_f$, then

$$\begin{bmatrix} x^0(t) \\ \lambda(t) \end{bmatrix} = \Phi_H(t, t_0)\begin{bmatrix} I \\ S(t_f, t_0; S_f) \end{bmatrix} x^0(t_0). \tag{40}$$

Substitution of (40) into (31) results in the general optimal control rule

$$u^0(t) = -R(t)^{-1}[C(t), B(t)]\Phi_H(t, t_0) \times \begin{bmatrix} I \\ S(t_f, t_0; S_f) \end{bmatrix} x^0(t_0). \tag{41}$$

This control rule can be interpreted as a sample data controller if $x^0(t_0)$ is the state measured at the last sample time and t, the present time, lies within the interval $[t_0, t_0 + \Delta]$, where Δ is the time between samples. If t_0 is considered to be the present time t, then (41) reduces to the continuous optimal control rule

$$u^0(t) = -R(t)^{-1}[C(t) + B(t)S(t_f, t; S_f)]x^0(t). \tag{42}$$

This linear control rule forms the basis for linear-quadratic control synthesis.

Our objective is to understand the properties of this control rule. More precisely, the character of $S(t_f, t; S_f)$ and the transition matrix $\Phi_H(t, t_0)$ are to be studied. Beginning in the next section, some properties peculiar to Hamiltonian systems are presented.

V. THE SYMPLECTIC PROPERTY OF THE TRANSITION MATRIX OF HAMILTONIAN SYSTEMS

The transition matrix of the Hamiltonian system (32) has the useful symplectic property [15,16], defined as

$$\Phi_H(t, t_0)\underline{J}\Phi_H(t, t_0)^T = \underline{J} \tag{43}$$

where

$$\underline{J} \triangleq \begin{bmatrix} 0 & I \\ -I & 0 \end{bmatrix}. \tag{44}$$

To show that the transition matrix of our Hamiltonian system satisfies (43), we time-differentiate (43) as

$$\dot{\Phi}_H(t, t_0)\underline{J}\Phi_H(t, t_0)^T + \Phi_H(t, t_0)\underline{J}\dot{\Phi}_H(t, t_0)^T = 0. \tag{45}$$

Substitution of the differential equation for $\Phi_H(t, t_0)$ [see footnote associated with (19)] into (45) results in

$$H(t)\Phi_H(t, t_0)\underline{J}\Phi_H(t, t_0)^T + \Phi_H(t, t_0)\underline{J}\Phi_H(t, t_0)^T H(t)^T = 0. \tag{46}$$

By using (43), (46) reduces to

$$H(t)\underline{J} + \underline{J}H(t)^T = 0 \tag{47}$$

where $H(t)$ defined by (33) clearly satisfies (47).

Note that since $\underline{J}^T = \underline{J}^{-1}$, then from (43)

$$\Phi_H(t, t_0)^{-1} = \underline{J}\Phi_H(t, t_0)^T\underline{J}^T. \tag{48}$$

Furthermore, the characteristic equations of $\Phi_H(t, t_0)$ and $\Phi_H(t, t_0)^{-1}$ are the same since

$$\begin{aligned} \mathrm{Det}\left(\Phi_H(t, t_0)^{-1} - \lambda I\right) &= \mathrm{Det}\left(\underline{J}\Phi_H(t, t_0)^T\underline{J}^T - \lambda I\right) \\ &= \mathrm{Det}\left(\underline{J}\Phi_H(t, t_0)^T\underline{J}^T - \lambda\underline{J}\underline{J}^T\right) \\ &= \mathrm{Det}\left(\Phi_H(t, t_0)^T - \lambda I\right). \end{aligned} \tag{49}$$

The implication of this is that since $\Phi_H(t, t_0)$ is a $2n \times 2n$ matrix and μ_i, $i = 1, \ldots, n$, are n eigenvalues of $\Phi_H(t, t_0)$, then the remaining n eigenvalues are

$$\mu_{i+n} = 1/\mu_i, \quad i = 1, \ldots, n. \tag{50}$$

By partitioning $\Phi_H(t, t_0)$ as in (34), the following relations are obtained from (43):

$$\Phi_{11}(t, t_0)\Phi_{12}(t, t_0)^T = \Phi_{12}(t, t_0)\Phi_{11}(t, t_0)^T, \tag{51}$$

$$\Phi_{21}(t, t_0)\Phi_{22}(t, t_0)^T = \Phi_{22}(t, t_0)\Phi_{21}(t, t_0)^T, \tag{52}$$

$$\Phi_{11}(t, t_0)\Phi_{22}(t, t_0)^T - \Phi_{12}(t, t_0)\Phi_{21}(t, t_0)^T = I. \tag{53}$$

These identities will be used later.

VI. THE RICCATI MATRIX DIFFERENTIAL EQUATION

Instead of forming $S(t_f, t; S_f)$ by calculating the transition matrix, in this section we show that $S(t_f, t; S_f)$ can be propagated directly by a quadratic matrix differential equation called the matrix Riccati equation. This equation plays a key role in all of the following sections.

A few preliminaries will help simplify this derivation as well as others in coming sections. First, note that since $\Phi_H(t, \tau)$ is symplectic, then

$$\bar{\Phi}_H(t, \tau) \triangleq L\Phi_H(t, \tau) \tag{54}$$

is also a symplectic matrix where

$$L \triangleq \begin{bmatrix} I & 0 \\ -S_f & I \end{bmatrix}. \tag{55}$$

Therefore, the partitioned form of $\bar{\Phi}_H(t, \tau)$ satisfies (51)-(53). Secondly, by using the propagation equation for the transition matrix [see footnote associated with (19)], differentiation of the identity

$$\Phi_H(t_f, t)\Phi_H(t, t_0) = \Phi_H(t_f, t_0) \tag{56}$$

with respect to t, where t_f and t_0 are two fixed times, gives the adjoint form for propagating the transition matrix as

$$(d/dt)\Phi_H(t_f, t) = -\Phi_H(t_f, t)H(t), \quad \Phi_H(t_f, t_f) = I \tag{57}$$

where input time is the independent variable and the output time is fixed. Therefore,

$$(d/dt)\overline{\Phi}_H(t_f, t) = -\overline{\Phi}_H(t_f, t)H(t), \quad \overline{\Phi}_H(t_f, t_f) = L. \tag{58}$$

Finally, note from (39) and (54) that

$$S(t_f, t; S_f) = -\overline{\Phi}_{22}(t_f, t)^{-1}\overline{\Phi}_{21}(t_f, t). \tag{59}$$

Theorem 2 [13]

Let $\Phi_H(t_f, t)$ be the transition matrix for the dynamic system (32) with partitioning given by (34). Then, a symmetric matrix $S(t_f, t; S_f)$ satisfies

$$\begin{aligned}(d/dt)S(t_f, t; S_f) = &-(A(t) - B(t)R(t)^{-1}C(t))^T S(t_f, t; S_f)\\ &- S(t_f, t; S_f)(A(t) - B(t)R(t)^{-1}C(t))\\ &- [Q(t) - C(t)^T R(t)^{-1}C(t)]\\ &+ S(t_f, t; S_f)B(t)R(t)^{-1}B(t)^T S(t_f, t; S_f);\end{aligned}$$

$$S(t_f, t_f; S_f) = S_f \tag{60}$$

if the indicated inverse of (59) exists and S_f is symmetric.

Proof. If (59) is rewritten as

$$-\overline{\Phi}_{21}(t_f, t) = \overline{\Phi}_{22}(t_f, t)S(t_f, t; S_f) \tag{61}$$

and differentiated with respect to t, then

$$-(d/dt)\left[\bar{\Phi}_{21}(t_f, t)\right]$$
$$= (d/dt)\left[\bar{\Phi}_{22}(t_f, t)\right]S(t_f, t; S_f)$$
$$+ \bar{\Phi}_{22}(t_f, t)(d/dt)[S(t_f, t; S_f)]. \quad (62)$$

The derivatives for $\bar{\Phi}_{21}(t_f, t)$ and $\bar{\Phi}_{22}(t_f, t)$ are obtained from the partitioning of (58) as

$$\bar{\Phi}_{21}(t_f, t)(A(t) - B(t)R(t)^{-1}C(t))$$
$$- \bar{\Phi}_{22}(t_f, t)(A(t) - C(t)^T R(t)^{-1}C(t))$$
$$= \left[\bar{\Phi}_{21}(t_f, t)B(t)R(t)^{-1}B(t)^T\right.$$
$$\left.+ \bar{\Phi}_{22}(t_f, t)(A(t) - B(t)R(t)^{-1}C(t))^T\right]$$
$$\times S(t_f, t; S_f) + \bar{\Phi}_{22}(t_f, t)\frac{dS(t_f, t; S_f)}{dt}. \quad (63)$$

Since $\bar{\Phi}_{22}(t_f, t)$ is assumed invertible, then by premultiplying by $\bar{\Phi}_{22}(t_f, t)^{-1}$ and using (59), the Riccati equation of (60) is obtained. Since S_f is symmetric, and

$$dS(t_f, t; S_f)/dt \triangleq \dot{S}(t_f, t; S_f) = \dot{S}(t_f, t; S_f)^T,$$

then $S(t_f, t; S_f)$ will be symmetric.

Remark 1. By the symplectic property (52) using (54)

$$S(t_f, t; S_f) = -\bar{\Phi}_{22}(t_f, t)^{-1}\bar{\Phi}_{21}(t_f, t)$$
$$= -\bar{\Phi}_{21}(t_f, t)^T\bar{\Phi}_{22}(t_f, t)^{-T} \quad (64)$$

implies that $S(t_f, t; 0)$ is symmetric.

Remark 2. Since the boundary condition on $\bar{\Phi}_{22}(t_f, t_f)$ is the identity matrix, a finite interval of time is needed before $\bar{\Phi}_{22}(t_f, t)$ may no longer be invertible and the control law of (42) is no longer meaningful. In the classical literature this is the focal point condition or Jacobi condition [6].

In the next section, it is shown that if the Riccati variable exists, then the Hamiltonian system can be transformed into another similar Hamiltonian system for which the feedback law appears directly in the dynamic system.

VII. A CANONICAL TRANSFORMATION OF THE HAMILTONIAN SYSTEM

Some additional insight into the character of this Hamiltonian system is obtained by a canonical similarity transformation of the variables $x^0(t)$ and $\lambda(t)$ into a new set of variables $x^0(t)$ and $\bar{\lambda}(t)$. A transformation $L(t)$ for Hamiltonian systems is said to be canonical if it satisfies the symplectic property

$$L(t)\underline{J}L(t)^T = \underline{J} \tag{65}$$

where $\underline{J}$ is defined in (44).

The canonical transformation that produces the desired result is

$$L(t) \triangleq \begin{bmatrix} I & 0 \\ -S(t_f,\ t;\ S_f) & I \end{bmatrix} \tag{66}$$

such that

$$\begin{bmatrix} x^0(t) \\ \bar{\lambda}(t) \end{bmatrix} = \begin{bmatrix} I & 0 \\ -S(t_f,\ t;\ S_f) & I \end{bmatrix} \begin{bmatrix} x^0(t) \\ \lambda(t) \end{bmatrix}. \tag{67}$$

L is a canonical transformation since $S(t_f,\ t;\ S_f)$ is symmetric. Note that the state variables are not being transformed. The propagation equation for the new variables is obtained by differentiating (67) and using (32) as

$$\begin{bmatrix} \dot{x}^0(t) \\ \dot{\overline{\lambda}}(t) \end{bmatrix} = \begin{bmatrix} A(t) - B(t)R(t)^{-1} \times \left(C(t) + B(t)^T S(t_f, t; S_f)\right), & -B(t)R(t)^{-1}B(t)^T \\ 0, & -\left[A(t) - B(t)R(t)^{-1} \times \left(C(t) + B(t)^T S(t_f, t; S_f)\right)\right]^T \end{bmatrix} \times \begin{bmatrix} x^0(t) \\ \overline{\lambda}(t) \end{bmatrix}; \tag{68}$$

$$\begin{bmatrix} x^0(t_f) \\ \overline{\lambda}(t_f) \end{bmatrix} = L(t_f)\begin{bmatrix} x^0(t_f) \\ S_f x^0(t_f) \end{bmatrix}$$

where use is made of the inverse of L(t):

$$L(t)^{-1} = \begin{bmatrix} I & 0 \\ S(t_f, t; S_f) & I \end{bmatrix}. \tag{69}$$

The zero matrix in the coefficient matrix of (68) is a direct consequence of $S(t_f, t; S_f)$ satisfying the Riccati equation (60).

Note that from the boundary condition of (68)

$$\overline{\lambda}(t_f) = [S_f - S(t_f, t_f; S_f)]x^0(t_f). \tag{70}$$

Since $S(t_f, t_f; S_f) = S_f$,

$$\overline{\lambda}(t_f) = 0. \tag{71}$$

Observe in (68) that $\overline{\lambda}(t)$ is propagated by a homogenous differential equation which by (71) has a solution $\overline{\lambda}(t) = 0$ for all t in the interval $[t_0, t_f]$. Therefore, (68) produces the differential equation for the state as

$$\dot{x}^0(t) = \Big[A(t) - B(t)R(t)^{-1} \times \Big(C(t) + B(t)^T S(t_f, t; S_f)\Big)\Big]x^0(t), \tag{72}$$

$$x^0(t_0) = x_0$$

which is the dynamic equation using the optimal control rule (42).

The existence of the Riccati variable is necessary for the existence of the linear control rule and the above canonical transformation. In the next section it is shown that the existence of the Riccati variable $S(t_f, t; S_f)$ is necessary and sufficient condition for the quadratic cost criterion to be positive definite, i.e., it is a necessary and sufficient condition for the linear controller to be the minimizing controller.

VIII. NECESSARY AND SUFFICIENT CONDITION FOR THE POSITIVITY OF THE QUADRATIC COST CRITERION

We show here that the quadratic cost criterion is actually positive for all controls which are not null when the initial condition is $x(t_0) = 0$. The essential assumption, besides $R(t) > 0$, is complete controllability. The essential ideas in this section were given in [11,12].

Assumption 4. The dynamic system (2) is completely controllable on the interval $[t_0, t']$, where $t_0 \le t' \le t_f$.

If the system is completely controllable, then a bounded control

$$\overline{u}(t) = B^T(t)\Phi_A^T(t', t)W_A\big(t', t_0\big)^{-1} x(t') \tag{73}$$

always exists which transfers the state $x(t_0) = 0$ to any desired state $x(t')$ at $t = t'$ where $W_A(t', t_0)$, the controllability Gramian matrix, is

$$W_A(t', t_0) = \int_{t_0}^{t'} \Phi_A(t', t)B(t)B^T(t)\Phi_A(t', t)^T\, dt > 0 \quad (74)$$

where

$$(d/dt)\Phi_A(t, \sigma) = A(t)\Phi_A(t, \sigma), \qquad \Phi_A(\sigma, \sigma) = I \quad (75)$$

for all t' in $(t_0, t_f]$.

Definition 1. $J[u(\cdot); 0, t_0]$ is said to be positive definite if for each $u(\cdot)$ in $\mathscr{U}$, $u(\cdot) \neq \emptyset$ (null function), $J[(\cdot); 0, t_0] > 0$.

We show first that if there exists for all t in $[t_0, t_f]$ an $S(t_f, t; S_f)$ which satisfies (54), then $J[u(\cdot); 0, t_0]$ is positive definite. Consider adding to $J[u(\cdot); x(t_0), t_0]$ of (1) the identically zero quantity

$$\frac{1}{2}\, x(t_0)^T S(t_f, t_0; S_f)x(t_0) - \frac{1}{2}\, x(t_f)^T S(t_f, t_f; S_f)x(t_f)$$
$$+ \int_{t_0}^{t_f} \frac{1}{2}\frac{d}{dt}\Big[x(t)^T S(t_f, t; S_f)x(t)\Big]\, dt = 0. \quad (76)$$

This can be rewritten using the Riccati equation (60) and the dynamics (2) as

$$\frac{1}{2}\, x(t_0)^T S(t_f, t_0; S_f)x(t_0) - \frac{1}{2}\, x(t_f)^T S_f x(t_f)$$
$$+ \int_{t_0}^{t_f} \Bigg\{ -\frac{1}{2}\, x(t)^T \Big[Q(t) + S(t_f, t; S_f)A(t) + A(t)^T S(t_f, t; S_f)$$
$$- \Big(C(t) + B(t)^T S(t_f, t; S_f)\Big)^T R(t)^{-1}$$
$$\times \Big(C(t) + B(t)^T S(t_f, t; S_f)\Big)\Big] x(t)$$

$$+ \frac{1}{2} x(t)^T \left[S(t_f, t; S_f)A(t) + A(t)^T S(t_f, t; S_f)\right] x(t)$$

$$+ 2x(t)^T S(t_f, t; S_f)B(t)u(t) \Big\} dt = 0. \tag{77}$$

If (77) is added to (1), the integrand can be manipulated into a perfect square where the cost takes the form

$$J[u(\cdot); x(t_0), t_0]$$

$$= \frac{1}{2} x(t_0)^T S(t_f, t_0; S_f) x(t_0)$$

$$+ \int_{t_0}^{t_f} \frac{1}{2}\Big[u(t) + R(t)^{-1}\Big(C(t)$$

$$+ B(t)^T S(t_f, t; S_f)\Big) x(t)\Big]^T R(t)$$

$$\times \Big[u(t) + R(t)^{-1}\Big(C(t) + B(t)^T S(t_f, t; S_f)\Big) x(t)\Big] dt. \tag{78}$$

Therefore, the cost takes on its minimum value when $u(t)$ takes the form of the optimal controller (42). If $x(t_0)$ is zero, then the optimal control is the null control. Any other control $u(\cdot) \neq u^0(\cdot)$ will give a positive value to $J[u(\cdot); 0, t_0]$.

If the cost $J[u(\cdot); 0, t_0]$ is positive definite, then the necessity of the existence of the Riccati variable $S(t_f, t; S_f)$ depends on Assumption 4. First note, from Section VI, that for some t' close enough to t_f, $S(t_f, t; S_f)$ exists for $t' \leq t \leq t_f$. Therefore, by using the optimal control from t' to t_f for some $x(t')$, the extremal cost is

$$J[u^0(\cdot); x(t'), t'] = \frac{1}{2} x(t')^T S(t_f, t'; S_f) x(t'). \tag{79}$$

We argue for the necessity of the existence of $S(t_f, t; S_f)$ for optimality by supposing the opposite; that $S(t_f, t; S_f)$ ceases to exist at some escape time,* t_e. If this occurs, then

Since the Riccati equation is nonlinear, then the solution may approach infinite values for finite values of time. This time is called the escape time.

either the cost criterion can be made as negative as we like, which violates the positive-definite assumption on the cost criterion, or as positive as desired, which violates the assumption of minimality. The cost, using the control defined as

$$\begin{aligned} u(t) &= \bar{u}(t), \qquad t_0 \le t \le t', \\ u(t) &= u^0(t), \qquad t' < t \le t_f, \end{aligned} \tag{80}$$

can be written as

$$J[u(\cdot);\ 0,\ t_0] = \int_{t_0}^{t'} \left[\frac{1}{2}\, x(t)^T Q(t) x(t) + \bar{u}(t)^T C(t) x(t) + \frac{1}{2}\, \bar{u}(t)^T R(t) \bar{u}(t) \right] dt + \frac{1}{2}\, x(t')^T S(t_f,\ t';\ S_f) x(t') \tag{81}$$

where by Assumption 4 there exists a control $\bar{u}(t)$ for $t \in [t_0, t']$ which transfers $x(t_0) = 0$ to any $x(t')$ at $t = t' > t_0$ such that $\|x(t')\| = 1$ and $\|\bar{u}(\cdot)\| \le \rho(t') < \infty$ where $\rho(\cdot)$ is a continuous function.

Since $\|\bar{u}(\cdot)\|$ is bounded by the controllability assumption, the integral in (81) is also bounded. If $x(t')^T S(t_f, t'; S_f) x(t') \to -\infty$ as $t' \to t_e (t_e < t')$ for some $x(t')$, then $J[u(\cdot); 0, t_0] \to -\infty$. But this violates the assumption that $J[u(\cdot); 0, t_0] \ge 0$. Furthermore, $x(t')^T S(t_f, t'; S_f) x(t')$ cannot go to positive infinity since this implies that the minimal cost $J[u^0(\cdot); x(t'), t']$ can be made infinite. But the controllability assumption implies that there is a finite control which gives a finite cost. Therefore, since the integral in (81) can be bounded, $x(t')^T S(t_f, t'; S_f) x(t')$ cannot go to ∞. Our arguments apply to the interval $(t_0, t_f]$. We appeal to Gelfand and Fomin [1] to verify that $S(t_f, t; S_f)$ exists for all t in $[t_0, t_f]$.

These results are summarized in the following theorem.

Theorem 3

Suppose that system (2) is completely controllable. A necessary and sufficient condition for $J[u(\cdot); 0, t_0]$ to be positive definite is that there exists a function $S(t_f, t; S_f)$ for all t in $[t_0, t_f]$ which satisfies the Riccati equation (60).

Note that since no smallness requirements are placed on $x(t)$ as in Section III, Theorem 3 is a statement of the global optimality of the solution to the linear quadratic problem.

IX. THE LINEAR-QUADRATIC PROBLEM WITH LINEAR TERMINAL CONSTRAINTS--A TRANSITION MATRIX APPROACH

The first-order necessary conditions of Theorem 1 are now used for the optimal control problem of (1)-(4) where the terminal constraints (4) and boundary condition

$$\lambda(t_f) = S_f x^0(t_f) + D^T\nu \tag{82}$$

are explicitly included. The two-point boundary value problem of Theorem 1 is solved in a manner similar to that of Section IV by using the transition matrix (35) as

$$x^0(t_f) = \Phi_{11}(t_f, t_0)x(t_0) + \Phi_{12}(t_f, t_0)\lambda(t_0), \tag{83}$$

$$\begin{aligned}\lambda(t_f) &= \Phi_{21}(t_f, t_0)x(t_0) + \Phi_{22}(t_f, t_0)\lambda(t_0)\\ &= D^T\nu + S_f x^0(t_f).\end{aligned} \tag{84}$$

From (84) the relation between $\lambda(t_0)$ and $(\nu, x(t_0))$, assuming that $\overline{\Phi}_{22}(t_f, t_0)$ defined in (54) is invertible, is

$$\begin{aligned}\lambda(t_0) = &-\overline{\Phi}_{22}(t_f, t_0)^{-1}\overline{\Phi}_{21}(t_f, t_0)x_0\\ &+ \overline{\Phi}_{22}(t_f, t_0)^{-1}D^T\nu.\end{aligned} \tag{85}$$

This is introduced into (83) which in turn is introduced into (4), producing

$$Dx^0(t_f) = D\left[\bar{\Phi}_{11}(t_f, t_0) - \bar{\Phi}_{12}(t_f, t_0)\bar{\Phi}_{22}(t_f, t_0)^{-1} \times \bar{\Phi}_{21}(t_f, t_0)\right]x_0 + D\bar{\Phi}_{12}(t_f, t_0)\bar{\Phi}_{22}(t_f, t_0)^{-1}D^T\nu = 0. \tag{86}$$

The symplectic property of the Hamiltonian transition matrix is used to reduce the coefficient of x_0 in (86). By using the symplectic identity (53) for the symplectic matrix $\bar{\Phi}_H(t_f, t_0)$ defined in (54)

$$\bar{\Phi}_{11}(t_f, t_0)\bar{\Phi}_{22}(t_f, t_0)^T - \bar{\Phi}_{12}(t_f, t_0)\bar{\Phi}_{21}(t_f, t_0)^T = I \tag{87}$$

and the assumed invertibility of $\bar{\Phi}_{22}(t_f, t_0)$, we obtain

$$\bar{\Phi}_{11}(t_f, t_0) - \bar{\Phi}_{12}(t_f, t_0)\bar{\Phi}_{21}(t_f, t_0)^T\bar{\Phi}_{22}(t_f, t_0)^{-T} = \bar{\Phi}_{22}(t_f, t_0)^{-T}. \tag{88}$$

By pre- and postmultiplying the symplectic identity (52)

$$\bar{\Phi}_{21}(t_f, t_0)\bar{\Phi}_{22}(t_f, t_0)^T = \bar{\Phi}_{22}(t_f, t_0)\bar{\Phi}_{21}(t_f, t_0)^T \tag{89}$$

by $\bar{\Phi}_{22}(t_f, t_0)^{-1}$ and $\bar{\Phi}_{22}(t_f, t_0)^{-T}$, respectively, we obtain

$$\bar{\Phi}_{22}(t_f, t_0)^{-1}\bar{\Phi}_{21}(t_f, t_0) = \bar{\Phi}_{21}(t_f, t_0)^T\bar{\Phi}_{22}(t_f, t_0)^{-T}. \tag{90}$$

By using (90) in (88), the coefficient of x_0 in (86) reduces to

$$\bar{\Phi}_{11}(t_f, t_0) - \bar{\Phi}_{12}(t_f, t_0)\bar{\Phi}_{22}(t_f, t_0)^{-1}\bar{\Phi}_{21}(t_f, t_0) = \bar{\Phi}_{22}(t_f, t_0)^{-T}. \tag{91}$$

Therefore, (85) and (86) can be written in the symmetric form

$$\begin{bmatrix} \lambda(t_0) \\ 0 \end{bmatrix} = \begin{bmatrix} -\bar{\Phi}_{22}(t_f, t_0)^{-1}\bar{\Phi}_{21}(t_f, t_0) & \bar{\Phi}_{22}(t_f, t_0)^{-1}D^T \\ D\bar{\Phi}_{22}(t_f, t_0)^{-T} & D\bar{\Phi}_{12}(t_f, t_0)\bar{\Phi}_{22}(t_f, t_0)^{-1}D^T \end{bmatrix} \times \begin{bmatrix} x_0 \\ \nu \end{bmatrix}. \tag{92}$$

At this point $\lambda(t_0)$ and ν can be determined as a function of $x(t_0)$. Substitution of this result into (31) will result in an optimal control rule for the terminal constrained optimal control problem. Before explicitly doing this, the elements of the coefficient matrix of (92), identified as

$$S(t_f, t; S_f) \triangleq -\bar{\Phi}_{22}(t_f, t)^{-1}\bar{\Phi}_{21}(t_f, t), \tag{93}$$

$$F(t_f, t)^T \triangleq \bar{\Phi}_{22}(t_f, t)^{-1}D^T, \tag{94}$$

$$G(t_f, t) \triangleq D\bar{\Phi}_{12}(t_f, t)\bar{\Phi}_{22}(t_f, t)^{-1}D^T, \tag{95}$$

are to be analyzed. Our objective is to find the propagation equations for the elements and discuss their properties. In particular, these elements will be seen to combine into a Riccati variable for the constrained control problem, and the coefficient matrix of (92) is shown to be a symmetric matrix.

As given in Theorem 2, $S(t_f, t; S_f)$ satisfies a Riccati differential equation. The differential equation for $F(t_f, t)$ is now developed by determining the differential equation for $\bar{\Phi}_{22}^{-1}(t_f, t)$, by noting

$$(d/dt)\left[\bar{\Phi}_{22}(t_f, t)^{-1}\right]\bar{\Phi}_{22}(t_f, t) + \bar{\Phi}_{22}(t_f, t)^{-1}\dot{\bar{\Phi}}_{22}(t_f, t) = 0. \tag{96}$$

From the adjoint differential equation for $\Phi_H(t_f, t)$ (58), (96) becomes

$$(d/dt)\left[\overline{\Phi}_{22}(t_f, t)^{-1}\right]\overline{\Phi}_{22}(t_f, t)$$
$$= -\overline{\Phi}_{22}(t_f, t)^{-1}\left[\overline{\Phi}_{21}(t_f, t)B(t)R(t)^{-1}B(t)^T + \overline{\Phi}_{22}(t_f, t)(A(t) - B(t)R(t)^{-1}C(t))^T\right]. \tag{97}$$

Then, by the assumed invertibility of $\overline{\Phi}_{22}(t_f, t)$,

$$(d/dt)\left[\overline{\Phi}_{22}(t_f, t)^{-1}\right] = -\left[(A(t) - B(t)R(t)^{-1}C(t))^T - S(t_f, t; S_f)B(t)R(t)^{-1}B(t)^T\right] \times \overline{\Phi}_{22}(t_f, t)^{-1}. \tag{98}$$

Noting that $(d/dt)\left[F(t_f, t)^T\right] = (d/dt)\left[\overline{\Phi}_{22}(t_f, t)^{-1}\right]D^T$, then

$$(d/dt)\left[F(t_f, t)^T\right] = -\left[(A(t) - B(t)R(t)^{-1}C(t))^T - S(t_f, t; S_f)B(t)R(t)^{-1}B(t)^T\right] \times F(t_f, t_f)^T, \tag{99}$$

$$F(t_f, t_f)^T = D^T.$$

In a similar manner, the differential equation for $G(t_f, t)$ is obtained by direct differentiation of $\overline{\Phi}_{12}(t_f, t)\overline{\Phi}_{22}(t_f, t)^{-1}$, as

$$(d/dt)\overline{\Phi}_{12}(t_f, t)\overline{\Phi}_{22}(t_f, t)^{-1} + \overline{\Phi}_{12}(t_f, t)(d/dt)\left[\overline{\Phi}_{22}(t_f, t)^{-1}\right]$$
$$= \left[\overline{\Phi}_{11}(t_f, t)B(t)R(t)^{-1}B(t)^T + \overline{\Phi}_{12}(t_f, t)(A(t) - B(t)R(t)^{-1}C(t))^T\right]\overline{\Phi}_{22}(t_f, t)^{-1}$$
$$- \overline{\Phi}_{12}(t_f, t)\left[(A(t) - B(t)R(t)^{-1}C(t))^T - S(t_f, t; S_f)B(t)R(t)^{-1}B(t)^T\right]\overline{\Phi}_{22}(t_f, t)^{-1}$$

$$= \left[\bar{\Phi}_{11}(t_f, t) - \bar{\Phi}_{12}(t_f, t)\bar{\Phi}_{22}(t_f, t)^{-1}\bar{\Phi}_{21}(t_f, t)\right]$$
$$\times B(t)R(t)^{-1}B(t)^T\bar{\Phi}_{22}(t_f, t)^{-1}. \qquad (100)$$

Equation (100) is reduced further, by using the symplectic identity of (91), to

$$(d/dt)\left[\bar{\Phi}_{12}(t_f, t)\bar{\Phi}_{22}(t_f, t)^{-1}\right]$$
$$= \bar{\Phi}_{22}(t_f, t)^{-T}B(t)R(t)^{-1}B(t)^T\bar{\Phi}_{22}(t_f, t)^{-1}. \qquad (101)$$

By pre- and postmultiplying (101) by D and D^T, respectively, and using the definition of $F(t_f, t)$ and $G(t_f, t)$, the differential equation for $G(t_f, t)$ is

$$\dot{G}(t_f, t) = F(t_f, t)B(t)R(t)^{-1}B(t)^TF(t_f, t)^T,$$
$$G(t_f, t_f) = 0. \qquad (102)$$

Note that $G(t_f, t)$ generated by (102) is symmetric. Since it was already shown that $S(t_f, t; S_f)$ is symmetric, the coefficient matrix of (92) is symmetric.

Our objective is to determine ν in terms of $x(t_0)$. This can only occur if $G(t_f, t)$ is invertible. For this to happen it is necessary for D to be of full rank. Assuming $G(t_f, t)$ is invertible, we get

$$\nu = -G(t_f, t_0)^{-1}F(t_f, t_0)x(t_0). \qquad (103)$$

The invertibility of $G(t_f, t_0)$ is known as a normality condition allowing ν to be finite for finite $x(t_0)$. By using (103) to eliminate ν in (85),

$$\lambda(t_0) = \bar{S}(t_f, t_0)x(t_0) \qquad (104)$$

where

$$\bar{S}(t_f, t) = S(t_f, t; S_f) - F(t_f, t)^TG(t_f, t)^{-1}F(t_f, t). \qquad (105)$$

The optimal control can now be written as an explicit function of the initial state. If t_0 is considered to be the present time t, then introducing (104) and (105) into (31) results in the optimal control rule for the terminal constrained optimal control problem as

$$u^0(t) = -R(t)^{-1}\left[C(t) + B(t)^T\bar{S}(t_f, t)\right]x(t). \tag{106}$$

That $\bar{S}(t_f, t)$ satisfies the same Riccati differential equation as (60) is seen by time differentiation of $\bar{S}(t_f, t)$ using (105). Furthermore, if all the terminal states are constrained, i.e., $D = I$, and (93)-(95) are used in (105), then by the symplectic identities, $\bar{S}(t_f, t)$ reduces to

$$\bar{S}(t_f, t) = -\bar{\Phi}_{12}(t_f, t)^{-1}\bar{\Phi}_{11}(t_f, t). \tag{107}$$

The major difficulty with propagating $\bar{S}(t_f, t)$ directly is in applying the proper boundary conditions at t_f. From (105), $\bar{S}(t_f, t_f)$ is not defined because $G(t_f, t_f)$ is not invertible. Note that the integration of $S(t_f, t; S_f)$, $F(t_f, t)$, and $G(t_f, t)$ indicates a computational savings over the integration of the transition matrix. Furthermore, $G(t_f, t)$ and $F(t_f, t)$ do not have to be integrated over the entire interval $[t_0, t_f]$ but only until $G(t_f, t)$ is invertible. This allows a proper initialization for $\bar{S}(t_f, t)$. Once $\bar{S}(t_f, t)$ is formed, only $\bar{S}(t_f, t)$ need be propagated backwards in time. The behavior of $\bar{S}(t_f, t)$ is reflected in the behavior of $u^0(t)$ near t_f. For large deviations away from the terminal manifold, $u^0(t)$ reacts by emphasizing the satisfaction of the constraints rather than reducing the performance criterion.

In the next section, we demonstrate that the invertibility of $G(t_f, t)$ is equivalent to a controllability requirement but only associated with the required terminal boundary restriction (4).

X. NORMALITY AND CONTROLLABILITY FOR THE LINEAR-QUADRATIC PROBLEM

We show here that the normality condition of Section IX is actually a controllability requirement. This is done by converting the original problem to one in which the quadratic cost criterion is only a function of a control variable. The minimization of this new performance criterion, subject to given initial conditions and the terminal constraints (4), requires a controllability condition which is just $G(t_f, t)$. The following theorem is similar to that of Brockett [13].

Theorem 4

Assume that the symmetric matrix $S(t_f, t; S_f)$, which is a solution to the Riccati equation (60), exists on the interval $t_0 \leq t \leq t_f$. Then there exists a control $u(\cdot)$ on the interval $t_0 \leq t \leq t_f$ which minimizes

$$J[u(\cdot); x(t_0), t_0] = \frac{1}{2} x(t_f)^T S_f x(t_f) + \frac{1}{2}\int_{t_0}^{t_f} [x(t)^T Q(t) x(t) + 2u(t)^T C(t) x(t) + u(t)^T R(t) u(t)]\, dt \tag{108}$$

subject to the differential constraint

$$\dot{x}(t) = A(t)x(t) + B(t)u(t), \tag{109}$$

the boundary conditions $x(t_0) = x_0$, and $Dx(t_f) = 0$, if and only if there exists a $v(\cdot)$ on the interval $t_0 \leq t \leq t_f$ which minimizes

$$J_1[v(\cdot); x_0, t] = \frac{1}{2}\int_{t_0}^{t_f} v^T(t) R(t) v(t)\, dt \tag{110}$$

subject to the differential constraint

$$\dot{x}(t) = \underline{A}(t)x(t) + B(t)v(t) \tag{111}$$

where

$$\underline{A}(t) \triangleq A(t) - B(t)R^{-1}(t)\left[C(t) + B(t)^T S(t_f, t; S_f)\right], \quad (112)$$

the boundary conditions $x(t_0) = x_0$, and $Dx(t_f) = 0$.

Proof. By proceeding exactly as was done to obtain (78), we note that if we let

$$v(t) = u(t) + R(t)^{-1}\left[C(t) + B(t)^T S(t_f, t; S_f)\right]x(t), \quad (113)$$

then the cost can be written as

$$J[v(\cdot); x(t_0), t_0] = \frac{1}{2} x^T(t_0)S(t_f, t_0; S_f)x(t_0) + \frac{1}{2}\int_{t_0}^{t_f} v(t)^T R(t)v(t)\, dt. \quad (114)$$

Since $x(t_0) = x_0$ is given, the cost function upon which $v(\cdot)$ has influence is

$$J_1[v(\cdot); x_0, t_0] = \frac{1}{2}\int_{t_0}^{t_f} v^T(t)R(t)v(t)\, dt \quad (115)$$

which is subject to the differential constraint (111) when (113) is substituted into (109).

We now proceed to solve this accessory problem of minimizing (110) subject to (111) using the technique of the previous section. First, the Riccati variable $S^*(t_f, t; 0)$ is propagated from (60) as

$$\dot{S}^*(t_f, t; 0) = -\underline{A}(t)^T S^*(t_f, t; 0) - S^*(t_f, t; 0)\underline{A}(t) + S^*(t_f, t; 0)B(t)R(t)^{-1}B(t)^T S^*(t_f, t; 0),$$

$$S^*(t_f, t_f; 0) = 0 \quad (116)$$

where the * superscript is used to denote dependence on the Riccati variable $S(t_f, t; S_f)$. For this problem, $Q(t)$ and $C(t)$ are now zero. The solution to this homogeneous Riccati equation with zero initial condition is $S^*(t_f, t; 0) = 0$ over the interval $t_0 \leq t \leq t_f$. The propagation of the linear differential equation (99) is

$$F(t_f, t)^T = \Phi_{\underline{A}}(t_f, t)D^T. \tag{117}$$

Using (117) in (102), the solution to $G(t_f, t_0)$ is

$$G(t_f, t_0) = DW_{\underline{A}}(t_f, t_0)D^T \tag{118}$$

where

$$W_{\underline{A}}(t_f, t_0) = \int_{t_0}^{t_f} \Phi_{\underline{A}}(t_f, t)B(t)R(t)^{-1}B(t)^T\Phi_{\underline{A}}(t_f, t)\, dt \tag{119}$$

is the controllability Gramian. Therefore, the invertibility does not depend upon controllability of the entire state space but only on the controllability to the desired terminal manifold. Clearly, the invertibility of $G(t_f, t_0)$ is a controllability condition for $v(t)$ to reach the terminal manifold; then by (113), $G(t_f, t_0)$ is also a controllability condition on $u(t)$. Note that $F(t_f, t)$ and $G(t_f, t_0)$ are the same as those that would be generated by the original problem.

Theorem 5

If

$$\dot{x}(t) = A(t)x(t) + B(t)u(t) \tag{120}$$

is controllable on the interval $[t_0, t_f]$ and if

$$u(t) - v(t) + \Lambda(t)x(t), \tag{121}$$

then

$$\begin{aligned}\dot{x}(t) &= (A(t) + B(t)\Lambda(t))x(t) + B(t)v(t) \\ &= \underline{A}(t)x(t) + B(t)v(t) \end{aligned} \tag{122}$$

is also controllable for any finite piecewise continuous $\Lambda(t)$ on the interval $[t_0, t_f]$.

Proof. We need to show that $x_0^T \Phi_{\underline{A}}(t_0, t) B(t) = 0$ for all t in the interval $[t_0, t_f]$ implies that $x_0^T \Phi_A(t_0, t) B(t) = 0$, a contradiction to the controllability assumption. To do this, note that the controllability Gramian

$$W_A(t_0, t_f) = \int_{t_0}^{t_f} \Phi_A(t_0, t) B(t) B^T(t) \Phi_A(t_0, t)^T \, dt \qquad (123)$$

can be obtained by integrating the linear matrix equation

$$\begin{aligned} \dot{W}_A(t, t_f) &= A(t) W_A(t, t_f) + W_A(t, t_f) A(t)^T - B(t) B(t)^T, \\ W_A(t_f, t_f) &= 0. \end{aligned} \qquad (124)$$

Similarly, the controllability Gramian for $\underline{A}(t)$ is obtained from

$$\begin{aligned} \dot{W}_{\underline{A}}(t, t_f) &= \underline{A}(t) W_{\underline{A}}(t, t_f) + W_{\underline{A}}(t, t_f) \underline{A}(t)^T - B(t) B(t)^T, \\ W_{\underline{A}}(t_f, t_f) &= 0. \end{aligned} \qquad (125)$$

Form the matrix

$$E(t) = W_{\underline{A}}(t, t_f) - W_A(t, t_f). \qquad (126)$$

This has a linear differential equation

$$\begin{aligned} \dot{E}(t) &= \underline{A}(t) E(t) + E(t) \underline{A}(t)^T - B(t) \Lambda(t) W_A(t, t_f) \\ &\quad - W_A(t, t_f) \Lambda(t)^T B(t)^T, \\ E(t_f) &= 0. \end{aligned} \qquad (127)$$

Then

$$\begin{aligned} E(t_0) = \int_{t_0}^{t_f} \Phi_{\underline{A}}(t_0, t) \Big[& B(t) \Lambda(t) W_A(t, t_f) \\ & + W_A(t, t_f) \Lambda(t)^T B(t)^T \Big] \Phi_{\underline{A}}(t_0, t)^T \, dt. \end{aligned} \qquad (128)$$

Since by hypothesis, $x_0^T \Phi_{\underline{A}}(t_0, t) B(t) = 0$, then $x_0^T E(t_0) x_0 = 0$

and $x_0^T W_{\underline{A}}(t_0, t_f)x_0 = 0$. But this implies that

$$x_0^T W_{\underline{A}}(t_0, t_f)x_0 = x_0^T W_A(t_0, t_f)x_0 = 0 \tag{129}$$

which is a contradiction of the assumed controllability of

$$\dot{x}(t) = A(t)x(t) + B(t)u(t). \tag{130}$$

From Theorem 5 we see that the controllability Assumption 3 implies the normality condition $G(t_f, t_0) < 0$. If the controllability Assumption 3 for reaching the manifold (4) is restricted to complete controllability as in Assumption 4, then

$$G(t_f, t) < 0 \quad \text{for} \quad t \in [t_0, t_f). \tag{131}$$

XI. NECESSARY AND SUFFICIENT CONDITION FOR THE POSITIVITY OF THE TERMINALLY CONSTRAINED QUADRATIC COST CRITERION

The objective of this section is to show that a necessary and sufficient condition for the quadratic cost criterion with linear terminal constraints (4) to be positive definite when $x(t_0) = 0$ is that the Riccati variable $\overline{S}(t_f, t)$ exist for all the t in the interval $[t_0, t_f)$. The results of this section closely parallel those of Section VIII for the unconstrained problem.

First, it is shown that if there exists for all t in the interval $[t_0, t_f]$ an $\overline{S}(t_f, t)$ defined by (105), then $J[u(\cdot); 0, t_0]$ is positive definite. Consider adding to $J[u(\cdot); 0, t_0]$ of (1) the identically zero quantity

$$-\frac{1}{2}[x(t)^T, \nu^T]\begin{bmatrix} S(t_f, t; S_f) & F(t_f, t)^T \\ F(t_f, t) & G(t_f, t)\end{bmatrix}\begin{bmatrix} x(t) \\ \nu \end{bmatrix}\Bigg|_{t_0}^{t_f}$$

$$+\frac{1}{2}\int_{t_0}^{t_f} \frac{d}{dt}\left\{[x(t)^T, \nu^T]\begin{bmatrix} S(t_f, t; S_f) & F(t_f, t)^T \\ F(t_f, t) & G(t_f, t)\end{bmatrix}\begin{bmatrix} x(t) \\ \nu \end{bmatrix}\right\} dt = \tag{132}$$

By using the Riccati equation (60), the propagation equation for $F(t_f, t)$ in (99) and that of $G(t_f, t)$ in (103), the cost criterion (1) can be manipulated into a perfect square as

$$
\begin{aligned}
J[u(\cdot);\, x(t_0),\, t_0]
&= \frac{1}{2}\, x(t_0)^T S(t_f, t_0; S_f) x(t_0) + x(t_0)^T F(t_f, t_0)^T \nu \\
&\quad + \frac{1}{2}\, \nu^T G(t_f, t_0)\nu - x(t_f)^T D^T \nu \\
&\quad + \int_{t_0}^{t_f} \Big\| R(t)^{-1}\Big[\Big(C(t) + B(t)^T S(t_f, t; S_f)\Big)x(t) \\
&\qquad + B(t)^T F(t_f, t)^T \nu\Big] + u(t)\Big\|^2_{R(t)}\, dt.
\end{aligned}
\tag{133}
$$

One difficulty occurs at $t = t_f$ where ν cannot be determined in terms of $x(t_f)$. Since the system is assumed completely controllable by Assumption 4, then $G(t_f, t_f - \Delta)$ is invertible for any $\Delta > 0$. For small enough Δ, $S(t_f, t_f - \Delta; S_f)$ exists. Therefore, the optimal control in an interval $t_f - \Delta \le t \le t_f$ is given by

$$
\begin{aligned}
u^0(t) &= \Bigg\{[C(t), B(t)]\Phi_H(t, t_f - \Delta)\begin{bmatrix} I \\ S(t_f, t_f - \Delta; 0)\end{bmatrix} \\
&\quad - B(t)^T F(t_f, t)^T G(t_f, t_f - \Delta)^{-1} F(t_f, t_f - \Delta)\Bigg\} \\
&\quad \times x(t_f - \Delta)
\end{aligned}
\tag{134}
$$

where ν is determined by (103) evaluated at $t_0 = t_f - \Delta$ and Assumption 4. Since all the factors in (134) remain finite in $[t_f - \Delta, t_f]$, $u^0(t)$ remains finite in that interval. In the interval $t_0 \le t \le t_f - \Delta$ the optimal control is given by (106). By using the optimal control given by both (134) and (106) to replace the control $u(\cdot)$, the integral part of the cost in (133) becomes zero and is its minimum value. With $x(t_0) = 0$, the optimal control is the null control. Any other control which satisfies the terminal coundary condition that $Dx(t_f) = 0$ and is unequal to $u^0(\cdot)$ will give a positive value to $J[u(\cdot);\ 0,\ t_0]$.

The arguments for the existence of $\overline{S}(t_f,\ t)$ over the interval $[t_0,\ t_f)$ *given* that the cost $J[u(\cdot);\ 0,\ t_0]$ is positive definite are the same as that given in Section VIII; that is, for some t' close enough to t_f, $\overline{S}(t_f,\ t)$ exists for $t' \le t < t_f$. Therefore, the optimal control laws (134) or (106) apply and the optimal cost starting at some $x(t')$ is

$$J[u^0(\cdot);\ x(t'),\ t'] = \frac{1}{2}\, x(t')^T \overline{S}\left(t_f,\ t'\right) x(t'). \tag{135}$$

By applying a control suggested by (80), controllability, and positivity of the cost for $x(t_0) = 0$, the arguments of Section VIII imply that since $x(t')^T \overline{S}\left(t_f,\ t'\right) x(t')$ can neither go to positive or negative infinity for all finite $x(t')$ and for any t' in the interval $[t_0,\ t_f)$, then $\overline{S}\left(t_f,\ t'\right)$ exists for all t' in $[t_0,\ t_f)$. These results are summarized in the following theorem.

Theorem 6

Given Assumption 4, a necessary and sufficient condition for $J[u(\cdot);\ 0,\ t_0]$ to be positive definite for the class of controls which satisfy the terminal constraint (4) is that there exist a function $\overline{S}(t_f,\ t)$ for all t in $[t_0,\ t_f)$ which satisfies the Riccati equation (60).

Remark 3. Evaluation of $\overline{S}(t_f,\ t)$ by (105) may not be possible everywhere since $S(t_f,\ t;\ S_f)$ may not exist for all $t \in [t_0,\ t_f)$ even if $\overline{S}(t_f,\ t)$ does exist.

XII. FURTHER PROPERTIES OF THE SOLUTION OF THE MATRIX RICCATI EQUATION

Three important properties of the solution to the matrix Riccati equation are given here. First, it is shown that if the terminal weighting in the cost criterion is increased, then the solution to the corresponding Riccati equation is also increased. This implies, for example, that $S(t_f, t; S_f) \leq \bar{S}(t_f, t)$. Secondly, by restricting certain matrices to be positive semidefinite, $S(t_f, t; S_f)$ is shown to be nonnegative definite and bounded. Finally, if $S_f = 0$ and the above restrictions hold, $S(t_f, t; 0)$ is monotonically increasing as t_f increases. This is extremely important for the next section where we analyze the infinite-time, linear-quadratic problem with constant coefficients.

Theorem 7

If S_f^1 and S_f^2 are two terminal weightings in the cost criterion, such that $S_f^1 - S_f^2 \geq 0$, then the difference $S\left(t_f, t; S_f^1\right) - S\left(t_f, t; S_f^2\right) \geq 0$ for all $t \leq t_f$ where $S\left(t_f, t; S_f^2\right)$ exists.

Proof. First, the unconstrained optimization problem of (1) and (2) is converted, as in Theorem 4, to an equivalent problem. This is done precisely in the manner used to obtain (78). However, now we are concerned with two problems having terminal weightings S_f^1 and S_f^2, respectively. Therefore, (76) is indexed with a superscript 2 and added to a cost criterion having a terminal weighting S_f^1. The result is that the optimal cost for weighting S_f^1 is

$$\frac{1}{2} x_0^T S\left(t_f, t_0; S_f^1\right)x_0$$
$$= \frac{1}{2} x_0^T S\left(t_f, t_0; S_f^2\right)x_0 + \min_{u(\cdot)}\left[\frac{1}{2} x(t_f)^T\left(S_f^1 - S_f^2\right)x(t_f)\right.$$
$$+ \frac{1}{2}\int_{t_0}^{t_f} \left(u(t) + R(t)^{-1}\left(C(t) + B(t)^T S\left(t_f, t; S_f^2\right)\right)^T x(t)\right)$$
$$\times R(t)\left(u(t) + R(t)^{-1}\left(C(t) + B(t)^T\right.\right.$$
$$\left.\left.\left.\times S\left(t_f, t; S_f^2\right)\right)x(t)\right) dt\right] \tag{136}$$

Clearly, a new problem results, if again

$$v(t) = u(t) + R^{-1}(t)\left(C(t) + B^T(t)S\left(t_f, t; S_f^2\right)\right)x(t) \tag{137}$$

where it is assumed that $S\left(t_f, t; S_f^2\right)$ exists, as

$$x_0^T\left[S\left(t_f, t_0; S_f^1\right) - S\left(t_f, t_0; S_f^2\right)\right]x_0$$
$$= \min_{v(\cdot)}\left[x(t_f)^T\left(S_f^1 - S_f^2\right)x(t_f) + \frac{1}{2}\int_{t_0}^{t_f} v(t)^T R(t)v(t)\, dt\right]. \tag{138}$$

Since $S_f^1 - S_f^2$ is nonnegative definite, then the optimal cost must be nonnegative, implying that

$$x_0^T\left[S\left(t_f, t_0; S_f^1\right) - S\left(t_f, t_0; S_f^2\right)\right]x_0 \geq 0 \tag{139}$$

for all x_0 and $t_0 \leq t_f$.

Remark 4. Since this new control problem (138) will have an optimal cost as $x_0^T S^*\left(t_f, t_0; S_f^1 - S_f^2\right)x_0$, then a relationship exists as

$$S\left(t_f, t_0; S_f^1\right) = S\left(t_f, t_0; S_f^2\right)$$
$$+ S^*\left(t_f, t_0; S_f^1 - S_f^2\right) \tag{140}$$

where $S^*\left(t_f, t; S_f^1 - S_f^2\right)$ satisfies the homogenous Riccati equation

$$(d/dt)S^*\left(t_f, t; S_f^1 - S_f^2\right)$$
$$= -\underline{A}(t)S^*\left(t_f, t; S_f^1 - S_f^2\right) - S^*\left(t_f, t; S_f^1 - S_f^2\right)\underline{A}(t)^T$$
$$+ S^*\left(t_f, t; S_f^1 - S_f^2\right)B(t)R(t)^{-1}B(t)^T S^*\left(t_f, t; S_f^1 - S_f^2\right),$$
$$S^*\left(t_f, t_f; S_f^1 - S_f^2\right) = S_f^1 - S_f^2, \tag{141}$$

where

$$\underline{A}(t) = A(t) - B(t)R(t)^{-1}C(t) - B(t)R(t)^{-1}B(t)^T S\left(t_f, t_0; S_f^2\right). \tag{142}$$

Note that if $S^*\left(t_f, t; S_f^1 - S_f^2\right)$ has an inverse, then a linear matrix differential equation for $S^*\left(t_f, t; S_f^1 - S_f^2\right)^{-1}$ results by simply differentiating $S^*\left(t_f, t; S_f^1 - S_f^2\right)S^*\left(t_f, t; S_f^1 - S_f^2\right)^{-1} = I$.

Remark 5. From (105), the difference between the constrained Riccati matrix $\overline{S}(t_f, t)$ and the unconstrained Riccati matrix $S(t_f, t; S_f)$ is

$$\overline{S}^*(t_f, t) \triangleq -F(t_f, t)^T G(t_f, t)^{-1} F(t_f, t) \geq 0 \tag{143}$$

for $t \in [t_0, t_f]$ since $G(t_f, t) \leq 0$ for $t \in [t_0, t_f)$ by virtue of Theorem 5. Furthermore, the differential equation for $\overline{S}^*(t_f, t)$ is that of (141), but the boundary condition at t_f is not defined. Intuitively, the constrained problem can be thought of as a limit of the unconstrained problem, where certain elements of the weighting function are allowed to go to infinity.

Existence of the solution to the Riccati equation is of central importance. Results using the following restrictive but useful assumption guarantees not only that $S(t_f, t; S_f)$ exists but that it is nonnegative definite.

Assumption 5. $S_f \geq 0$ and $Q(t) - C^T(t)R^{-1}(t)C(t) \geq 0$ for all t in the interval $[t_0, t_f]$.

Theorem 8

Given Assumptions 4 and 5, the solution to the Riccati equation, $S(t_f, t; S_f)$ exists on the interval $t_0 \leq t \leq t_f$ regardless of t_0, and is nonnegative definite.

Proof. From (79) the minimum cost is related to the Riccati variable for arbitrary state as

$$\frac{1}{2} x(t_0)^T S(t_f, t_0; S_f) x(t_0)$$
$$= \min_{u(\cdot)} \left\{ \frac{1}{2} x(t_f)^T S_f x(t_f) + \frac{1}{2} \int_{t_0}^{t_f} [u(t)^T R(t) u(t) + 2u(t)^T C(t) x(t) + x(t)^T Q(t) x(t)]\, dt \right\}. \tag{144}$$

Let us make a change in controls of the form

$$u(t) = v(t) - R(t)^{-1} C(t) x(t). \tag{145}$$

The cost can now be converted to the equivalent form

$$\frac{1}{2} x_0^T S(t_f, t_0; S_f) x_0$$
$$= \min_{v(\cdot)} \left\{ \frac{1}{2} x(t_f)^T S_f x(t_f) + \frac{1}{2} \int_{t_0}^{t_f} [x(t)^T (Q(t) - C(t)^T R(t)^{-1} C(t)) x(t) + v(t)^T R(t) v(t)]\, dt \right\} \tag{146}$$

where the cross term between u(t) and x(t) is now eliminated. Since R(t) is positive definite and by Assumption 5, S_f and

$Q(t) - C(t)^T R(t)^{-1} C(t)$ are nonnegative definite, the cost must be nonnegative definite for all x_0, i.e.,

$$x(t_0)^T S(t_f, t_0; S_f) x(t_0) \geq 0 \Rightarrow S(t_f, t_0; S_f) \geq 0 \tag{147}$$

regardless of t_0. Furthermore, since the original system is controllable with respect to u, the new system

$$\dot{x}(t) = (A(t) - B(t)R(t)^{-1}C(t))x(t) + B(t)v(t) \tag{148}$$

must be controllable with respect to v(t) by Theorem 5. Therefore, the cost $x_0^T S(t_f, t_0; S_f) x_0$ is bounded from above and below, even if t_0 goes to $-\infty$.

The final two theorems deal with the monotonic and asymptotic behavior of the Riccati equation under Assumptions 4 and 5. First, it is shown that when $S_f = 0$, $S(t_f, t_0; 0)$ is a monotonically increasing function of t_f. Then, it is shown that $S^*(t_f, t; S_f)$ goes asymptotically to zero regardless of the boundary condition, S_f. This means that $S(t_f, t_0; S_f)$ or $\overline{S}(t_f, t_0)$ approach $S(t_f, t_0; 0)$ as the difference $t_f - t_0$ goes to infinity.

Theorem 9

Given Assumptions 4 and 5,

$$S(t_f, t_0; 0) \geq S(t_1, t_0; 0) \quad \text{for} \quad t_0 \leq t_1 \leq t_f. \tag{149}$$

Proof. The optimal cost criterion can be written as

$$\frac{1}{2} x_0^T S(t_f, t_0; 0) x_0$$
$$= \min_{u(\cdot)} \left[\frac{1}{2} \int_{t_0}^{t_f} (x(t)^T Q(t) x(t) + 2u(t)^T C(t) x(t) + u(t)^T R(t) u(t) \right] dt \tag{150}$$

The optimal cost criterion can be decomposed further as

$$\frac{1}{2} x_0^T S(t_f, t_0; 0) x_0$$

$$= \min_{u(\cdot)} \left[\frac{1}{2} \int_{t_0}^{t_1} (x(t)^T Q(t) x(t) + 2u(t)^T C(t) x(t) + u(t)^T R(t) u(t))\, dt + \frac{1}{2} x(t_1)^T S(t_f, t_1; 0) x(t_1) \right]$$

$$= \frac{1}{2} x_0^T S(t_1, t_0; S(t_f, t_1; 0)) x_0. \qquad (151)$$

From (140)

$$x_0^T S(t_f, t_0; 0) x_0 = x_0^T S(t_1, t_0; S(t_f, t_1; 0)) x_0$$
$$= x_0^T \left[S(t_1, t_0; 0) + S^*(t_1, t_0; S(t_f, t_1; 0)) \right] x_0. \qquad (152)$$

Since $S(t_f, t_1; 0) \geq 0$ by Theorem 8, then $S^*(t_1, t_0; S(t_f, t_1; 0)) \geq 0$. Therefore,

$$x_0^T S(t_f, t_0; 0) x_0 \geq x_0^T S(t_1, t_0; 0) x_0 \qquad (153)$$

By Assumption 4, $x_0^T S(t_f, t_0; 0) x_0$ is bounded for all x_0 regardless of $t_0 \leq t_f$, implying

$$S(t_f, t_0; 0) \geq S(t_1, t_0; 0). \qquad (154)$$

In our final result we show that $S^*(t_f, t_0; S_f)$ goes to zero for all $S_f \geq 0$ as t_0 goes to $-\infty$ by requiring an observability assumption. If the cost without a terminal weighting is nonzero for all $x(t_0) \neq 0$, $t_0 < t_f$, then $x_0^T S(t_f, t_0; 0) x_0 > 0$ for all $x_0 \neq 0$. This condition will be shown to be guaranteed by ensuring that $x(t)$ given the observation

$$y(t) = N(t) x(t) \qquad (155)$$

is observable where $N(t)$ is the square root of the matrix $\underline{Q} \triangleq Q(t) - C(t)^T R(t)^{-1} C((t))$ such that $y(t)^T y(t) = x(t)^T \underline{Q}(t) x(t)$.

Assumption 6. The dynamic system

$$\dot{x}(t) = A(t)x(t), \quad x(t_0) = x_0, \quad y(t) = N(t)x(t) \tag{156}$$

is completely observable on the interval $[t_0, t']$, where $t_0 < t' \le t_f$.

If the system is completely observable, then the initial state can be determined as

$$x(t_0) = M^{-1}\left(t_0, t'\right) \int_{t_0}^{t'} \Phi_A(t, t_0)^T N(t)^T y(t)\, dt \tag{157}$$

where the observability Gramian matrix

$$M\left(t_0, t'\right) = \int_{t_0}^{t'} \Phi_A(t, t_0)^T N(t)^T N(t) \Phi_A(t, t_0)\, dt \tag{158}$$

is invertible for all t' in the interval $t_0 < t' \le t_f$. This means that

$$\int_{t_0}^{t'} x(t)^T \underline{Q}(t) x(t)\, dt = \int_{t_0}^{t'} y(t)^T y(t)\, dt$$

$$= x_0^T M\left(t_0, t'\right) x_0 > 0 \tag{159}$$

for all $x_0 \neq 0$, $t' \in (t_0, t_f]$, and $u(\cdot) = 0$. Therefore, $J[u(\cdot); x_0, t_0] > 0$.

Theorem 10

Given Assumptions 4-6, and $\underline{A}(t)$ defined in (142) with $S_f^2 = 0$, the following hold:

(a) $S(t_f, t_0; 0) > 0$ for all t_0 in $-\infty < t_0 < t_f$,

(b) $\dot{x} = \underline{A}(t)x$, $x(t_0) = x_0$ is asymptotically stable,

(c) $S^*(t_f, t_0; S_f) \to 0$ as $t_0 \to -\infty$ for all $S_f \ge 0$.

Proof. From Theorem 8 $S(t_f, t_0; 0) \geq 0$ and bounded. By Assumption 6, using (146), for all $x_0 \neq 0$,

$$x_0^T S(t_f, t_0; 0) x_0 > 0 \quad \text{for all} \quad t_0 \text{ in } -\infty < t_0 < t_f \tag{160}$$

resulting in $S(t_f, t_0; 0) > 0$. Let us now use the optimal cost function (160) as a Lyapunov function to determine if $x(t)$ in condition (b) is asymptotically stable. First, determine if the rate of change of the optimal cost function is negative definite. Therefore,

$$\begin{aligned}(d/dt)&\left[x(t)^T S(t_f, t; 0) x(t)\right] \\ &= x(t)^T\left[\underline{A}(t)^T S(t_f, t; 0) + S(t_f, t; 0)\underline{A}(t) \right. \\ &\qquad \left. + \dot{S}(t_f, t; 0)\right] x(t).\end{aligned} \tag{161}$$

By using (60) with $S_f = 0$,

$$\begin{aligned}(d/dt)\ &x(t)^T S(t_f, t; 0) x(t) \\ &= -x(t)^T\left[\underline{Q}(t) + S(t_f, t; 0) B(t) R(t)^{-1} B(t)^T \right. \\ &\qquad \left. \times S(t_f, t; 0)\right] x(t).\end{aligned} \tag{162}$$

Therefore, $(d/dt)\left[x(t)^T S(t_f, t; 0) x(t)\right] \leq 0$ and the optimal cost function (160) is a Lyapunov function for $t < t_f$. By integrating (162),

$$\begin{aligned}x_0^T &S(t_f, t_0; 0) x_0 - x(t_1)^T S(t_f, t_1; 0) x(t_1) \\ &= \int_{t_0}^{t_1} x(t)^T\left[\underline{Q}(t) + S(t_f, t; 0) B(t) R(t)^{-1} B(t)^T \right. \\ &\qquad \left. \times S(t_f, t; 0) x(t)\right] dt\end{aligned} \tag{163}$$

where $t_0 \leq t_1 < t_f$ such that $S(t_f, t_1; 0) > 0$. If $\|x(t_1)\| \neq 0$, then $\|x(t)\| \neq 0$ for all $t \in [t_1, t_0]$ since $x(t)^T S(t_f, t; 0) x(t)$ is a Lyapunov function. Therefore, by Assumption 6, as $t_1 - t_0 \to \infty$ the right-hand side of (163) goes to ∞, implying that

$x_0^T S(t_f, t_0; 0)x_0 \to \infty$. But this contradicts the fact that $S(t_f, t_0; 0) < \infty$ by Theorem 8 and x_0 is given and assumed finite. Therefore, $\|x(t_1)\| \to 0$ as $t_1 - t_0 \to \infty$ for any $S_f \geq 0$.

In Remark 5 after Theorem 7, it is noted that $\bar{S}^*(t_f, t)$, defined in (143), satisfies the homogeneous Riccati equation (141). However, if the boundary conditions for $F(t_f, t_f)$ and $G(t_f, t_f)$ are chosen to be consistent with $S^*(t_f, t_f; S_f) = S_f$, then the solution and the behavior of $S(t_f, t; S_f)$ can be determined from $F(t_f, t)$ and $G(t_f, t)$. By writing

$$S_f = KK^T, \tag{164}$$

then

$$F(t_f, t_f) = K, \quad G(t_f, t_f) = -I. \tag{165}$$

Note that $F(t_f, t)$ satisfies, from (99), the differential equation

$$\dot{F}(t_f, t) = -F(t_f, t)\underline{A}(t)^T, \quad F(t_f, t_f) = K. \tag{166}$$

From conditions (b) of the theorem, $F(t_f, t)$ is stable and approaches zero as t goes to $-\infty$. From (102) and (165), the evaluation of $G(t_f, t)$ must always be negative definite for $t \leq t_f$, implying that $G(t_f, t)^{-1}$ exists for all $t \leq t_f$. Since $F(t_f, t) \to 0$ as $t \to -\infty$, $S^*(t_f, t; S_f) \to 0$ as $t \to -\infty$.

Remark 6. Note that $S(t_f, t; S_f) \to S(t_f, t; 0)$ as $t \to -\infty$ for all $S_f \geq 0$.

Remark 7. The assumptions of controllability and observability are stronger conditions than are usually needed. For example, if certain states are not controllable but naturally decay, then stabilizability of $x(t)$ is sufficient for condition (b) of Theorem 10 to still hold.

XIII. THE LINEAR REGULATOR PROBLEM

The linear-quadratic control problem is restricted in this section to a constant coefficient dynamic system and cost criterion. Furthermore, the time interval over which the cost criterion is to be minimized is assumed to be infinite. As might be suspected by the previous results, a linear constant gain controller results from this restricted formulation. This specialized problem is sometimes referred to as the linear regulator problem.

The optimal control problem of Section II is specialized to the linear regulator problem by requiring that t_f be infinite and A, B, Q, C, R are all constant matrices.

Theorem 11

For the linear regulator problem, given Assumptions 4-6, there is a unique, symmetric, positive-definite solution S to the algebraic Riccati equation

$$(A - BR^{-1}C)^T S + S(A - BR^{-1}C) + (Q - C^T R^{-1} C) - SBR^{-1}B^T S = 0 \quad (167)$$

such that $(A - BR^{-1}C - BR^{-1}B^T S)$ has only eigenvalues with negative real parts.

Proof. From Theorem 9, $S(t_f, t_0; 0)$ is monotonic in t_f. Since the parameters are not time dependent, then $S(t_f, t_0; 0)$ only depends upon $t_f - t_0$ and is monotonically increasing with respect to $t_f - t_0$. Since from Theorem 8, $S(t_f, t_0; 0)$ is bounded for all $t_f - t_0$, then as $t_f - t_0 \to \infty$, $S(t_f, t_0; 0)$ reaches an upper limit of S. As $S(t_f, t_0; 0)$ approaches S, $\dot{S}(t_f, t; 0)$ approaches zero, implying that S must satisfy the algebraic Riccati equation (167). That is, for some $\Delta > 0$,

$$S(t_f, t_0 - \Delta; 0) = S(t_f, t_0; S(t_0, t_0 - \Delta; 0)). \tag{168}$$

Continuity of the solution with respect to the initial conditions implies that as $\Delta \to \infty$, $S(t_f, t_0 - \Delta; 0)$ and $S(t_0, t_0 - \Delta; 0)$ go to S such that (168) becomes

$$S = S(t_f, t_0; S) \tag{169}$$

and S is a fixed-point solution to the autonomous Riccati equation. Furthermore, by condition (c) of Theorem 10, $S(t_f, t_0; S_f)$ approaches the same limit regardless of $S_f \geq 0$ and, therefore, S is unique. By conditions (a) and (b) of Theorem 10, S is positive definite and x(t) is asymptotically stable. Since S is a constant, this implies that the eigenvalues of the constant matrix

$$\underline{A} \triangleq A - BR^{-1}C - BR^{-1}B^TS \tag{170}$$

have only negative real parts.

The relationship between the Hamiltonian matrix H, of (36), and the feedback dynamic matrix $\underline{A}$ of (170) is vividly obtained by use of the canonical transformation introduced in Section VII. First, additional properties of Hamiltonian systems are obtained for the constant Hamiltonian matrix by rewriting (47):

$$H = -\underline{J}H^T\underline{J}^T. \tag{171}$$

The characteristic equations for H and -H can be obtained by subtracting λI from both sides of (171) and taking the determinant as

$$\begin{aligned} \mathrm{Det}(H - \lambda I) &= \mathrm{Det}(-\underline{J}H^T\underline{J}^T - \lambda I) \\ &= \mathrm{Det}(-\underline{J}H^T\underline{J}^T - \lambda \underline{J}\underline{J}^T) \\ &= \mathrm{Det}\ \underline{J}\ \mathrm{Det}(-H - \lambda I)\ \mathrm{Det}\ \underline{J}^T \\ &= \mathrm{Det}(-H - \lambda I). \end{aligned} \tag{172}$$

Since the characteristic equations for H and -H are equal, the eigenvalues of the $2n \times 2n$ matrix H are not only symmetric about the real axis but also about the imaginary axis. If n eigenvalues are λ_i, $i = 1, \ldots, n$, then the remaining n eigenvalues are

$$\lambda_{i+n} = -\lambda_i, \quad i = 1, \ldots, n. \tag{173}$$

From (173), it is seen that there are just as many stable eigenvalues as unstable ones. Furthermore, there is a question as to how many eigenvalues lie on the imaginary axis. To understand the spectral content of H better, the canonical transformation of (66) is used, but with S the solution to the algebraic Riccati equation (167). By using this canonical transformation, the transformed Hamiltonian matrix $\underline{H}$ is

$$LHL^{-1} \triangleq \underline{H} = \begin{bmatrix} \underline{A} & -BR^{-1}B^T \\ 0 & -\underline{A}^T \end{bmatrix}. \tag{174}$$

This form is particularly interesting because $\underline{A}$ and $-\underline{A}^T$ contain all the spectral information of both $\underline{H}$ and H since L is a similarity transformation. Note that from Theorem 11, the real parts of the eigenvalues of $\underline{A}$ are negative. Therefore, the feedback dynamic matrix $\underline{A}$ contains all the left-half poles in $\underline{H}$. The numerous solutions to the algebraic Riccati equation will give various groupings of the eigenvalues of the Hamiltonian matrix.

If the Hamiltonian matrix has *no* eigenvalues on the imaginary axis, then there is at most only one solution to the matrix Riccati equation which will decompose the matrix such that the eigenvalues of $\underline{A}$ have only negative real parts. This will be the case even if we are *not* restricted to Assumptions 4-6. The following theorem from Brockett [13] demonstrates directly that if the real parts of the eigenvalues of $\underline{A}$ are negative, then S is unique.

Theorem 12

For the linear regulator problem, there is at most one symmetric solution of $SA + A^TS - SBR^{-1}B^TS + Q = 0$ having the property that the eigenvalues of $A - BR^{-1}B^TS$ have only negative real parts.

Proof. Assume, to the contrary, that there are two symmetric solutions S_1 and S_2 such that both the eigenvalues of $A_1 = A - BR^{-1}B^TS_1$ and $A_2 = A - BR^{-1}B^TS_2$ have only negative real parts. By proceeding as in (76)-(78), the cost can be written

$$
\begin{aligned}
J[u(\cdot);\ x(t_0), t_0]
&= \frac{1}{2}\left[x(t_0)^TS_1x(t_0) - x(t_f)^TS_1x(t_f)\right] \\
&\quad + \int_{t_0}^{t_f} \frac{1}{2}\left[u(t) + R^{-1}\left(C + B^TS_1\right)x(t)\right]^T \\
&\qquad \times R\left[u(t) + R^{-1}\left(C + B^TS_1\right)x(t)\right] dt \\
&= \frac{1}{2}\left[x(t_0)^TS_2x(t_0)^T - x(t_f)^TS_2x(t_f)\right] \\
&\quad + \int_{t_0}^{t_f} \frac{1}{2}\left[u(t) + R^{-1}\left(C + B^TS_2\right)x(t)\right]^T \\
&\qquad \times R\left[u(t) + R^{-1}\left(C + B^TS_2\right)x(t)\right] dt.
\end{aligned}
\tag{175}
$$

Since S_1 and S_2 are symmetric and $S_1 \neq S_2$, then there exists an x_0 such that $x_0^TS_1x_0 \neq x_0^TS_2x_0$. Suppose that $x_0^TS_1x_0 \geq x_0^TS_2x_0$ and let $u(t) = -R^{-1}\left(C + B^TS_2\right)x(t)$. By taking the limit as t_f goes to infinity means $x(t_f)$ goes to zero by assumption, and the cost can be written as

$$J[u(\cdot);\ x(t_0),\ t_0]$$

$$= \frac{1}{2}\, x^T(t_0) S_2 x(t_0)$$

$$= \frac{1}{2}\, x^T(t_0) S_1 x(t_0)$$

$$+ \int_{t_0}^{\infty} \frac{1}{2}\left[B^T(S_1 - S_2)x(t)\right]^T R^{-1} \times \left[B^T(S_1 - S_2)x(t)\right] dt \tag{176}$$

which contradicts the hypothesis that $x_0^T S_1 x_0 \geq x_0^T S_2 x_0$ and, therefore, the hypothesis that there can be two distinct solutions to the algebraic Riccati equation which both produce stable dynamic matrices $\underline{A}_1$ and $\underline{A}_2$.

Remark 8. Since Assumptions 4-6 are not required, then the solution to the algebraic Riccati equation is not necessarily nonnegative definite. Furthermore, requiring Assumptions 4-6 implies that as $t \to -\infty$, $\overline{S}(t_f, t) \to S(t_f, t;\ 0)$. This is not generally the case. From Theorem 6, $\overline{S}(t_f, t) \geq S(t_f, t;\ 0)$. It can well occur that $S(t_f, t;\ 0)$ can have a finite escape time, whereas $\overline{S}(t_f, t)$ remains bounded even as $t \to -\infty$. For the regulator problem, the unconstrained terminal control problem may not have a finite cost. However, by requiring that $\lim_{t_f \to \infty} x(t_f) \to 0$, the terminal constrained problem may have a finite cost where $\lim_{t \to -\infty} \overline{S}(t_f, t) \to S$.

Remark 9. It is clear from the canonical transformation of the Hamiltonian matrix H into $\underline{H}$ of (174) that a necessary condition for all the eigenvalues of $\underline{A}$ to have negative real parts is for H to have no eigenvalues which have zero real parts.

XIV. SUMMARY AND EXTENSIONS

A consistent theory is given for a rather general formulation of the linear-quadratic problem. The theory has emphasized the time-varying formulation of the linear-quadratic problem with linear terminal constraints. The relationship between the transition matrix of the Hamiltonian system and the solution to the matrix Riccati differential equation is vividly shown using the symplectic property of Hamiltonian systems. Initially, no requirement was placed on the state weighting in the cost function, although the control weighting was assumed to be positive definite. By using this cost criterion, the existence of the solution to the Riccati differential equation is required for the cost criterion to be positive definite. If this problem were interpreted as the accessory problem in the calculus of variations [7], then the requirement that the cost criterion be positive definite is not enough. As shown in [6,12] the cost criterion is required to be "strongly positive" to ensure that the second variation dominates over higher-order terms.

A few additional extensions of the theory are mentioned. First, if the control weighting is required to be only positive semidefinite, then the control is required to be bounded since the optimal control will either lie on the boundary forming "bang-bang" arcs or "singular" arcs. Important results for the singular optimal control problem are given in [1,12,17]. Secondly, sufficiency for optimality for this class of problems is obtained directly through Hamilton-Jacobi-Bellman theory. However, for the terminal control problem, decomposition of the solution of the Riccati differntial equation is still required. This difficulty, expressed in [9], is overcome in [1,10,11].

Finally, the algebraic Riccati equation studied in Section XIII need not be restricted to positive-semidefinite $(Q - C^T F^{-1} C)$ matrices. Fundamental results for this more general case are given in [18,19].

ACKNOWLEDGMENT

The author is indebted to Dr. David Hull of the University of Texas at Austin for a critical review.

REFERENCES

1. A. E. BRYSON and Y. C. HO, "Applied Optimal Control," Blaisdell, Waltham, Massachusetts, 1969.

2. B. D. O. ANDERSON and J. B. MOORE, "Linear Optimal Control," Prentice-Hall, Englewood Cliffs, New Jersey, 1971.

3. H. KWAKERNAAK and R. SIVAN, "Linear Optimal Control Systems," Wiley (Interscience), New York, 1972.

4. M. ATHANS (ed.), "Special Issue on The Linear-Quadratic-Gaussian Problem," *IEEE Trans. Autom. Control AC-16* (December 1971).

5. M. SAIN (ed.), "Special Issue on Multivariable Control," *IEEE Trans. Autom. Control AC-26*, No. 1 (February 1981).

6. I. M. GELFAND and S. V. FOMIN, "Calculus of Variations," Prentice-Hall, Englewood Cliffs, New Jersey, 1963.

7. G. A. BLISS, "Lectures on the Calculus of Variations," Univ. of Chicago Press, Chicago, 1946.

8. M. R. HESTENES, "Calculus of Variations and Optimal Control Theory," Wiley, New York, 1966.

9. S. E. DREYFUS, "Dynamic Programming and the Calculus of Variations," Academic Press, New York, 1965.

10. D. H. JACOBSON and D. Q. MAYNE, "Differential Dynamic Programming," Elsevier, New York, 1970.

11. P. DYER and S. R. McREYNOLDS, "The Computation and Theory of Optimal Control," Academic Press, New York, 1970.

12. D. J. BELL and D. H. JACOBSON, "Singular Optimal Control Problem," Academic Press, New York, 1975.

13. R. W. BROCKETT, "Finite Dimensional Linear Systems," Wiley, New York, 1975.

14. E. CODDINGTON and N. LEVINSON, "Theory of Ordinary Differential Equations," McGraw-Hill, New York, 1958.

15. L. PARS, "A Treatise on Analytical Dynamics," Wiley, New York, 1965.

16. A. WINTNER, "The Analytical Foundations of Celestial Mechanics," Princeton Univ. Press, Princeton, New Jersey, 1947.

17. D. J. CLEMENTS and B. D. O. ANDERSON, "Singular Optimal Control: The Linear-Quadratic Problem," Springer-Verlag, New York, 1978.

18. J. D. WILLEMS, "Least Squares Stationary Optimal Control and the Algebraic Riccati Equation," *IEEE Trans. Autom. Control AC-16*, 621-634 (1971).

19. J. RODRIGUEZ-CANABAL, "The Geometry of the Riccati Equation," *Stochastics 1*, 129-143 (1973).

A Ritz-Type Optimization Method for Optimal Control Problems and Its Application to Hierarchical Final-Value Controllers*

BERNHARD ASSELMEYER

Illingen, West Germany

I. INTRODUCTION

The final-value control problem considered here can be stated as follows:

A system, whose model is described by a set of ordinary, nonlinear differential equations of first order (state equations),

$$\dot{\underline{x}}_{mod}(t) = \underline{g}_{mod}(\underline{x}_{mod}(t), \underline{u}(t), t) \tag{1}$$

This work was done at the Technische Hochschule in Darmstadt, West Germany with financial support from the DFG (Deutsche Forschungsgemeinschaft).

where $\underline{g}$ is an $n \times 1$ function vector, $\underline{x}$ an $n \times 1$ state vector, and $\underline{u}$ an $r \times 1$ control vector, is to be brought from an initial state given by

$$\underline{x}(t_0) = \underline{a} \tag{2}$$

where $\underline{a}$ is an $n \times 1$ constant vector to a final state, which must fulfill a set of final conditions

$$\underline{q}(\underline{x}(t_f), t_f) = 0 \tag{3}$$

where $\underline{q}$ is an $l \times 1$ function vector, $l \leqq n$. This is done by choosing an appropriate control vector $\underline{u}(t)$. The control strategy is called optimal, if this vector is chosen to minimize a cost criterion

$$P(\underline{x}(t_f), t_f) \to \min. \tag{4}$$

This formulation of the problem shows that two different tasks have to be accomplished. First, an optimal control function for the model describing the real system must be determined. Second, the solution is then applied to the real system; since this system may differ slightly from the model, deviations of the real-system behavior from the optimal behavior may occur and must be taken care of. According to these two different tasks a hierarchical control system is considered here.

In Section II a simple dynamic optimization algorithm is presented, which computes the optimal control functions for a model as described previously. This algorithm is based on a steepest descent method, as has been used by Kelley [1] or Bryson *et al.* [2]. In order to be able to do the necessary calculations on a small computer (i.e., on a computer with a limited amount of R/W memory and a relatively low execution speed) a Ritz-type parametrization of the control functions is introduced:

$$u_i(t) = \sum_{j=1}^{m} p_{ij} f_{ij}(t) \tag{5}$$

where $f_{ij}(t)$ are suitably chosen functions of time and p_{ij} are the parameters to be determined by the optimization process. This method was first introduced by Ritz [3] in the calculus of variations. For the calculation of optimal control, this method has been proposed by Rosenbrock [4] and has been used by Williamson [5] for linear models. Hicks and Ray [6] have discussed several aspects, without treating the problem as generally as it has been stated here. Brusch and Peletier [7-9] use a generalized parametrization

$$u_i = f_i(\underline{p}_i, t) \tag{5a}$$

where $\underline{p}$ is an $m \times 1$ vector, but they determine the change in these parameters using the so-called influence functions (see Section II.A). Sirisena *et al.* [10-12] and Mellefont and Sargent [13] treat special types of parametrizations. In this chapter the Ritz method will be used for the derivation of an iterative solution scheme for the general problem stated in (1)-(5) from the well-known gradient method in optimal control. Connections to the gradient projection method presented by Rosen [14] for nonlinear programming problems are shown. In Section III special properties will be discussed, which make this approach desirable with respect to on-line applications.

I want to point out that this approach yields suboptimal solutions in the sense that only the optimal control functions within the chosen function base are found. The choice of this function base of course influences the quality of the approximation of the real optimal control functions in the unrestricted function space. Convergence to the optimal control functions has been studied by Sirisena [12].

Other possible methods, where approximations are also used for the state equations [15-18] or where difference equations were used instead [19-20], are not discussed here. The generality of the problem considered also makes the application of the methods discussed in [21-24] for linear systems with quadratic cost criteria (with some extensions) impossible.

The result of this optimization procedure is a set of open-loop optimal control functions for the model only. Their application to the real system yields deviations due to differences between the behavior of the real system and the model and due to disturbances. Therefore in Section III a two-level closed-loop control is considered, where the optimization algorithm produces on-line improved control functions, depending on measurements of the system states at sampling points (upper level), while a model-following control reduces the differences between the model states and those of the real system. Such model-following controllers for nonlinear systems have been considered in [25-26]. Since optimal control makes sense only if the model is a good representation of the real system, it is assumed here that the deviations between the two can be described by a linear model, for which a controller is designed using quadratic cost criteria. So design of the controller and its application can be separated, contrary to method proposed in [27]. I want to emphasize that the control functions applied to the real system are not optimal there; however, they are suboptimal in the sense that they are the best obtainable with a given model. How close they are to the "real" optimal control for the system depends on how good a representation the model is. In the ideal case the model-following control does not influence the behavior of the overall control system; however, in real cases it is designed in such a way to force the real system to behave like the model.

Extensions to other levels in the hierarchy are possible but will be not considered here. For instance, an adaptation of the model could be done on a hierarchically higher level or a state observer could be introduced on a lower level to estimate states not directly measurable.

In Section IV a technical example is described. Some simulation results are shown and the applicability of the method described here with respect to available computer hardware is discussed.

II. OPTIMIZATION PROCEDURE

For control applications feedback solutions are desirable. The calculus of variations provides two different sets of necessary conditions. According to the theory of Hamilton-Jacoby-Bellman a partial differential equation must be solved and directly yields

$$\underline{u}(\underline{x}(t), t)$$

as a feedback solution. However, the solution is numerically feasible only for systems of low order (i.e., the number of states plus the number of control functions should be <5); the best known method for the solution is Bellman's dynamic programming [28]. For most technical systems the models are of higher order; therefore, only the approach according to Euler-Lagrange yields feasible numerical algorithms, which still require a lot of computational effort. The results obtained by this approach are just open-loop control functions $\underline{u}(t)$.

Two different numerical solution approaches are possible: an indirect one, which iteratively fulfills the optimization conditions, and a direct one, which reduces the cost criterion by changing the control functions [29]. The gradient technique used in the next section is a direct solution.

A. DERIVATION OF THE ITERATION SCHEME

We define the adjoint system

$$\dot{\underline{\lambda}} = (\partial \underline{g}/\partial \underline{x})\,\underline{\lambda} \tag{6}$$

where $\underline{\lambda}$ is an $n \times 1$ adjoint vector. For using direct methods, a relation describing how changes in a control function influence (4) and (3) has to be found. On following [28] this is

$$dF = \int_{t_0}^{t_f} \sum_{i=1}^{r} \underbrace{\left((\partial \underline{g}/\partial u_i)^T \underline{\lambda}\ \delta u_i\right)}_{\lambda^F_{u_i}} dt \tag{7}$$

where F stands for P from (5) or any of the q from (4), respectively. The $\lambda^F_{u_i}$ are called influence functions. F defines the boundary conditions for (6),

$$\underline{\lambda}(t_f) = (\partial F/\partial \underline{x})\big|_{t_f}. \tag{8}$$

For the sake of simplicity in presentation, from now on only one control function is considered. The transition to more than one is straight forward but implies rather lengthy formulas. A change in this control function, if the parametrization from (6) is used, is defined by

$$\delta u = \sum_{j=1}^{m} \delta p_j\ f_j(t) = \underline{\delta p}^T\ \underline{f}(t). \tag{9}$$

If (9) is introduced into (6) this yields

$$dF|_{t_f} = \int_{t_0}^{t_f} \lambda_u^F \, \underline{\delta p}^T \, \underline{f}(t) \, dt. \tag{7a}$$

If we now consider an infinitesimal change in just one of the parameters, we find

$$\partial F/\partial p_i = \int_{t_0}^{t_f} \lambda_u^F f_i(t) \, dt. \tag{10}$$

Note that if $f_i(t)$ is part of a complete set of orthonormal functions, these partial derivatives also give the coefficients for a series expansion of the influence function

$$\lambda_u^F \approx \sum_{j=1}^{m} (\partial F/\partial p_j) f_j(t) \tag{11}$$

using just these functions. Use of this approximation and following Bryson's suggestion [3] for determining the change of the control would lead to the same iteration formula as will be derived here [30].

Here we follow Kelley [1] and look for the maximal change of the cost criterion for a given "step length" Δs, while in addition certain changes in the final conditions are prescribed. This Δs is defined for the control function (6),

$$\begin{aligned} \Delta s^2 &= \underline{\delta p}^T \int_{t_0}^{t_f} (\underline{f}(t) * k(t) * \underline{f}(t)^T) \, dt \, \underline{\delta p} \\ &= \underline{\delta p}^T \, K \, \underline{\delta p}, \end{aligned} \tag{12}$$

i.e., it gives a prescribed change in the parameters, where K is a $(m \times m)$ positive-definite weighting matrix, and $k(t)$ is an arbitrary positive weighting function. If the change in the cost criterion according to (6) with $F = P$ with (12) and (6) with $F = q$ as constraints is to be maximized with respect to the change in the parameters, this yields

$$\frac{\partial\left(\overbrace{\int_{t_0}^{t_f} \lambda_u^P (\delta\underline{p}^T \ \underline{f}(t)) \ dt}^{1}\right.}{\partial\delta\underline{p}}$$

$$+ \frac{\left.\overbrace{\sum_{i=1}^{r} \nu_i \left(\Delta q_i - \int_{t_0}^{t_f} \lambda_u^{q_i} (\delta\underline{p}^T \ \underline{f}(t)) \ dt\right)}^{2} + \overbrace{\mu(\Delta s^2 - \delta\underline{p}^T \ K \ \delta\underline{p})}^{3}\right)}{\partial\delta\underline{p}}$$

$$= 0. \tag{13}$$

The prescribed change in q_i is given here by Δq_i. Constraints (2) and (3) are weighted by the Lagrangian multipliers ν_i and μ, respectively. Performing the differentiation we get

$$\int_{t_0}^{t_f} \lambda_u^P \underline{f}(t) \ dt - \sum_{i=1}^{r} \nu_i \int_{t_0}^{t_f} \left(\lambda_u^{q_i} \underline{f}(t)\right) dt$$

$$- 2\mu K \ \delta\underline{p} = 0. \tag{14}$$

If we use (11) for the integrals and introduce grad $F = (\partial F/\partial p_1, \ldots, \partial F/\partial p_m)$ for the partial derivatives, then (14) can be written as

$$\text{grad } P - \sum_{i=1}^{r} \nu_i \text{ grad } q_i - 2\mu K \ \delta\underline{p} = 0. \tag{15}$$

This equation can be solved for $\delta\underline{p}$,

$$\delta\underline{p} = \frac{1}{(2\mu)} K^{-1}\left(\text{grad } P - \sum_{i=1}^{r} \nu_i \text{ grad } q_i\right). \tag{16}$$

Still unknown are the Lagrangian multipliers ν_i and μ. From prescribing a desired change $\Delta\underline{q}$ in the final conditions ν_i can be determined using (7) and introducing (16) there. We define a gradient matrix G as G = (grad q_1, ..., grad q_l) and combine the ν_i in a vector $\underline{\nu} = (\nu_1, \ldots, \nu_l)$. Then (7) can be written

$$\Delta\underline{q} = G^T \delta\underline{p} \qquad (17)$$

and (16) solved for

$$\underline{\nu} = (G^T K^{-1} G)(GK^{-1} \text{ grad } P - 2\mu\, \Delta\underline{q}). \qquad (18)$$

Note that the $(r \times r)$ matrix $(G^T K^{-1} G)$ must be invertible. This is true, if $l < m$ (i.e., the number of parameters is larger than the number of final conditions) and if G has rank r [i.e., the gradients grad q_i are linearly independent, which implies that the final conditions q_i as well as the basis functions $f_j(t)$ are linearly independent]. K had been introduced as a positive-definite matrix.

The multiplier μ still remaining can be calculated by evaluating (12) or can be left open for a one-dimensional search. It has to be negative to find a minimum of P as can be seen quickly by differentiating (14) a second time with respect to $\delta\underline{p}$. The resulting matrix $-2\mu K$ is to be positive definite, which can be assured by choosing $\mu < 0$.

The iteration formula for $\delta\underline{p}$ then follows from (15) by introducing (18) there,

$$\delta\underline{p} = (1/(2\mu))(K^{-1} \text{ grad } P - K^{-1}G(G^T K^{-1} G)^{-1} G^T K^{-1} \text{ grad } P) + K^{-1}G(G^T K^{-1} G)^{-1} \Delta\underline{q}. \qquad (19)$$

The iteration can now be done:

Step 0. Choose initial values of the parameters.

Step 1. Determine P and $\underline{q}$ from nominal solution of the differential equations of the system.

Step 2. Determine grad P and grad q_i by numerical differentiation using m solutions of the system's differential equations with changes in the parameters.

Step 3. Choose suitable $\Delta\underline{q}$ and determine μ by a one-dimensional search.

Step 4. Determine a new set of parameters using (19) and a new nominal solution.

Step 5. Check if P has converged to the optimum. If so, stop; otherwise continue with Step 2.

B. CONNECTIONS TO NONLINEAR PROGRAMMING

In Section A a method for finding suboptimal control functions has been presented. The iteration formula (19) for the parameters of the Ritz parametrization (5) has been derived from gradient methods in optimal control theory. It corresponds to the iteration formula known from nonlinear programming, described by Rosen [22]. The cost criterion (4) is the function to be minimized; the final conditions $\underline{q}$ can be seen as equality constraints, which are considered using a gradient projection approach. Note that for each function evaluation the state equations (1) have to be solved.

The matrix K introduced in (12) has not yet been defined. For the simple steepest descent method K would just be the unity matrix. A more general form of K could be used for faster convergence; for instance, if we look at the second derivatives of the cost criterion with respect to $\delta\underline{p}$, this matrix is positive definite in a sufficiently small neighborhood of the minimum. If we define

$$K = \partial^2 P/(\partial\delta\underline{p})^2 \tag{20}$$

then (19) could be interpreted as a parametrized form of the so-called min-H method as has been described in [31].

Other possible definitions for K are the ones used in the conjugate gradient or variable metric method. A unified approach has been presented in [32]. Here K is computed iteratively, which means normally that more than one consecutive step of the iteration is to be done; in Step 3 of the iteration scheme from Section A the updating of the weighting matrix is also necessary.

III. FINAL VALUE CONTROL

In Section II a special algorithm for finding a suboptimal solution of the optimal control problem has been presented. This problem has the same formulation as the final-value control problem stated in Section I, except that in (6) the subscripts "mod" are deleted. For application of these control functions to a real system a feedback strategy is desirable.

A. ON-LINE OPTIMIZATION

As has been pointed out in Section II, only the calculation of open-loop optimal control is numerically feasible. One method to obtain a closed-loop strategy, nevertheless, is to introduce a sampled data control system. Here the real-system states are measured at the sampling points; starting from these values the optimization scheme calculates the optimal control functions for the rest of the control interval, which are applied to the real system during the next sampling interval.

The algorithm presented here has several features which make it particularly well suited for this task:

(a) Being a simplification of the gradient method for optimal control calculation, it typically requires less than 10% of the computation time of the general method.

(b) It is furthermore not necessary to solve the complete optimization problem during each sampling interval. As a direct method it calculates improvements of the control functions with respect to reducing the cost criterion and fulfilling the final conditions in each step. So after each iteration step an improved control function can be applied to the real system.

(c) Control boundaries, which can be prescribed for instance as

$$U_{min} \leqq u(t) \leqq U_{max}, \tag{21}$$

can be taken directly into account by choosing appropriate basis functions $\underline{f}(t)$.

(d) Gradient techniques are known to have the biggest absolute improvement in the first steps. Therefore for many technical applications just these steps are the most important ones.

The disadvantage of the method described here is that nearly all convergence improvement techniques as indicated in Section II.A cannot be used here, if only one iteration step per sampling interval is performed. The reason for that is that in most of these methods K is calculated iteratively, which implies that more than one consecutive iteration step is required. In addition, only suboptimal control functions are found even in the ideal case; this, however, does not seem a very severe restriction to me in most cases, since it is not very reasonable to compute an optimal solution with high accuracy using a model which may deviate slightly from the actual system, which is the one we really want to control.

During the sampling intervals the previously calculated control functions are applied to the system. This means that during such an interval only open-loop control is done. Disturbances, which occur in the meantime, can be recognized at

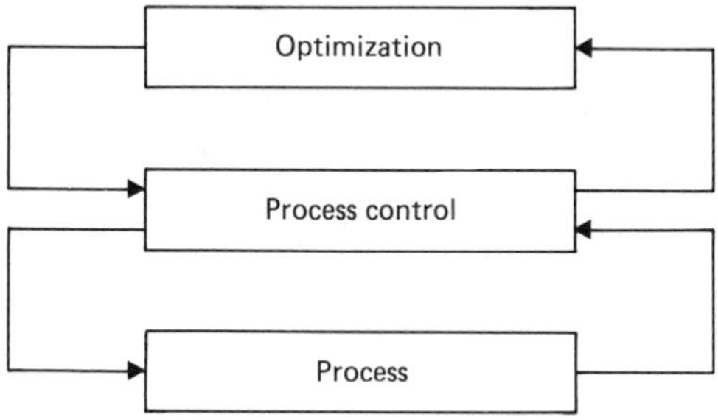

Fig. 1. Scheme of the hierarchical controller.

the next sampling point only and can be counteracted one more interval later. Since the computational burden for calculating the control functions is considerable despite the simplifications used, one tends to make the sampling intervals as long as possible. This, however, may produce difficulties especially with unstable systems. They can be reduced using a model-following controller on a hierarchically lower level, which forces the system to behave like the model used for optimization (Fig. 1).

Of course, the control functions calculated then are not optimal for the system. They are suboptimal, however, in the sense that they are the best which can be calculated with the model at hand.

B. MODEL-FOLLOWING CONTROL

For closed-loop control of the real system during the sampling interval reference values are needed in order to recognize disturbances and to control the system in such a way that it behaves like a prescribed model. The structure of such an explicit model-following control is shown in Fig. 2. It is called "explicit" since the model must be calculated explicitly during the actual control (whereas implicit model-following controllers use the model only for the design of the controller).

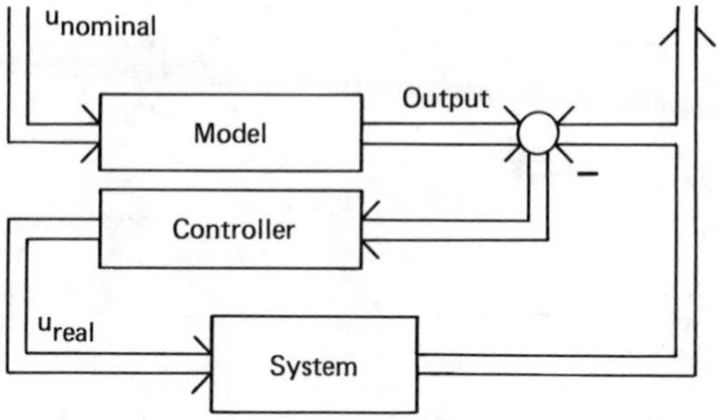

Fig. 2. Scheme of the model-following controller.

For the design of the controller we assume that the model is a good representation of the system. This is reasonable here, because otherwise optimal control would be obsolete anyway. Now a Taylor series is expanded around the present states x_{so} and controls u_{so} of the system, which yields

$$\dot{\underline{x}}_{s/m} = \underline{g}(\underline{x}_{so}, \underline{u}_{so}, t) + \underbrace{(\partial \underline{g}/\partial \underline{x})}_{A}(\underline{x}_{s/m} - \underline{x}_{so})$$

$$+ \underbrace{(\partial \underline{g}/\partial \underline{u})}_{B}(\underline{u}_{s/m} - \underline{u}_{so}) \tag{22}$$

where A [(n × n) matrix] and B [(n × r) matrix] are assumed to be the same for the model and the real system and where the subscripts m and s stand for the states of the model and the real system, respectively. If we now subtract the two forms of (22) from one another this results in

$$\underbrace{\left(\dot{\underline{x}}_s - \dot{\underline{x}}_m\right)}_{\Delta\dot{\underline{x}}} = A\underbrace{(\underline{x}_s - \underline{x}_m)}_{\Delta\underline{x}} + \underbrace{B(u_s - u_m)}_{\Delta\underline{u}} \tag{23}$$

which is a linear equation for the state differences $\Delta\underline{x}$. Here we can apply standard linear control techniques as linear optimal control for designing the model-following controller as

$$\Delta\underline{u} = F\ \Delta\underline{x} \tag{24}$$

where F is a (r × n) feedback matrix. This yields the controller structure shown in Fig. 3.

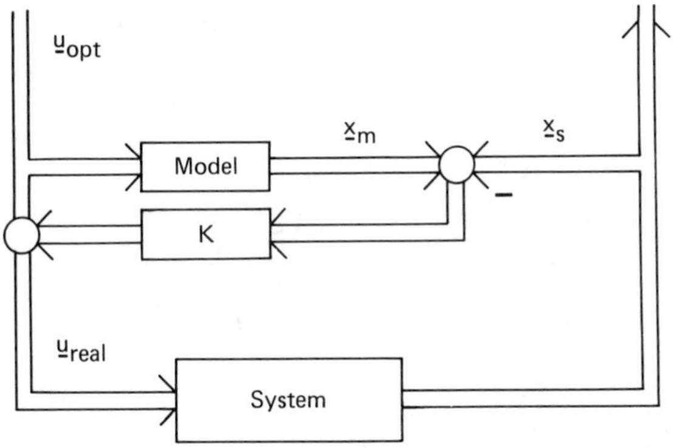

Fig. 3. Model-following control using linear state feedback.

This controller reduces the differences between the real system and the model by providing a correction term Δu, which must be added to the control functions calculated by the optimization scheme. Of course other design strategies for this controller are also possible. One approach could be to use design techniques developed for the state observers; this is possible because the structure of the model-following controller is the very same as for a system with a Luenberger observer, the only difference is that the model and the system are exchanged.

IV. EXAMPLE

As an example for the application of the proposed control method we consider the model of an upper stage of a rocket in a central gravitational field outside an atmosphere. Rotation of this rocket around its own center of gravity due to the excentric thrust is not considered here. The system is shown in Fig. 4.

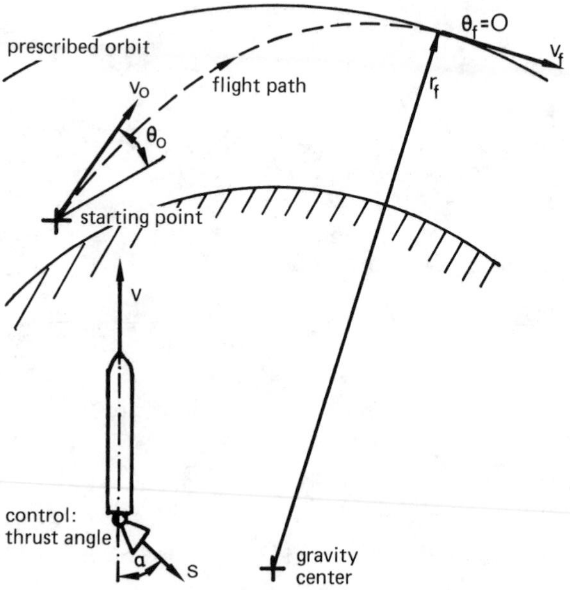

Fig. 4. Description of the movements of a rocket.

The differential equations describing this model in a form as described in (1) are given here without derivation (see [30]):

$$\dot{x}_1 = \dot{r} = v \sin \theta \qquad \text{(radius)}, \tag{25}$$

$$\dot{x}_2 = \dot{v} = (\mu/r) \sin \theta + (S/m) \cos \alpha \qquad \text{(velocity)}, \tag{26}$$

$$\dot{x}_3 = \dot{\theta} = ((v/r) - (\mu/r^2 v)) \cos \theta + (S/mv) \sin \alpha \qquad \text{(flight angle)}, \tag{27}$$

$$\dot{x}_4 = \dot{m} = -d \qquad \text{(mass)}, \tag{28}$$

$$\dot{x}_5 = \dot{\phi} = (v/r) \cos \theta \qquad \text{(angle)} \tag{29}$$

where μ, d, and S are constants describing the system under consideration. The control function is the thrust angle α.

The final conditions according to (3) prescribe a radius

$$x_1(t_f) = r_f \tag{30}$$

and a flight angle

$$x_3(t_f) = 0 \tag{31}$$

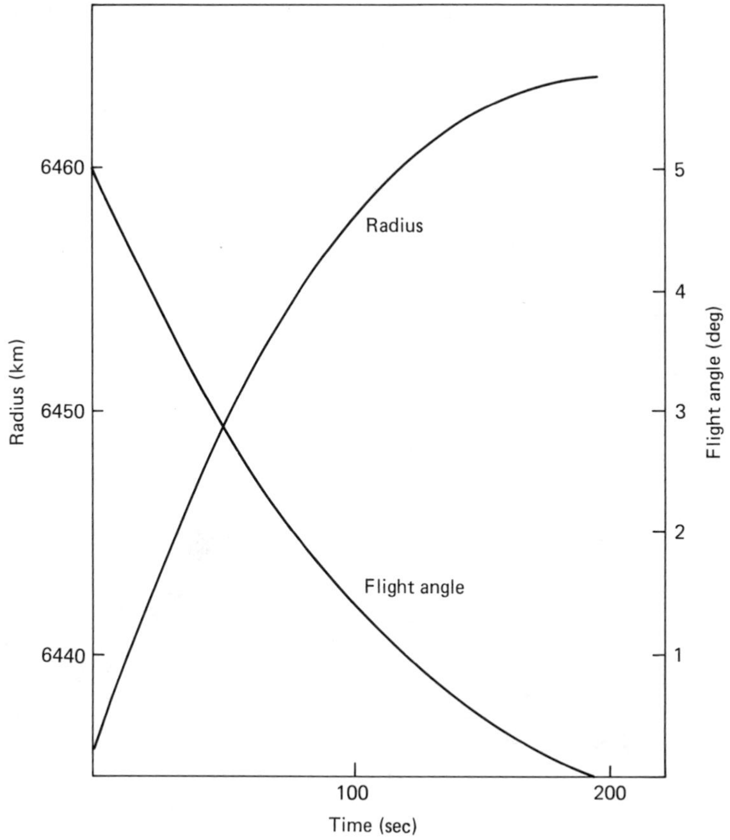

Fig. 5. Simulated trajectory.

at final time and a final energy

$$-\frac{1}{2}x_2^2(t_e) + \frac{\mu}{r(t_E)} - E_W = 0 \qquad (32)$$

where E_W is the desired energy, which all together determine the orbit into which the rocket is aimed.

Figure 5 shows a simulation of the optimal trajectories of the states x_1 and x_3, in the gravitation field of the earth. The control function found by the optimization algorithm with different sets of basis functions is given in Fig. 6. The example indicates that the choice of the function base is not a

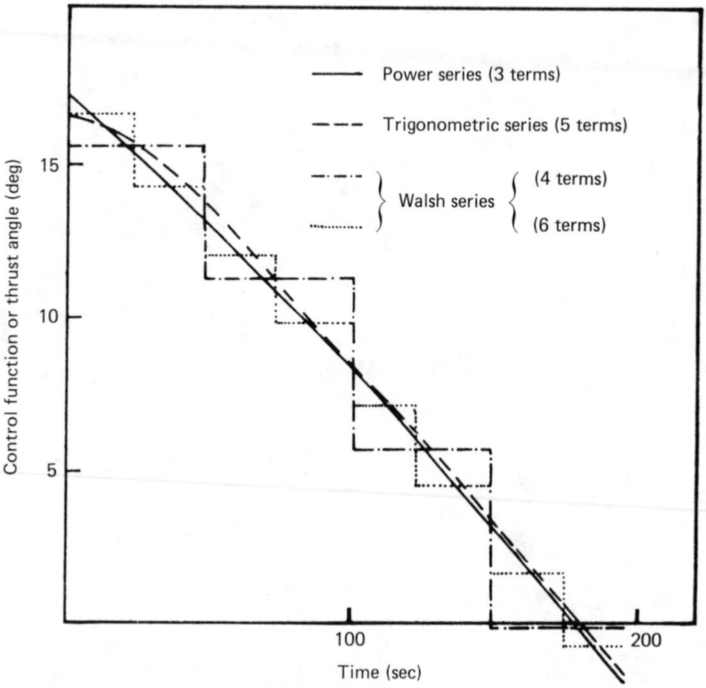

Fig. 6. Suboptimal control functions, calculated with different function bases.

very critical one, providing a sufficient number of functions is used. Several other examples have shown basically the same result.

For the simulation of the controlled system the model was realized by an analog computer, while the controller was a two-level computer structure with a desktop calculator for the optimization and a dedicated microcomputer for the model-following control. Figure 7 shows a simulation result of the control functions with on-line optimization only. The initial control function was not correct [there were some deviations in $\underline{x}(t_0)$] and the analog model was slightly different from the one used for optimization. The controller finds a suboptimal control function within a few intervals. The large steps in the curve

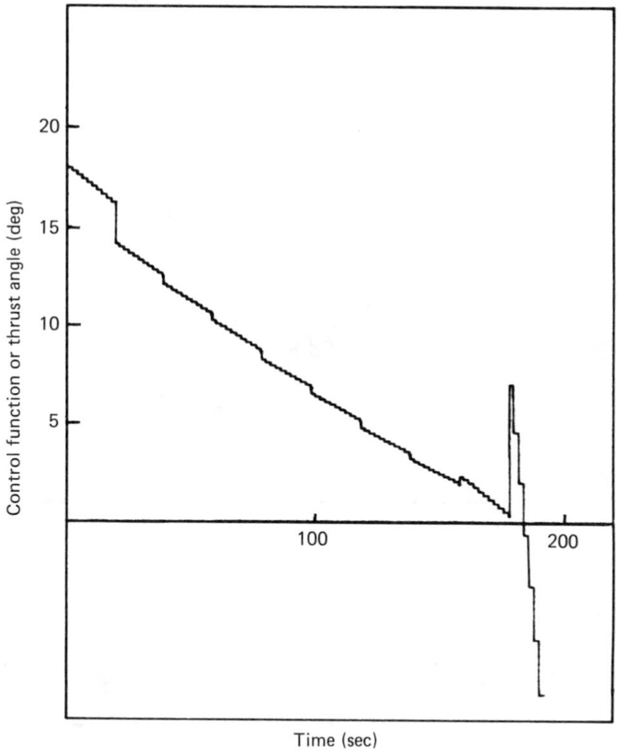

Fig. 7. Simulation of the control functions (feedback control using on-line optimization).

at the sampling points thereafter are due to the differences in the models (the smaller steps indicate the minor sampling intervals). Toward the end of the control period these steps get larger, because the controller has less time to counteract deviations in the states. If additionally a model-following control on the lower level is introduced, the output of this controller is added to the previous control function as shown in Fig. 8. The system (here presented by the analog model) is forced to behave like the model used for optimization despite disturbances (which cause the "ripple" in the curve) and model deviations.

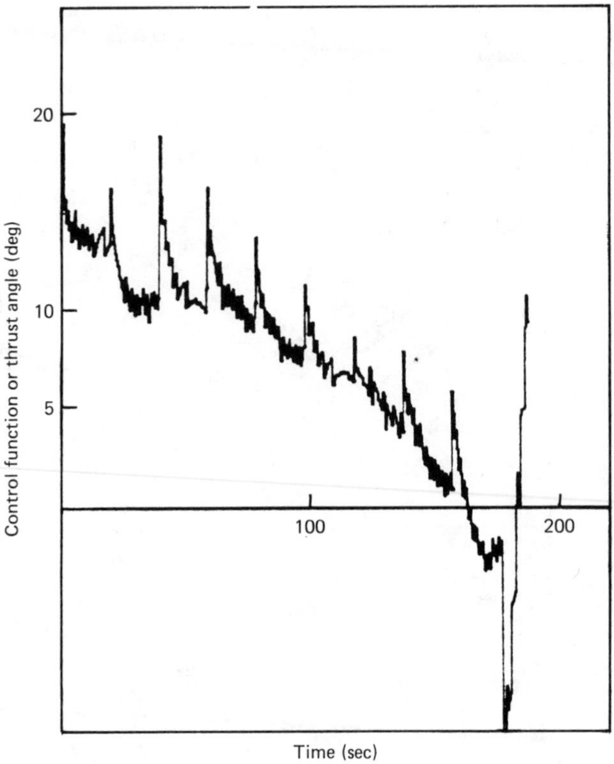

Fig. 8. Simulation of the control function (as in Fig. 7 but with additional model-following control).

The sampling interval lengths are limited by the necessary computation time. A microcomputer like an LSI 11/23 would need about a minute or less for an optimization step for the problem at hand and less than a second for a model-following control step. These times indicate that this control scheme is applicable at the moment for relatively slow systems only despite the simplifications used. An example with sufficiently slow time constants was discussed in [30].

V. CONCLUSION

Optimal final-value control is a special control problem; it aims at bringing a system from a given initial state to prescribed final values. It is called optimal, since the control functions are chosen to minimize a cost criterion.

For the application of final-value control several aspects have been discussed. A numerically efficient algorithm for the calculation of suboptimal control functions is given and its application in a sampled data control loop is proposed. Because of all the simplifications introduced, sampling intervals of under a minute can be obtained using a microcomputer. This indicates that the proposed control method is directly applicable at the moment only with relatively slow plants, as found for instance in chemical engineering.

In order to allow longer sampling intervals and to improve the overall behavior of the controlled system, a second control level has been introduced. Here a model-following control was applied to force the real system (which is normally not known exactly) to behave like the model used in the optimization processes. Of course it is necessary that the model is a good representation of the real system, if optimization is to make sense at all. For the design of the controller, linear quadratic design techniques were used. A hierarchical control like this is not limited to the configuration here; it can be used advantageously with other control schemes which require relatively long sampling intervals.

REFERENCES

1. H. KELLEY, "Gradient Theory of Optimal Flight Path," *ARS J. 30*, 947 (1960).

2. A. BRYSON, W. DENHAM, E. CARROLL, and K. MIKAMI, "Determination of the Lift or Drag Program That Minimizes Reentry Heating with Acceleration Constraints," IAS Paper No. 61-6 (1961).

3. W. RITZ, "Über eine Neue Methode zur Lösung gewisser Variationsprobleme der Mathematischen Physik," *J. Reine Angew. Math. 135*, 1 (1908).

4. H. ROSENBROCK and C. STOREY, "Computational Techniques for Chemical Engineers," Pergamon, New York, 1966.

5. W. WILLIAMSON, "Use of Polynomial Approximations to Calculate Suboptimal Controls," *J. Am. Inst. Aer. Astron. 9*, No. 11, 2271 (1971).

6. G. HICKS and W. RAY, "Approximation Methods for Optimal Control Synthesis," *Can. J. Chem. Eng. 49*, 522 (1971).

7. R. BRUSCH, "A Nonlinear Programming Approach to Space Shuttle Trajectory Optimization," *J. Optimization Theory Appl. 13*, No. 1, 94 (1974).

8. R. BRUSCH and J. PELTIER, "Parametric Control Models and Gradient Generation by Impulsive Response," *24th Congr. IAF, Baku*, p. 1 (1973).

9. R. BRUSCH and J. PELTIER, "Gradient Generation of Parametric Control Models," *Acta Astronautica 1*, 1453 (1974).

10. H. SISIRENA, "Computation of Optimal Controls Using a Piecewise Polynomial Approximation," *IEEE Trans. Autom. Control 18*, 409 (1973).

11. H. SISIRENA and K. TAN, "Computation of Constrained Optimal Control Using Parametrization Techniques," *IEEE Trans. Autom. Control 19*, 431 (1974).

12. H. SISIRENA and F. CHOU, "Convergence of the Control Parametrization Ritz Method for Nonlinear Optimal Control Problems," *J. Optimization Theory Appl. 29*, No. 3, 369 (1979).

13. D. MELLEFONT and R. SARGENT, "Calculation of Optimal Controls of Specified Accuracy," *J. Optimization Theory Appl. 25*, No. 3, 407 (1978).

14. J. ROSEN, "The Gradient Projection Method for Nonlinear Programming. Part 1," *SIAM J. 8*, No. 1, 181 (1960); *idem* Part 2," *SIAM J. 9*, No. 4, 514 (1961).

15. E. DICKMANNS and K. WELL, "Parametrization of Optimal Control Problems Using Piecewise Polynomial Approximation," AIAA Paper No. 74-822 (1974).

16. C. NEUMAN and A. SEN, "A Suboptimal Control Algorithm for Constrained Problems Using Cubic Splines," *Automatica 9*, 601 (1973).

17. T. TSANG, P. HIMMELBLAU, and T. EDGAR, "Optimal Control via Collocation and Nonlinear Programming," *Int. J. Control 21*, No. 5, 763 (1975).

18. K. FEGLEY, S. BLUM, J. BERGHOLM, A. CALISE, J. MAROWITZ, G. PORCELLI, and L. SINKA, "Stochastic and Deterministic Design and Control via Linear and Quadratic Programming," *Int. J. Control 21*, 197 (1975).

19. M. CANON, C. CULLUM, and E. POLAK, "Constrained Minimization Problems in Finite Dimensional Spaces," *SIAM J. Control 7*, 528 (1966).

20. J. CULLUM, "Discrete Approximations to Continuous Optimal Control Problems," *SIAM J. Control 7*, 32 (1969).

21. H. NOUR-ELDIN, "A Report on Convex Feedback Methods," Preprints IFAC Symp. Optimization Methods, Applied Aspects, Varna (1979).

22. M. GHONAIMY and R. BERNHOLTZ, "On a Direct Method of Optimization of Linear Control Systems," *Proc. 3rd IFAC World Congress*, Book 1, Paper 13F (1966).

23. W. BOSARGE and O. JOHNSON, "Direct Method Approximation to the State Regulator Control Problem," *IEEE Trans. Autom. Control 15*, 627 (1970).

24. C. CHEN and C. HSIAO, "Walsh Series Analysis in Optimal Control," *Int. J. Control 21*, No. 6, 881 (1975).

25. M. HASSAN and G. SINGH, "Synchronous Machine Control Using a Two-Level Model Follower," *Automatica 13*, 173 (1977).

26. N. ROSE and R. BROWN, "On Optimal Terminal Control," *IEEE Trans. Autom. Control 14*, 501 (1969).

27. E. KIENZLE and G. SCHMIDT, "A New Approach to a Model-Following Control for Nonlinear, Multivariable Systems," *IFAC Symp. Multivariable Control Systems, Duesseldorf*, Paper 2-1-2 (1971).

28. E. DREYFUS, "Dynamic Programming and the Calculus of Variations," Academic Press, New York, 1965.

29. H. TOLLE, "Optimization Methods," Springer-Verlag, New York, 1975.

30. B. ASSELMEYER, "On Optimal Final Value Control of Nonlinear Systems with Small Computers [in German]," Dissertation, Technische Hochschule Darmstadt, Darmstadt, West Germany.

31. G. GOTTLIEB, "Rapid Convergence to Optimal Solutions Using a Min.-H Strategy," *AIAA J.* (1976).

32. H. HUANG, "Unified Approach to Quadratically Convergent Algorithms for Function Minimization," *J. Optimization Theory Appl.* *5*, 405 (1970).

INDEX

L

M

N

O

P

Q

R